STRICTLY (Mining) BOARDROOM
VOLUME II

A Practitioner's Guide for Next Generation DIRECTORS

ALLAN TRENCH & JOHN SYKES

First published in 2016 by Major Street Publishing Pty Ltd
Contact: e: info@majorstreet.com.au | Ph: +61 421 707 983

© Allan Trench and John Sykes 2016

This book draws upon material first published in the *Strictly Boardroom* columns that appear in Aspermont Limited's MiningNewsPremium.net. The moral rights of the authors have been asserted.

National Library of Australia Cataloguing-in-Publication data:

Creator: Trench, Allan, author.
Title: Strictly (mining) boardroom volume II: a practitioner's guide for next generation directors / Allan Trench, John Sykes.
ISBN: 9780994542410 (paperback)
Subjects: Mines and mineral resources – Australia – Management.
Executives – Training of – Australia.
Other Creators/Contributors: Sykes, John, author.
Dewey Number: 338.20994

All rights reserved. Except as permitted under the Australian Copyright Act 1968 (for example, a fair dealing for the purposes of study, research, criticism or review), no part of this book may be reproduced, stored in a retrieval system, communicated or transmitted in any form or by any means without prior written permission. All inquiries should be made to the publisher.

Internal design by Production Works
Cover design by Simone Geary
Printed in Australia by Griffin Press

10 9 8 7 6 5 4 3 2 1

Disclaimer: The material in this publication is of in the nature of general comment only, and neither purports nor intends to be advice. Readers should not act on the basis of any matter in this publication without considering (and if appropriate taking) professional advice with due regard to their own particular circumstances. The authors and publisher expressly disclaim all and any liability to any person, whether a purchaser of this publication or not, in respect of anything and the consequences of anything done or omitted to be done by any such person in reliance, whether whole or partial, upon the whole or any part of the contents of this publication.

CRU International Limited accepts no liability to third parties, howsoever arising, for CRU International excerpts contained within this book. Although reasonable care and diligence has been used in the preparation of this book, we do not guarantee the accuracy of any data, assumptions, forecasts or other forward-looking statements.

© CRU International Ltd. 2016. All rights reserved.

Praise for *Strictly (Mining) Boardroom*

"Trench and Sykes are two incredibly well learned professionals presenting an insightful illustration of the formulation and implementation of mining company strategy backed by academic, empirical and experiential evidence. Strictly (Mining) Boardroom is a well-balanced text and a very useful addition to my bookshelf."

Tim Andrews, Contracts and Procurement Professional and The University of Western Australia MBA Graduate 2016

"An entertaining dialogue, covering many aspects of the business of mining from the board's perspective. The mention of low (STEM) gender diversity at the board level is well timed now that innovation is clearly linked to a long-term mindset and divergent thinking. This book has reminded me of some key concepts from my MBA(Fin) and their relevance to every strategic decision, with a focus on what must go right, asking the right questions at the right time and with an awareness of availability heuristics. This book sheds light on value-adding strategies and current commodities of choice, exploring the risk-return relationship in exploration, development and M&A! The book also touches on social licence to operate and the industry's duty to share some of the wealth it generates with the community through government "rents". There's a nice argument at the end on the need for a review of the royalties and tax regime in Australia and the need for long-term policy stability. A nice book!"

Alex Atkins, Manager in Risk Advisory at Deloitte Touche Tohmatsu, Director for the Australian Institute of Mining and Metallurgy (AusIMM) and Earth Science Western Australia (ESWA)

"Trench and Sykes are storytellers who bring issues that mire our industry to the forefront in an engaging style. I found myself thinking 'I know this person', maybe because at least once or twice it was me."

Steve Beresford, Exploration Geologist, Adjunct Professor at the Centre for Exploration Targeting, The University of Western Australia, and Chair of Geoscience, UNCOVER

"Managers, directors, students and teachers can benefit from this book. I am definitely recommending it; particularly to "my" WASM students of Mine Management and Corporate Governance. Examples throughout are incredibly illustrative and a great combination of the concepts that drive successful strategic management in the resources sector and practical advice on its implementation. This is more effective than deciphering theories. I had fun reading it – and hope to see more women on mining boardrooms, before 2040!"

Dr Carla Boehl, Senior Lecturer, Western Australian School of Mines (WASM), Curtin University

"Trench and Sykes deliver a valuable resource to practitioners and students of the boardroom alike, by stripping away theoretical overburden and providing intelligent, entertaining and practical insights on the full gamut of issues faced by boards of mining companies."

Oli Charlesworth, MBA Graduate

"*Strictly (Mining) Boardroom* is a delight, with lots of truth and advice for everyone. Don't read it from the front, just dive in anywhere. Maybe flag the key insights at the end of every chapter for memorising unless you can read the whole book three times. Have Post-It notes handy."

Chris Davis, Mining Industry Consultant

"Balanced with the perfect amount of humour, *Strictly (Mining) Boardroom* presents practical and progressive scenarios and case studies, which challenge the reader to consider historical assumptions of the industry when looking to the future."

Libby Gatti, MBA Graduate

"Trench and Sykes' informative and entertaining new book *Strictly (Mining) Boardroom* is a savvy guide for decision-makers in the mining industry. Using real-world examples and scenarios that illustrate the issues facing the boards members of mining companies it provides insights on where we as an industry can do better."

Matthew Greentree, Principal Consultant (Geology & Project Evaluation), SRK Consulting

"A thought-provoking read packed with anecdotes, *Strictly (Mining) Boardroom* encourages strategic and lateral thinking in the mining industry. Trench and Sykes present a forward-thinking and fresh perspective on what it takes for companies and professionals to succeed in the mining industry of the 21st century."

Jessica Harman, MBA Graduate and Project Manager

"Allan Trench and John Sykes have mastered what few are able to do with their publication *Strictly (Mining) Boardroom* by delivering an incredibly insightful and informative text in a very engaging and readable format. The use of personal anecdotes and thought pieces underlined by a subtly humorous narrative makes for a very enjoyable and equally thought-provoking read."

Matthew Horgan, MBA Candidate & Process Engineer at Alcoa

"Whatever your current or aspiring role in the mining industry – whether director, investor, analyst, specialist, accountant or other stakeholder, this collection of case studies, theoretical examples and thought-provoking scenarios offers real insight into the decision-making processes that should occur around the table at boardrooms. The authors and contributors draw on a range of direct experiences in the mining and exploration industry rarely achievable for any individual, gained through years of client contact, board positions, management consulting and armchair speculation. If you're serious about the mining and exploration industry, particularly in its current state, make sure you know about the issues and ideas raised here. Buy the book!"

Gareth Northam, Consultant Chief Geologist

"*Strictly (Mining) Board*room focuses on issues prevalent in the mining industry – ranging from the obvious to the ignored. It will serve as an essential guide for everyone: from the next generation of mining executives, to technical leaders and anyone interested in mining and mineral exploration strategy. There are likely other such resources, but this will eclipse them due to the simple, practical and entertaining presentation of its insights."

Ahmad Saleem, Exploration geologist and PhD Researcher (Mineral economics)

"Entertaining and thought-provoking in equal measures, *Strictly (Mining) Boardroom* is an invaluable resource for the next generation of leaders; alongside offering practical advice for directors, the book sets itself apart by challenging those conventions that may not be as clear-cut as they first appear."

Natalie Staffurth, Consulting Geologist (Mineral Exploration)

"The authors' chatty style and witty metaphors form a highly entertaining backdrop to their compelling insights into 'real' issues confronting resources industry boards. This is highly recommended to aspiring board members, those seeking to improve their emotional intelligence in a board setting, and anyone seeking an entertaining read."

Jessica Volich, Resources Sustainability Specialist

"Trench and Sykes revisit the Strictly Boardroom columns to provide us with the do's and don't's for any would-be mining exec. The questions posed give the reader a taste of the many business conundrums that boards may face and offer tips for strategy and planning in various hypothetical scenarios. A nice informal read for a serious, business-orientated genre."

Josh Wright, Minerals Consultant and Director of Rowton Consolidated

ACKNOWLEDGMENTS

The authors and publisher wish to acknowledge MiningNews.net staff at Aspermont, in particular Kristie Batten, editor of MiningNews.net.

This book contains contributions as co-authors to specific short chapters from Graham Arvidson, Doug Brewster, Chris Gemell, Ian Hiscock, Jon Hronsky, Matthew Kanakis, Vikki Lauritsen, Campbell McCuaig, Paul Robinson, Jose Saavedra-Rosas and Morgan Trench. All such contributions are gratefully acknowledged.

In addition to the contributors, the authors would like to thank the following people:

Michael Anderson, Tim Andrews, Alex Atkins, Jon Bell, Sandy Bell, Steve Beresford, Rob Bills, Murray Black, Carla Boehl, Barry Bourne, Doug Bowie, Ken Brinsden, Mark Burridge, Oli Charlesworth, Tim Craske, David Crook, Mike Curtis, Vanessa Davidson, Sam Davies, Chris Davis, Joao Carlos de Assuncao, Mike Dentith, Richard Dewhirst, Alan Dickson, Helen Dillon, Christian Easterday, Pat Ellis, Jim Everett, Will Featherstone, Nick Gardiner, Libby Gatti, Mike Gershon, Maxine Green, Matthew Greentree, David Groves, Pietro Guj, Stefan Hagemann, Paul Hallam, Jessica Harman, Matthew Horgan, Susan Hunter, Mark Jessell, Caroline Johnson, Simon Jowitt, Peter Kettle, Dudley Kingsnorth, Cho Khong, Richard Krasnoff, Melanie Leighton, Cui Lin, Mark Lindsay, Bryan Maybee, Craig McGown, Andrew McIlwain, Paul Miller, Tom Mulqueen, Mark Munro, Rob Murdoch, John Nitschke, Gareth Northam, Dan Packey, Pas Perazzelli, Alison Preston, Julia Ralph, Rafael Ramirez, Genevieve Riviere, Laurence Robb, Michele Roberts, Paul Robinson, Dermot Ryan, Ahmad Saleem, Ian Satchwell, Richard Schodde, Cynthia Selin, John Sendziuk, Philip Sewell, Jose Ignacio Silva, Natalie Staffurth, Kataryna Sykes, Nicolas Thebaud, Alex Tonks, Cameron Trench, Lauren Trench, Sam Ulrich, Kees van der Hiejden, John Vann, Tony Venables, Jessica Volich, Richard Walkland, Tom Wesby, Julie Wolseley, Matthew Wonnacott, Josh Wright and Mike Young.

ABOUT THE AUTHORS

Allan Trench is research professor (Value & Risk) at the Centre for Exploration Targeting, The University of Western Australia (UWA), Professor at the UWA Business School, a non-executive director of Emmerson Resources, Enterprise Metals, Hot Chili and Pioneer Resources – and the Perth representative for CRU Consulting, a division of independent metals and mining advisory CRU Group. Allan is a Fellow of the Australian Institute of Company Directors (FAICD) and the Australasian Institute of Mining and Metallurgy (FAusIMM) (allan.trench@uwa.edu.au).

John Sykes is undertaking a multidisciplinary doctorate at the Centre for Exploration Targeting, UWA. The research combines geological, economic, sustainable development and strategic assessments of the future of copper mining and exploration. He is also director of Greenfields Research, a consultancy specialising in the analysis of mining and exploration across the base, precious and specialty metals sectors. John is a Fellow of the Geological Society of London (FGS), a Chartered Scientist (CSci) and a member of the Institute of Materials, Minerals and Mining (MIMMM), Australasian Institute of Mining and Metallurgy (MAusIMM) and the Australian Institute of Geoscientists (MAIG) (john.sykes@greenfieldsresearch.com).

CONTRIBUTORS

Graham Arvidson is a mechanical engineer currently working as a Maintenance Manager for Independence Group. He has worked on mineral projects in Australia, Canada, China and West Africa. He recently completed an MBA and MSc in Mineral Economics at Curtin University. He is a Chartered Professional Engineer (CPEng) on the National Professional Engineering Register of Australia (NPER), a Chartered Professional (CP) for Metallurgy and Mineral Processing and a member of the Australasian Institute of Mining and Metallurgy and Engineers Australia (MIEAust) (graham.arvidson@gmail.com).

Douglas Brewster is an experienced exploration geologist and manager based in Brisbane. Educated as a geologist in Sydney and apprenticed across Australia, including a seminal posting at the venerable Broken Hill, he learned the practicalities, philosophy, history and excitement of mineral exploration and discovery. Multifarious companies, places, people, technicalities, professional roles, discoveries and too frequent harsh disruptions to the hunt have further imbued the journey. Buttressed by his patient family while on another "industry-sabbatical", he is exploring efficacious ways to go exploring yet again (brewster@powerup.com.au).

Chris Gemell has worked in a variety of roles in the mining industry over the last ten years. Starting his career as a project engineer for Rio Tinto, he worked across several commodities and sites. He then moved into consulting, working both independently as well as being part of larger consulting teams. He currently works as a commercial consultant focusing on the resources sector and is based in Sydney.

Ian Hiscock is author and former editor of the CRU Group Uranium Market Outlook and Uranium Mining Cost Service. Ian has undertaken primary research at uranium mines around the world and has spoken at a number of industry conferences. He remains an adviser and contributor to CRU's research in this area. Ian works across the mining and metals industry within CRU's management consultancy division and has advised numerous companies and governments on commodity market issues (ian.hiscock@crugroup.com).

Jon Hronsky is a principal of Western Mining Services and a non-executive director of Cassini Resources and Encounter Resources. He previously worked for BHP Billiton and WMC Resources in geoscience and strategy leadership roles. He is chairman of the board of the Centre for Exploration Targeting at The University of Western Australia (UWA), chairman of the Australian Geoscience Council and an adjunct professor at both UWA and Macquarie University (jon.hronsky@wesminllc.com).

Matthew Kanakis is currently a consultant within the research and development incentives group of KPMG. He has previously worked as a geoscientist for Sipa Resources, Insight Geology and Mackie Research Capital. He recently completed a joint BSc in Geosciences and BCom in Commerce at The University of Western Australia. His major research project focused on the link between gold deposit geology and operating costs, the results of which feature in this book (kanakis45@hotmail.com).

Vikki Lauritsen is a chartered accountant currently working as a senior business analyst for Minara Resources. She has previously worked in accountancy roles for Teck Resources, Gold Fields and Tyco. She recently completed a joint MBA and MSc in Mineral Economics at Curtin University. Her major research project focused on gender diversity in the Australian minerals sector and features in this book.

Campbell McCuaig is a professor at in the School of Earth and Environment at The University of Western Australia. He is the director of the Centre for Exploration Targeting and the node director for the ARC Centre of Excellence for Core to Crust Fluid Systems. Previously he was a principal consultant for SRK Consulting (campbell.mccuaig@uwa.edu.au).

Paul Robinson is a director at CRU Group with responsibility for CRU's economics, information, knowledge management and multi-commodity services. He joined CRU in 2005 following a 12-year career in the power sector. Paul is also a member of CRU's group executive team (paul.robinson@crugroup.com).

Jose Saavedra-Rosas is a mathematical engineer currently working as a principal consultant for Optika Solutions, Perth. Previously he worked as a senior lecturer in the Department of Mineral and Energy Economics and the Centre for Exploration Targeting at Curtin University. He has an MSc in Operations Management and a PhD in Natural Resources Engineering (charango.chile@gmail.com).

Morgan Trench recently completed a degree in physics and computational science at the Australian National University (morgan.trench@gmail.com).

"There are many arts and sciences of which a miner should not be ignorant. First, there is philosophy, that he may discern the origin, cause and nature of subterranean things; for then he will be able to dig out the veins easily and advantageously, and to obtain more abundant results from his mining. Secondly, there is medicine, that he may be able to look after his diggers and other workmen...Thirdly, follows astronomy, that he may know the divisions of the heavens and from them judge the directions of the veins. Fourthly, there is the science of surveying that he may be able to estimate how deep a shaft should be sunk... Fifthly, his knowledge of arithmetical science should be such that he may calculate the cost to be incurred in the machinery and the working of the mine. Sixthly, his learning must comprise architecture, that he himself may construct the various machines and timber work required underground... Next, he must have knowledge of drawing, that he can draw plans of his machinery. Lastly, there is the law, especially that dealing with metals, that he may claim his own rights, that he may undertake the duty of giving others his opinion on legal matters, that he may not take another man's property and so make trouble for himself, and that he may fulfil his obligations to others according to the law."

—Georgius Agricola, *De Re Metallica* (1556), trans. H. C. and L. H. Hoover (1950), 3-4

CONTENTS

Foreword 1
About this book 3

Part 1: In the Minerals Boardroom 7

1. Boardroom spill at Aussie gold miner: Vote now 9
2. The purpose of exploration and mining company boards 12
3. The Magna Carta of exploration governance – concise edition 15
4. Women on mining boards – a brief background check 18
5. Ten mining boardroom conundrums 20
6. Boardroom confinement without parole 22
7. Wise counsel for women (and men) on mining company boards 24
8. How to make a compelling argument for anything 26
9. Boardroom spill motions defeated at Aussie gold miner 28
10. Ten quotable steps towards boardroom effectiveness 31

Key Insights: In the Minerals Boardroom 34

Part 2: On Strategic Management 37

11. Robin Hood meets the rapidly receding mining boom 39
12. Top ten strategy essentials 41
13. Strategy deliberations – take CARE 44
14. Beware non-core assets 46
15. Promoting mining heresy – not once but twice 48
16. A $200 million boardroom dilemma 51
17. $200 million acquisition voted down 53
18. Creating value in emerging resources companies – think exploration 56
19. Towards the 'DNA' of emerging mineral resources companies 58
20. Poker in the exploration boardroom 60
21. Another $200M mining strategy conundrum 62

22. Three paths to mining industry growth – buy, sell, explore! 64
23. Innovation strategies: Beyond slow pizzas 67
Key Insights: On Strategic Management 70

Part 3: Looking to the Future 73

24. Beyond FUBAR forecasts 75
25. Why equity analysts are always wrong 79
26. The future of mining 'GDP' 82
27. Women on mining boards hits all-time high 83
28. Return of the mid-tier miner? 85
29. Mining 2040: An industry under siege 87
30. Mining 2040: The commodity crusades 91
31. Mining 2040: Major miners as counting houses 95
32. Mining 2040: Peasants' revolt 99
33. Tales from the past: The reinvention of mineral exploration 103
Key Insights: Looking to the Future 106

Part 4: At the Coal Face 107

34. Mark Twain on mine management 109
35. Avoiding Keystone Cops syndrome 112
36. Mining professional or strategy consultant? 114
37. Mining costs demystified 116
38. Cost focus – be careful what you wish for 119
39. Mining cost escalation – lest we forget 121
40. High morale fosters high achievers 123
41. A little more conversation… 125
42. Ask not what your company can do for you… 127
43. The undercover KPI 129
44. Managing through the downturn 132
Key Insights: At the Coal Face 135

Part 5: On Competitiveness and Mining Excellence 137

45. From mediocrity to capability 139
46. Mining emperors wear few clothes 141
47. Mining World Cup 2014 – Australia thrashed 143
48. All is not well with gold 146

49. Large mining companies: Capability lost? 148
50. On mining juniors: A view from the city 150
51. The best way is up: Crafting a winning strategy 152
52. Lateral thinking – there is always a way 154
53. Grade: The king – or serf – of gold orebodies 156
54. Struggling with bureaucracy? Introduce adhocracy 158
55. The Real Housewives of Mining 161
Key Insights: On Competitiveness and Mining Excellence 164

Part 6: On Exploration Strategy 165

56. Why big companies should explore 167
57. Is exploration truly high risk? 170
58. Where are the mines of tomorrow? Hiding in plain sight 172
59. Towards 'Big Exploration' 175
60. The X-Files on mineral exploration: Building a perfect team 177
61. The X-Files on new exploration search space 180
62. Corporate excellence in exploration 185
63. Large company volunteer required: Exploration champion 187
64. Mystery in the exploration boardroom 190
Key Insights: On Exploration Strategy 192

Part 7: On Exploration Management 195

65. Goldilocks on exploration portfolio management 197
66. The wheat from the chaff of overseas exploration 199
67. What explorers should ask brokers 201
68. Battleships – the all-new exploration game 203
69. Exploration drill targeting – the sequel 205
70. Sequencing of exploration techniques matters 208
71. My Prospect (Kitchen) Rules 210
72. Trivial Pursuit – special mineral explorers' edition 212
73. Which exploration personality are you? 214
74. Measuring success – in sport and exploration 218
75. "Make a discovery stupid": On measuring exploration company MD performance 220
76. On exploration remuneration – the hard line 222
Key Insights: On Exploration Management 225

Part 8: Of Mineral Economics and Finance 227
77. The commodity cycle sundial 228
78. Beyond China – why some commodities are profitable (and others not) 231
79. Getting into bismuth 235
80. Reasons to love uranium 239
81. The ultimate hot metal – radium 242
82. Mining investment myth busters 244
83. Gearing up for mining's future leaders 246
84. The market is abysmal – so what must change? 249

Key Insights: Of Mineral Economics and Finance 251

Part 9: Of Mineral Policy and Mining Regulation 253
85. Three rules to build a resources economy 255
86. The forgotten economic potential of new mineral discovery 257
87. Quiz time: Where in the world is your state? 259
88. Global competition for the exploration dollar 262
89. Towards the most competitive exploration on Earth 264
90. A report card to Australia's mining ministers on exploration: Could do better 267
91. The emperor's new royalties 269
92. The three golden rules of mining royalties 271
93. Countdown to a new Western Australian gold royalty: 4, 3, 2, 1... 273
94. The perception of mining – a social licence reality check 275
95. Social licence – a NIMBY perspective 277

Key Insights: Of Mineral Policy and Mining Regulation 280

Bibliography 283
Index 287

FOREWORD

If you are a decision-maker in the mineral resources sector, whether from the private or the public sector, or else if you aspire to become one in the foreseeable future, perhaps in the boardroom of a listed resources company, then you are on the right track by having picked up a copy of this book.

I commend it to you as a valuable read. It is a book that will entertain you whilst also potentially influencing your business thinking and perspective. It is therefore a pleasure to write a brief foreword to *Strictly (Mining) Boardroom – A Practitioner's Guide for Next Generation Directors*.

Mineral commodity markets undergo constant change, requiring that all companies respond very rapidly to mitigate business risk and to seize potential opportunities. Companies must act fast to anticipate market developments and then maximise opportunities therefrom. With hindsight we observe that all too few companies prepare themselves sufficiently or have the capability and culture to seize market opportunities in a timely fashion. Such challenges are not limited to the private sector. Governments the world over, from Australia to Zambia, are also constantly working hard to unlock the full economic potential and the flow-on community benefits that a dynamic resources sector can bring.

For the minerals sector to enjoy greater success into the future both companies and governments need to constantly seek out ways to improve. Making great strides forward in the minerals sector, consistent with the philosophies discussed in this book, requires that companies and governments are successful in 'growing the economic pie' that is the global resources sector rather than each stakeholder aiming to just take a larger slice at the expense of others.

This book forms a useful companion to all those industry stakeholders who wish to think a little deeper on how 'business gets done around here' and how it might improve in numerous ways into the future. From the best practices in the boardroom right through to the way that you choose to interact with your frontline workforce, this book has the potential to act as a catalyst towards finding better ways of doing things. If reading it merely causes you to pause and to think about doing something differently in your workplace it has already succeeded in its aim.

Allan Trench is a Professor at The University of Western Australia (UWA) Business School where his "Strategic Management of Resources Companies" Masters of Business Administration (MBA) course, delivered jointly with John Sykes, receives very positive reviews. Future MBA students at UWA and beyond now have a valuable new book to accompany their strategy development thinking that is a far more entertaining read than the vast majority of academic tomes they will encounter during their studies.

Enjoy the read and think about new ways to improve the way we do business in the minerals sector as a consequence.

Mark Barnaba
AM, CitWA, BCom (Hons) (UWA), MBA (Harvard)

Mark Barnaba is Chairman, The University of Western Australia (UWA) Business School Board; Adjunct Professor, Investment Banking & Finance, UWA Business School; Chairman, Macquarie Group, Western Australia; Chairman, Global Resources Group, Macquarie Capital; Non-Executive Director, Fortescue Metals Group; Chairman, Black Swan State Theatre Company

ABOUT THIS BOOK

It has now been over three years since the publication of the companion book to this one *Strictly (Mining) Boardroom – Management Insights from Inside the Resources Sector*. Those three years have proven to be very difficult ones for the resources industry in general – and especially for the smaller exploration companies within the sector who have struggled to maintain meaningful activity in the face of dwindling investor support. Excessive pessimism prevails across the sector at the time of writing. With that backdrop however, there is perhaps no better time to release this book as a form of call-to-arms to the entire resources sector at both an individual and collective level to 'lift our game'. The challenges from lower commodity prices only serve to amplify both the need and opportunity for us to improve as an industry.

The infamous Warren Buffett quote that "only when the tide goes out do you discover who has been swimming naked" is apt. This book contains information on the strategic equivalent of a minerals sector 'wetsuit' – or perhaps, bearing in mind the Renaissance man turned miner described by Georgius Agricola at the beginning of this book, even 'preliminary drawings for a future life-boat'.

Despite the tough market conditions, the first *Strictly (Mining) Boardroom* book is quite popular – albeit that the text has yet to 'go viral' so-to-speak. Indeed, it is a standing joke amongst our closest academic colleagues that the Kindle version of *Strictly (Mining) Boardroom* has been the number one best-seller on amazon.com for books with that exact same title for each of the last three years. Joking aside, *Strictly (Mining) Boardroom* has proven to be an invaluable text to accompany a number of executive short courses, fulfilling the role of thought-companion to discussions held with industry groups and with various post-graduate classes. Participants in such courses have hailed from many different parts of the world – including over 10 African countries, Brazil, Chile, Colombia, Peru and Uruguay in South America, plus the likes of China, Fiji, Indonesia, Kazakhstan, Laos, Mongolia, Papua New Guinea, the Philippines, South Korea, Thailand, Vietnam and Uzbekistan across the developed and developing countries of Asia and Oceania. Of course minerals professionals from Australia, the United Kingdom, Canada, the United States and New Zealand have added valuable perspectives too. The common goal of all those attending such courses has been to seek to better understand the varied factors that drive success and failure in our industry, all the way from the boardroom to the frontline workforce. Critically, course participants have come from both the private sector and public sectors. It is only with innovative co-operation between mining companies and governments that the true potential of the minerals sector can be realised. As yet, we are not even close to contemplating that full potential, let alone capturing it.

The aim of the book you are reading now is similar to that of the previous *Strictly (Mining) Boardroom*. In a nutshell, this book's intent is to act as a catalyst to those charged with authority for decision-making within our industry and in governments to 'think smart' in arriving at future decisions under inevitable conditions of significant uncertainty.

Risks abound in the commodities industries as they do for all business activity. Understanding those risks is a prerequisite to becoming an effective decision-maker. In a small way, this book will help you to understand risk in the sector – including those risks that are specific to an asset and company – and equally those risks that are principally systemic in their nature.

This is neither a technical nor an academic book. It reflects a collection of experiences derived from interactions with senior decision-makers whilst aiming to improve the strategy and effectiveness of minerals sector organisations.

My colleague John Sykes joins as an author in this book – recognising John's co-authorship of many of the articles that have come together to form *Strictly (Mining) Boardroom – A Practitioner's Guide for Next Generation Directors*. The (short) chapters in this book have been published as the *Strictly Boardroom* columns on the Miningnews.net industry portal throughout late 2012 to 2016. No doubt John himself is one of those next generation directors to which the book's title refers. He already leads a successful mineral economics consultancy, serving executives and other industry decision-makers, providing an outsider's and bottom-up perspective on the minerals industry boardroom, to complement my experiences.

We would like to thank all those readers who have provided feedback over the years – and in some cases pushback too – in respect of the thoughts and takeaways championed in these pages. Such debate is very healthy. The overarching message on which all seem in agreement is that as an industry we need to get a whole lot better at what we do – and to do so we must constantly entertain the thought that there are no doubt far more efficient and effective ways to deliver upon stakeholder needs and expectations.

So let's just do that.

The book's content has been arranged into nine parts – which, in a manner reminiscent of Agricola, collectively span the many subject areas that intertwine to present challenges to the successful management of resources companies. That is, decision-makers in the sector must have the requisite skill-sets to make contributions In the Minerals Boardroom (Part One); On Strategic Management (Part Two), be forward-thinking (Looking to the Future, Part Three), and yet also relate to the day-to-day challenges of working the sector – discussed in At the Coal Face (Part Four). The way in which some companies are more successful than others in creating value in the resources sector is discussed in Competitiveness and Mining Excellence (Part Five). Further, On Exploration Strategy (Part Six) and On Exploration Management (Part Seven) are of particular relevance to the plethora of smaller resources companies aiming to become next generation larger minerals and energy companies. An understanding Of Mineral Economics and Finance

(Part Eight) and last but not least also a working knowledge Of Mineral Policy and Mining Regulation (Part Nine) seek to round out the knowledge-base required for minerals companies to deliver excellence performance.

Dr Allan Trench
Perth, 2016

NOTE: Throughout the book we sometimes refer to the author as "Your scribe", by which we mean either Allan Trench or John Sykes or both.

PART 1
In the Minerals Boardroom

Part One of this book finds us "In the Minerals Boardroom", with the aim to document and challenge current practices with a view to improving boardroom effectiveness. We start with a case study conundrum for you relating to the right composition of a board for a fictional Australian gold miner. In "Boardroom spill at Aussie gold miner: Vote now" the incumbent board is subject to a spill motion by a discontented major shareholder aiming to improve board effectiveness by introducing a new generation of directors. Should shareholders side with the current board, or is it time for change? There is of course no definitive answer to this question – but the conundrum aims to draw out your own initial impressions on the ideal minerals sector board of directors.

To improve boardroom effectiveness we must first understand what it is that boards actually do. With the assistance of some industry-hardened MBA and mineral economics students we next tackle "The purpose of exploration and mining company boards". Corporate governance, individual expertise, management mentoring, stakeholder engagement and strategic guidance emerge as the key roles of industry directors.

We first consider governance in "The Magna Carta of exploration governance – concise edition". Efficient and effective governance is of course good governance too – allowing the board to devote its collective skills and expertise towards guiding the company forward.

It is 'what you know', not just 'who you know' that gets you into the boardroom in the first place. The short chapter "Women on mining boards – a brief background check" seeks to discover the skillsets and experiences the next generation of directors are bringing to mining company boards, and to consider the role of gender balance in boardroom effectiveness.

"Ten mining boardroom conundrums" gives a flavour of some of the many leadership, strategic, shareholder, analytical, technical and commercial challenges a minerals industry director should be prepared for.

The many challenges facing mineral industry directors are then raised in "Boardroom confinement without parole" which shares some personal experiences on effective directorship. Respect, patience, hard-work, honesty, thrift, a shareholder mindset and a commitment to doing 'real work' all make an appearance.

"Wise counsel for women (and men) on mining company boards" then seeks out the advice of an older and wiser colleague who offers supportive words for women (and new male directors) entering the boardroom. The key messages are that in practice boardroom communication is not as good as it should be – and that if steps are taken to improve the situation then everyone will be better off.

Similar logic comes to the fore in "How to make a compelling argument for anything" – in that a successful director is one who is a capable, indeed a compelling, communicator.

We return to the conundrum set at the beginning of Part One to find the "Boardroom spill motions defeated at Aussie gold miner". The short chapter then looks at some of the skills and experiences the next generation of minerals industry directors need to develop, and some that incumbent executives need to extend their longevity.

Last but not least we seek out boardroom advice from a number of iconic figures from Napoleon through to Dale Carnegie on subjects such as process, communication and financing in "Ten quotable steps towards boardroom effectiveness".

1. BOARDROOM SPILL AT AUSSIE GOLD MINER: VOTE NOW

8 Feb 2016 Strictly Boardroom asks you to choose between two competing sets of directors seeking election to the board of an Aussie gold miner. Will you vote for the incumbents or the challengers?

How should a minerals company optimise the collective skillset of its board for success? The answer to that question remains far from clear. To illustrate, here is a case study* of a boardroom spill at an emerging Australian gold miner to showcase some of the practical difficulties.

Strictly Boardroom has developed two sets of pen pictures for directors competing to occupy the same boardroom roles – the incumbents and the challengers. The company fully owns a gold mine in the Goldfields region of Western Australia producing around 120,000 ounces of gold per annum from both open pit and underground sources.

A disgruntled significant shareholder has called an extraordinary general meeting (EGM) seeking to elect a new board. The resolutions call for the replacement of all non-executive directors (NEDs) – with the expectation that a new 'managing director (MD) in waiting' would be appointed to replace the sitting MD, should the board spill succeed.

Both sets of directors have positive attributes – but each also has clear knowledge gaps. So which set of directors would you vote for? First, let's profile the incumbent board.

Percy – "Chairman and Lawyer, FAICD" – A semi-retired lawyer with over 25 years' boardroom experience, Percy has pretty much 'seen it all before' – with the many scars to prove it. Percy made a fortune in the first nickel boom and has taken an interest in the minerals sector ever since. Percy chairs two other boards; one a speculative technology play and more recently a new lithium exploration hopeful.

Roger – "The High-Profile MD" – A mining engineer of over 20 years' experience, Roger is amongst the first to set up his company conference booth and take to centre stage at mining conferences worldwide. Promoting the company is clearly a key strength. Attention to operational detail is a potential area for concern, however. The mine manager last saw Roger in August of last year when he brought a gaggle of brokers to the company's sole operating gold mine *en route* to the annual Diggers and Dealers conference. Roger first worked for Percy in the 1990s and has helmed a number of his companies since.

Hilary – "The Banker" – An early career on Wall Street for Hilary ended abruptly in the '87 crash. Returning to Australia, a period at a strategy consulting firm saw Hilary lead organisational restructures across the banking, retail and utilities sectors. Hilary is a lead independent director on two other company boards; one in online retail and a second focused on transport/logistics provision. Hilary's technical knowledge of gold mining is not as strong as her financial acumen and governance expertise. Hilary provides corporate advice to some of the other companies Percy is involved with.

Miles – "The Explorer" – Miles is a geologist – who hails from the days before computers were invented. Miles undertakes regular far-flung mine and field visits linked to international conferences and has written several papers on the nuances of gold deposits. Miles reads and comments upon the geological sections of the board papers in detail – and is a staunch advocate for maintaining a strong exploration budget but he shows little interest in the detail of the company's finances. Miles likes Roger as he is always keen to promote exploration successes.

Now for the challengers:

Angela – "Proposed Chair, Self-Made Investor" – Angela made her first fortune in New York as a boutique fund manager shorting technology stocks in the tech-wreck. Angela holds degrees in Commerce and Economics. Turning her attention to mineral commodities she then ran a successful commodities desk at a major bank in London before returning to Australia to spend more time with her parents. Angela holds a portfolio of significant shareholdings in technology and mining stocks but has not previously served on a minerals company board. The shareholder who has called the EGM is a business acquaintance who asked Angela to stand for board election. Angela may just be the busiest person you have ever met.

Rebecca – "MD-in-waiting" – One of the first generation female mine managers, Rebecca has successfully held on-site general manager roles at gold and base metals mining operations both in Africa and Australia for global diversified mining companies. Now considering a career move from a larger company to an emerging miner, Rebecca has indicated to Angela that she would be keen to take on the challenge of her first MD role should the 'challengers' unseat the 'incumbents' to win board control.

Joshua – "Corporate Adviser" – Joshua is a chartered accountant, initially gaining experience with a global firm before leaving to set up a boutique corporate advisory business. Joshua flourished in the post-global financial crisis (GFC) resurgence of the mining sector, playing a role in numerous exploration initial public offerings (IPOs) and backdoor listings. Joshua also recently completed his part-time MBA and has just returned from a study tour of technology start-ups in Silicon Valley. Josh is a renowned deal-maker and has both friends and enemies in the junior mining sector resulting from past transactions.

Chris – "The Geoscientist" – Chris worked in state geological surveys for a decade after graduating as a geologist. He is credited with developing an innovative online interface for minerals explorers to access open file and other public domain geoscience data. Chris has also worked as a contract exploration geologist for a geological services firm and was involved in some minor gold discoveries in the Northern Territory. For the last two years he has managed his own very successful geological consultancy. Chris has never worked outside Australia.

So there you have it. In practice, the choice would be to simply vote for one board 'ticket' or for the other. In this fictitious case study however you have far more voting freedom to select a 'pick and mix' board.

So do you back Percy and his experienced incumbents? Or Angela and the next generation challengers? Or some combination of both perhaps? Are there additional key skill-sets that are missing from both set of directors?

Calls for a poll of proxies are most welcome.

---

* Any resemblance to a real company and to specific individuals is unintentional.

2. THE PURPOSE OF EXPLORATION AND MINING COMPANY BOARDS

12 Oct 2015 Strictly Boardroom reports the results of an informal survey into the *raison d'être* of resources sector company boards and directors. The results will surprise you.

With annual general meeting (AGM) season looming large, the role of boards on both exploration and mining companies will once again hit the spotlight. Shareholders will vote on remuneration reports, on director re-elections and in some cases on the likes of option packages and other incentive schemes. Questions from the floor as to whether the boards are 'doing something' about the current difficult market conditions will no doubt be ubiquitous.

Recently, we had the opportunity to work with a group of masters' students on the topic of the resource sector management* – and the question of the purposes of the board inevitably became front and centre during part of the class discussion. The group was largely drawn from professionals within the minerals and energy sectors, typically with up to ten years' experience and sometimes more.

Rather than espouse from the textbook as to the role of the board, we chose to turn around the discussion somewhat. We asked the group to decide what the role of the board was themselves and to rank the strategic importance of the various facets of board remit in terms of the board's contribution to the company, firstly for exploration companies and also for mining companies.

The results surprised us – and we suspect may surprise you too.

For example, here are the answers from two different teams within the group as to the 'Top 5' value-adding duties performed by a board of an exploration company starting with the most important.

Team 1: Exploration board value-add

1. Governance
2. Networking
3. Specific individual expertise
4. Funding (both facilitating and buying shares themselves)
5. Motivating the team.

Team 2: Exploration board value-add

1. Represent shareholder interests
2. Governance
3. Fact-based assessment
4. A willingness to make decisions
5. Mentor support for management.

Now to the corresponding answers for a mining company board as opposed to an explorer. The lists from two other teams in the group on this question read as follows:

Team 3: Mining board value-add

1. 'What they know' – their experience
2. Independent objective counsel
3. Governance
4. Engagement with management
5. Instilling values.

Team 4: Mining board value-add
1. Set strategy
2. Auditing
3. Taking a shareholder perspective
4. Investor relations
5. Stakeholder management.

So what do you make of that lot? For Strictly Boardroom the takeaways are as follows:

- Firstly that governance in its various forms is more prominent on the lists and ranked higher than we initially anticipated. One might have considered governance as something of a 'given' whereas the groups clearly see this as particularly valuable. Perhaps this explains the popularity of the various board governance professional short courses now available.

- Secondly that 'what you know' (bringing a key skill-set including decision-making) ranks equally and potentially higher than 'who you know' (networking). For those seeking to get into directorial roles this seems important too, as sometimes the career development dialogue is more often focused on networking, when in reality it seems more likely you will be appointed for your skills and experience.

- Thirdly that tight engagement with management in a supportive context looms large as a value-add, in particular mentorship, which it is worth noting is at least as beneficial to senior management as it is recent graduates.

- Finally, that the role of the board does not stop at the boardroom door. Stakeholder management, investor relations and involvement in funding all rate a mention. Again for those interested in the world of directorships, this is a point worth consideration – the expectation that directors will subscribe to share placements in the company can mean that directing becomes an expensive activity, especially in a struggling exploration sector when share prices are falling.

What particularly surprised Strictly Boardroom was the infrequent appearance of strategy development on the lists (aside from Team 4), although decision-making and fact-based assessment are no doubt both inclusive of strategy. Also there was no obvious split of duties between an exploration board and mining board. You might have expected that relevant technical skills would be highlighted more in the case of exploration boards. Nor was there mention of the role and impact of the level of board diversity upon decision-making.

So there you have it. Being a good resources sector director includes governing to best practice levels, bringing your individual skills to the table, acting as a mentor to management and also 'getting out there' on behalf of the company. Shareholders will decide whether they are getting good value from their respective boards in these areas (and others too?) when voting at their respective AGMs.

---

* With due to credit to the 2015 "Resource Sector Management" class on the Curtin University MSc Mineral Economics and MBA. You know who you are.

3. THE MAGNA CARTA OF EXPLORATION GOVERNANCE – CONCISE EDITION

16 Feb 2015 Strictly Boardroom looks at best practice corporate governance for exploration companies and distils over 35 pages of compliance into what really matters – a few bullet-points.

Strictly Boardroom has just spent the best part of an evening reading a legal draft corporate governance document for a junior explorer that proved to be highly amusing, albeit unintentionally so. Despite being flagged as a short-form document, the prose still stretched to over 35 pages of 10 point-font.

Why so amusing then? The humorous side of the tome requires an academic bent to comprehend. Basically, the governance document had no clear hierarchy to it – at least none that was evident to this reader. The apparently random introduction of undefined but prescriptive governance concepts in the document made it a witty read. The "Where's Wally?" approach became to guess just where and when another out-of-context piece of governance counsel would appear amongst the many pages.

Also making random entrances were bland definitions of governance concepts and protocols that were not relevant to the part of the document either immediately preceding or just following the insertion of the definitions.

Next, the extensive descriptions of board committees would have made perhaps justifiable reading for the internal audit function at a major miner but had far less relevance to a micro-cap explorer.

Eventually it all became too much for Strictly Boardroom. Your scribe gave up on the red-lining world of tracked-change editing and opted instead for the red-wine world with a bottle of Cape Mentelle Shiraz.

Strictly Boardroom suspects that he is not the only director of a mineral explorer who has suffered glazed eyes upon reading generic corporate governance material.

Targeted governance guidance to overseeing the mineral exploration sector is needed. So without further ado here are ten suggested corporate governance 'commandments' suitable for Australian Securities Exchange (ASX)-listed minerals exploration companies:

1. The company never rips-off its shareholders: The board ensures that all monies invested in the company are spent judiciously, with funds directed towards mineral exploration discovery as the principal focus of all budgets – whether capital or operating expenditure.

2. The company maintains a suitably qualified, experienced and competent board: The board will always be of a size (and thus cost) appropriate for the stage of development and activity level of the company and be linked in to the company's exploration business by knowledge of, and contacts in, the industry.

3. The board of the company will continuously work hard for its shareholders: As guidance, non-executive directors will

commit the equivalent of a minimum of two full days per month to advancing the company and substantially more time should events so dictate.
4. The board of the company invests in the company on the same terms as other shareholders when such opportunities present.
5. The board will ensure that management does the job they are employed for, being mineral exploration and not principally administrative management.
6. The company board will contribute to the company's technical thinking over and above just maintaining best practice corporate governance standards.
7. The board will not unduly interfere with management doing their job. If, however, the management team proves unable to complete jobs adequately, the board will replace it in a timely fashion.
8. The board will ensure that the company does not run out of money, leaving no stone unturned in so doing, however being "market aware" in the method of capital raising.
9. The board will appoint a suitably qualified and competent company secretary to do what competent company secretaries always do.
10. The company will always comply: The compliance commandment is simply one commandment of a total of ten – no more. That is, the tenth commandment reads that the board will ensure the company acts ethically, adheres to all laws including disclosure and reporting, remunerates fairly based on performance, limits wherever possible the company's environmental impact, does not discriminate in any way, engages appropriately with community and stakeholders, values and manages all forms of diversity, has due regard for the health and safety of employees and actively identifies and then appropriately manages business risks and any conflicts of interest, whether perceived or real.

Simple really. So what is missing? Is there a case for an eleventh commandment? How about that the company will (one day) make a mineral discovery?

4. WOMEN ON MINING BOARDS – A BRIEF BACKGROUND CHECK

30 Dec 2013 Strictly Boardroom seeks out the professional backgrounds of women on mining company boards and finds that finance places first, with 'daylight' second.

Your scribe has a lot of work ahead, with one research study (subject to funding) aiming to review the backgrounds of more than 800 company directors across the mining and metals sector.

The study will, among other things, look at the respective roles of geologists, mining engineers, metallurgists and also commerce, legal and finance professionals in guiding the mining sector forward.

Analysing 800 biographies will take quite some time.

The research is yet to be completed, however, a small snapshot of what is to come is provided using the more manageable dataset of women on mining sector boards.

Here are some preliminary findings of that short-form study which quickly reviews the curriculum vitae (CVs) of the 45 female directors that sit across the largest 150 minerals and mining companies (excluding oil and gas).

Before revealing the findings of the study some obvious caveats apply.

Like most senior professionals, the female directors in this study have added many strings to their bow during very distinguished careers. So pigeonholing their professional backgrounds as hailing either singularly from finance, legal, geology, engineering and the like oversimplifies the diversity of skill-sets these directors bring to the boardroom table.

Many have not one but several degrees, for example, and many have also enjoyed a number of career changes on their way to the boardroom table.

That said, some career themes are nevertheless very clear in the data – with the original university background of the director used as the principal means to classify professional background.

Judgment calls are needed in assigning categories. In some cases the brief biographical information on company web pages proved insufficient to even make a generic call. These directors were assigned an 'unclear' professional background.

So to the results then – observers of boardroom composition may or may not be surprised by the findings.

Here are the backgrounds of the 45 women on mining company boards:

- Finance (investment banking and accounting): 16
- Lawyers: 6
- Economics/commerce: 5
- Other science (not geology): 5
- Engineer: 2
- Geology: 2
- Metallurgist: 2
- Education: 1
- Politics: 1
- Unclear: 5

The insights? To some degree, those must await the larger dataset, which in many ways is a control dataset to the micro-snapshot presented here.

Clearly the first finding is that when it comes to professional background, it is finance first and then daylight second.

Lawyers are no great surprise in placing second, with those from a commerce and economics background rounding out the numbers on the commercial side of the boardroom table.

That graduates of other sciences (physics, biology, chemistry) outnumber geologists is perhaps a surprise.

Similarly, the relative lack of engineers is a surprise too.

When it comes to women in the boardroom, those from a commercial, legal and finance background far outnumber those with technical training.

If women on boards were compared to a form of parliament, the "Finance Party" would clearly have the numbers – especially if governing in coalition with those from a legal and commerce background.

So will the numbers change materially when the men join the dataset? That question awaits a far larger study but if Strictly Boardroom were asked to guess at the answer it would be a no rather than a yes.

What do you think?

5. TEN MINING BOARDROOM CONUNDRUMS

21 Jul 2014 Strictly Boardroom picks out ten tricky questions of relevance to the contemporary minerals sector and asks you to avoid sitting on the fence in choosing your answers to each.

Strictly Boardroom had the pleasure of spending a week on a course with a group of resources sector managers who came from several professional disciplines and who also brought recent experience across a variety of mineral commodities.

The week was great fun – especially with the freedom to explore the many nuances of management theory and practices and to also look closely at different minerals industry corporate strategies, whether successful or otherwise.

The intensive course closed off with a brief exam in which ten short questions were asked of each participant. Questions were specifically designed such that the 'right' answer to each one was somewhat debatable. For some questions, a right answer may not even exist. Nevertheless, each person was asked to take sides and to be definitive with an answer to each question.

The ten questions are reproduced below and you are invited to form your own view on each. As stated above, a number of the questions have highly debatable 'right' answers – whereas other questions appear to have clear consensus answer across our industry. Not that Strictly Boardroom's answers are better than any others but for the record these are revealed at the end. What do you think?

1. Does a mining company need an inspirational leader? *Yes* or *No*.
2. "Our vision is to deliver superior shareholder returns through mining and exploration while maintaining our social licence to operate." Is this a good vision statement? *Yes* or *No*.
3. "A good share register is a very open one, with no single shareholder holding above 5% equity." *Agree* or *Disagree*.
4. Should mine-site key performance indicator (KPI) bonus systems be predominantly annual, quarterly, monthly or weekly?
5. "Board members of small explorers are appointed predominantly for corporate governance purposes." *Agree* or *Disagree*.
6. "An emerging mining company (with one to three mines) is best served by appointing a commercial professional as its managing director." Do you agree? Answer *Yes* or *No*.
7. "Australian mining and exploration public company boards need more gender balance than at present." Do you agree? Answer *Yes* or *No*.
8. "Mining companies should proactively embrace 'lean mining' principles as a means to lower production costs." Do you agree? Answer *Yes* or *No*.
9. Which of the following is most important for an emerging single mine gold producer (~$100 million cap)? a) operational excellence; b) commercial/financial excellence?
10. "Scenario planning as a corporate strategy tool should be widely adopted in the minerals sector." *Yes* or *No*.

Strictly Boardroom's answers
1. No (but it helps).
2. No (too generic).
3. Disagree (several cornerstone shareholders can be a big help – but only if they behave themselves!)

4. Monthly (clearly there is no single answer here – but if forced to pick one then monthly).
5. Disagree (small company directors need a lot more than governance skills).
6. No (an operator with commercial acumen would be my pick).
7. Yes (the stats don't lie).
8. Yes (mining is decades behind other industries).
9. A (operational excellence – related to the answer in question 6).
10. Yes (we live in an uncertain world).

How many do we agree upon?

6. BOARDROOM CONFINEMENT WITHOUT PAROLE

17 Mar 2014 Strictly Boardroom suggests some lessons learnt in the minerals boardroom from the last decade of mining's booms and busts.

Asked to deliver an evening seminar to a Master of Business Administration (MBA) audience recently, your scribe opted to go with a 'lessons learnt' dialogue. Speaking to a seminar title of "Entering the corporate boardroom – be careful what you wish for", here are some of the suggested business takeaways of what the MBA audience can expect to experience in future across the boardroom table:

1. **On relationships:** Boardroom relationships grow very strong, which is a great upside to being a director but carries with it a potential downside akin to "doing business with friends".
2. **On conduct:** You will, on occasions, see the worst in people's behaviours – even from respected industry figures. Try your utmost not to reciprocate with equally poor behaviour when under personal pressure. Apologise to your boardroom colleagues when you fail!

3. **On workload:** Always aim to do more than is expected of you, without unduly stepping on the toes of the managing director or chair if in a non-executive director capacity. It is better for the board to not adopt your input than for you not to contribute.
4. **On detail:** Always ask when you are unclear on a particular issue. Chances are everyone else is unclear too!
5. **On appraisal:** Adopt a "no passengers" rule with candid board appraisal. This is a major challenge and, in my experience, most boards fail it.
6. **On mindset:** Always think like a shareholder – a small one – and you won't be too far off the mark.
7. **On austerity:** Be extra frugal with a company's money. Will your small shareholders really appreciate proliferation of company pens, hats, polo-shirts and jackets?
8. **More on austerity:** Fly economy (meaning cattle class) except (in some cases) on international flights that cross either of the poles or the equator.
9. **On meetings:** Do "real work" in board meetings – beyond best practice administration, regulation, risk management and governance.
10. **On feedback:** Expect to receive external criticism of key decisions you make. Listen, but do not let uninformed criticism influence you unduly. Finally, whatever you do, do not answer abusive texts from shareholders!

7. WISE COUNSEL FOR WOMEN (AND MEN) ON MINING COMPANY BOARDS

08 Apr 2013 The share of women in the mining sector, particularly in the boardroom, remains a hot topic – and one that will continue until boardroom gender balance further evolves. Strictly Boardroom has some sage counsel for women in the mining sector boardroom – courtesy of a wise old (male) friend.

Boardroom gender statistics is a topic that Strictly Boardroom has commented upon previously as it pertains to the minerals sector[1] – and a topic to which conversation returned recently with an old mentor and friend who is a veteran of numerous mining sector boards.

Rather than ask the same old questions of his friend (who wishes to remain anonymous) – such as should gender balance in the boardroom be mandated by quota – Strictly Boardroom thought to ask what one hopes is a more useful question. Specifically, what counsel would a veteran board member offer to an incoming female colleague in the minerals sector boardroom?

The answers surprised your scribe at first but upon reflection they seem spot on.

Here are the two principal pieces of advice.

> *"Don't ever take it that if you feel you are being ignored in the boardroom dialogue that it is a gender thing. It is perfectly normal and indeed quite usual for male non-executive directors to feel they are not being listened too also. For example, the managing director may ignore your comment and answer another question entirely. Similarly, the chairman may either ignore your comment in favour of keeping the meeting moving along – else may pay lip service to it and rapidly move on. Neither effect is gender driven – but neither makes for very good board performance either!"*

Next, on the technical aspects of exploration, mining and mineral processing[2] your scribe's mentor offered the following:

"Don't ever think that because some technical issue seems incomprehensible, obscure and odd that it may reflect the fact that you have not in your career had first-hand experience of [insert some specific aspect of geology, mining or metallurgy here]. Board members with lots more 'mine-time' than yourself are probably equally as confused as you are. Your lack of understanding is not your fault – so speak up. It more likely reflects management's inability to either: a) understand the issue themselves; or b) communicate even their limited understanding effectively."

Both the above snippets of counsel ring true.

Why? Despite having both an X and a Y chromosome, your scribe has often been ignored in the boardroom – as too it appears has my older colleague.

Similarly, your scribe admits to being confused on many occasions in the boardroom too, even in areas where his technical experience places him in a relatively strong position. As an example, ask your managing director to explain the relative benefits of various frequency domain versus time domain electromagnetic systems in ground versus airborne sulphide exploration and see what comes back!

A conclusion: how about the suggestion that increasing the number of X chromosomes in the minerals boardroom will not, of itself, lift company performance levels – despite research claiming that three or more females in the boardroom can achieve higher company performance in the general case. Aiming to improve intra-board communication may well do, however.

---

1 See "Exploration boardrooms slow to discover female directors" and "Women on mining boards – the top 100 companies" in Trench, A., (2013), *Strictly (Mining) Boardroom – Management Insights from Inside the Resources Sector*. Major Street Publishing, Highett, Vic., p27-31.

2 As short chapter 4 "Women on mining boards – a brief background check" earlier in Part One notes, the majority of women on mining boards have a non-technical background. Strictly Boardroom, of course, acknowledges that there are also many women in the mining sector working in technical roles (and even a few female directors with technical backgrounds) to which this second piece of counsel is less applicable.

8. HOW TO MAKE A COMPELLING ARGUMENT FOR ANYTHING

18 May 2015 Strictly Boardroom looks at the topic of negotiation – in the boardroom and beyond – and suggests a five-point plan might help.

There are some arguments you face in life that you can never win. For example, no amount of logic will get you into a late night establishment if the bouncers have taken a dislike to your overly casual attire or to your somewhat sporty footwear. Similarly, Strictly Boardroom last won a domestic argument back in 1991, getting to watch the rugby just as the game neared its end as his team lost.

In business however, the outcome of discussions at which contrasting and opposing viewpoints are tabled can often go in your favour – if your position is strong enough that is. Your chances will be maximised by using a framework known as referring the discussion to the "PANEL" – where the PANEL acronym calls for the judicious use of Precedent, Analogy, Numbers, Empathy and Logic. Good proponents of the PANEL framework prepare each of these attributes to support their viewpoint ahead of time – often winning the battle in the 'pre-meetings' before the actual negotiation takes place. So let's look a little deeper:

- **Precedent:** Those from a legal background are expert here. In formal terms, a precedent is a legal case establishing a principle or rule that a court or other judicial body adopts when deciding later cases with similar issues or facts based upon earlier trial results. Applied to business the use of precedent simply means researching the trigger points for previous decision-making and reminding decision-makers of key calls made in the past. For example, if projects are typically approved when the proponents volunteer to follow through and manage the next stage of advancement then building this into the proposal is a no-brainer.

- **Analogy:** Many people confuse analogy with precedent. Those proficient at the use of analogies realise that the rules are relaxed significantly from those pertaining to precedents.

Similes and metaphors can be wheeled out here too but should not be overdone else they can become distracting. Likewise, an analogy that doesn't stack up or requires too great a stretch of the imagination should be avoided. One of Apple's most basic analogies is so commonplace that we forget it was an analogy to begin with: your computer's desktop.

- **Numbers:** No business case will succeed in the absence of numbers. Avoiding garbage-in-garbage-out is critical of course. Good decision-makers apply a smell test to numbers – quickly identifying those that make little sense. Over-contriving a financial analysis to hit a corporate hurdle rate is to be avoided. Making overtly conservative assumptions and still achieving greater than a 15% return on investment is the way to go.

- **Empathy:** Understanding what makes those around the boardroom table tick is best practice in any negotiation or investment proposal. Some things will be sticking points to some people (usually those with the scars still showing from previous bad experience), whereas flexibility will exist in other areas in these very same people. Putting yourself in the position of those charged with making a final call on an issue helps.

- **Logic:** Logic, perhaps surprisingly, is the last element in the PANEL framework. Contrary to initial thinking it can both be the last and the least important aspect of the PANEL framework too. Dale Carnegie's *How to Win Friends and Influence People** has insightful and memorable words on the use of logic to win others over to your views. It pays to remember Carnegie's sage advice that "you can't win an argument (with logic)" – so aim not to start one in the first place.

---

* Carnegie, D. 1936. *How to Win Friends and Influence People*. Simon and Schuster, New York.

9. BOARDROOM SPILL MOTIONS DEFEATED AT AUSSIE GOLD MINER

15 Feb 2016 Strictly Boardroom reveals the votes on the spill motion resolutions to unseat the board of an Aussie gold miner.

A sincere thanks to all those who provided feedback[1] to the conundrum in Chapter 1 on whether to unseat or retain the board at a 120,000 ounce per annum Australian gold miner[2]. With the votes all now counted – the incumbent board will remain in place – but nevertheless with some interesting insights as to how the board might be improved in future.

A brief reminder of the sitting board:

Percy – "Chairman, FAICD" – A semi-retired lawyer with over 25 years' boardroom experience.

Roger – "The High-Profile MD" – A mining engineer of over 20 years' experience. Strong at company promotion; hands-off on operating matters.

Hilary – "The NED Banker" – Lead independent director on two other companies: governance and strategy expertise.

Miles – "The Explorer" – The geologist who hails from the days before computers were invented.

Now to the challengers:

Angela – "Proposed Chair, Self-Made Investor" – Angela holds a portfolio of significant shareholdings in technology and mining stocks but has not previously served on a minerals company board.

Rebecca – "MD-in-waiting" – One of the first generation female mine managers, Rebecca has successfully held on-site general manager roles at gold and base metals mining operations both in Africa and Australia for global diversified mining companies.

Joshua – "Corporate Adviser" – Joshua is a chartered accountant and also is a renowned deal-maker. He has both friends and enemies in the junior mining sector, resulting from past transactions.

Chris – "The Geoscientist" – Chris worked in state geological surveys for a decade. For the last two years he has managed his own very successful geological consultancy. Chris has never worked outside Australia.

Miles attracted the equal highest votes, seven, alongside Rebecca. The strong vote for Miles recognises his worldly geological knowledge and detailed understanding of gold geology – easily outpointing his younger rival Chris who polled the least of all potential directors with Angela at just three votes. Chris clearly needs more experience under his belt and might consider taking on a role to expand his exploration experience beyond Australia. Miles on the other hand should do what he does best – which is to help Roger spot exploration upside at the mine and ensure high quality mine geology. Miles should be more diligent in reviewing the financials – but with Percy and Hilary covering that base well he can perhaps be forgiven his lack of great interest in the accounting numbers. Whilst it was unstated, the company will no doubt be performing strongly in financial terms in the current gold price environment coupled with a relatively weak Australian dollar and little cost pressure.

Percy, at six votes, scored twice the votes of his challenger for the chair, Angela. Percy is a wily old dog who won't be unseated easily. No doubt he cosied up to the dissident shareholder who called the spill motion in the lead-up to the shareholder meeting (and in practice would have most likely avoided the issue reaching the actual meeting itself). Percy will now be on his toes to avoid a repeat occurrence of a spill.

Roger received strong support – likely reflecting his prowess at investor relations. But he was actually out-polled by MD-in-waiting Rebecca, who looks a great catch if she were to join the company, perhaps in the role of executive director and '2IC' to Roger; although instigating such a move would seem harsh on the incumbent mine manager at the company who is responsible for the company's sole cash generating asset. Perhaps bringing Rebecca aboard would be a forerunner to the company seeking to acquire a second operating asset either in Australia or abroad (given her background in operations management in Africa for example).

Hilary polled five votes – two more than Angela, the financially astute challenger for chair who failed to woo shareholders being seen as the principal instigator of the uncertainty at board level. Hilary also outpolled Joshua, who has many too many enemies to be universally popular as a new director. Shareholders and fellow directors may be wary of Joshua's motives as a prolific dealer in junior companies. Notwithstanding her strong showing, Hilary should nevertheless seek to improve her technical knowledge of geology, mining and metallurgy.

The suggestion of appointing an outside director unconnected to either board 'ticket' has merit and wily Percy may have discussed just this with the dissident significant shareholder. In such board-level tussles, it is not uncommon for an additional director to appear 'from nowhere' – but likely be linked to the dissident shareholder in some form or other as their representative, independent of their own suitability on an individual merit basis.

As to any skill-sets missing from the board, there is no director with specific environmental, community management or heritage credentials (Percy's generic legal skill-set aside). The area of community engagement and best practice environmental management is becoming ever more critical to companies to maintain a social licence to operate. As such it is a likely area of growth in terms of the background of next generation minerals sector board members.

So there you have it. Percy and his experienced incumbents survive and Angela and the next generation challengers must lick their wounds and wait another day. Their time will come but both Joshua and Chris in particular need a few more years' experience under their belt to be fully 'boardroom ready'. The challenger board could also seek to form their own minerals company – where the financial acumen of Angela, Joshua's deal-making capability and the technical credentials of Rebecca and Chris would lay the foundations of success.

Would the result have been a different one in a far tougher market? Had the company been either an iron ore or nickel miner in the current climate would the board have then survived? Real-world examples may yet eventuate in the near future that may provide further insight into that question.

---

[1] Thanks in particular to votes and comments from Alex Atkins, Steve Beresford, Doug Brewster, Michael Collins, John Doepel, Steve Heather, Colin Jackson, Josh Wright and 'Roger'.

[2] Any resemblance to a real company and to specific individuals is unintentional.

10. TEN QUOTABLE STEPS TOWARDS BOARDROOM EFFECTIVENESS

21 Sep 2015 Strictly Boardroom seeks some quotable help towards boardroom excellence.

Keen to be a more effective director? Strictly Boardroom has compiled some of the wisest short-form counsel from a diversity of erudite sources. To excel in the boardroom, getting the following ten things right should ensure that you are on the right track:

1. **First, get a seat at the table**
   "It's not who you know, it's who knows you." (Anonymous)

2. **Think strategically but take action**
   "Take time to deliberate, but when the time for action comes, stop thinking and go in." (Napoleon Bonaparte)

3. **Make clear, decisive decisions**
   For those in any doubt avoid the syndrome that is
   "My Indecision is Final." (Jake Eberts and Terry Ilott[1])

4. **Challenge the status quo early**
   "The reasonable man adapts himself to the conditions that surround him. The unreasonable man adapts surrounding conditions to himself… All progress depends on the unreasonable man." (George Bernard Shaw)

5. **Streamline the board committee process**
   "If Columbus had an advisory committee he would probably still be at the dock." (Arthur Goldberg)

6. **Focus board communications towards the point**
   "This paper, by its very length, defends itself from ever being read." (Winston Churchill)

7. **Bring the right skill-sets to the boardroom table**
   "How many board members does it take to change a light bulb? Answer: It really depends on the composition and skill-set of the particular board." (Anonymous[2])

8. **Whatever you do, don't run out of cash**
   "A banker lends you his umbrella when it's sunny and wants it back when it rains." (Mark Twain)

9. **Avoid conflicts of interest, whether perceived or real**
   "The world is full of people who are grabbing and self-seeking. So the rare individual who unselfishly tries to serve others has an enormous advantage." (Dale Carnegie[3])

10. **Realise that you don't know everything**
    "There are known knowns. These are things we know that we know. There are known unknowns. That is to say, there are things that we know we don't know. But there are also unknown unknowns. There are things we don't know we don't know." (Donald Rumsfeld)

So there it is: ten steps to become an effective director. That said, your scribe is not totally convinced as yet that a boardroom that comprises Columbus, Churchill, Napoleon, Mark Twain, Dale Carnegie, Donald Rumsfeld and George Bernard Shaw will constitute an effective corporate team?[4]

What do you think?

1 Eberts, J. and Ilott, T. 1990. *My Indecision is Final – The Rise and Fall of Goldcrest Films*. Faber and Faber, London.

2 With thanks to Nonprofitwithballs.com

3 Carnegie, D. 1936. *How to Win Friends and Influence People*. Simon and Schuster, New York.

4 Note that such a board would also lack gender balance which contemporary research suggests is correlated with higher performance outcomes at companies. See, for example: Thomson, P. and Graham, J. 2005. *A Women's Place is in the Boardroom*. Palgrave MacMillan, London.

KEY INSIGHTS:
IN THE MINERALS BOARDROOM

- An improvement mindset requires that the next generation of minerals industry directors will have skills over and above the existing generation. The ability to guide minerals companies through sustainability issues and the many facets of social licence to operate both loom large. 'New' approaches to 'old' industry challenges, such as effective operations management and winning strategies are always welcome.

- New directors with governance skills, individual expertise and the ability to mentor management will always be required across the minerals sector. Add in leadership skills, effective stakeholder engagement and strategic guidance and the boardroom door will open.

- Boardroom culture and practices can differ substantially between companies. Do not expect the boardroom of one company to resemble that of any other. Like individuals, boards as a whole have their own unique personality.

- Learning about the boardroom is not just a case of reading corporate governance texts and tomes. Governance knowledge is typically only a qualifier to be considered for a boardroom role.

- Effective boardroom activity requires a diverse range of knowledge on technical subjects such as geology, engineering and science, but also economics, finance, law, commerce and socio-political engagement.

- Interestingly, non-technical expertise is currently the most common route for women to enter the mining boardroom, as proportionally more female directors have non-technical backgrounds. Further progress is, however, required in this area to achieve more gender-balanced and diversified boardrooms, which ultimately will be more effective boardrooms.

- Effective directors exhibit a range of attributes including respect, patience, motivation, honesty, thrift, a shareholder mindset and work prioritisation skills. That said, personalities abound in the boardroom – with all their human frailties. Expect to encounter 'directors behaving badly' on occasions, especially in the heat of argument. Try not to reciprocate.

- Boardroom decisions are seldom so simple that every director is immediately aligned to a single viewpoint. Persuasive communication skills are important if you wish to see your own perspective adopted.

- Boardroom communication is still not as effective as it could be. If each director commits to improve communication channels it will be of benefit to everyone – and to the company.

- Directors can make a significant difference to the performance of a company – both for good and bad!

PART 2
On Strategic Management

Part Two of the book "On Strategic Management", starts out with a short chapter entitled "Robin Hood meets the rapidly receding mining boom" which outlines the difficult strategic playing field that boards face in the present mining industry – declining business conditions, competing objectives, declining competitive advantage and unsustainable past growth rates. The rest of Part Two looks at the strategic options boards have to extract their companies from these tough market conditions.

All mining industry executives should be familiar with a basic toolkit of strategic frameworks. "Top ten strategy essentials" provides such a toolkit for the mining industry, combining the most suitable general strategy frameworks with a few mining industry specific strategy tools. "Strategy deliberations – take CARE" aims to summarise the key areas for decision-making. A successful minerals sector strategy requires corporate and asset-level solutions, an understanding of the specific technical and non-technical risks facing the mining sector, and a watching brief on developments in mineral economics.

"Beware non-core assets" looks at the world of mergers and acquisitions (M&A) and in particular the concept of 'natural ownership' and how to ensure an asset's location, resource and inherent risks align with those of the owner. The next short chapter "Promoting mining heresy – not once but twice" then challenges the common mantra that companies should target low-cost assets, by reminding readers that a low-cost asset acquired at a high-price is actually a high-cost asset. Readers can then test their strategic M&A decision-making with "A $200 million boardroom dilemma" of whether to purchase an asset for a hefty premium. Readers can then review their answers in "$200 million acquisition voted down" which looks at why most would avoid such an acquisition, but a brave few might still choose to take it on.

Beyond M&A, organic growth is also critical to strategy development in the mining industry. Such growth requires both exploration and development of new assets, discussed in "Creating value in emerging resource companies – think exploration".

Successful exploration can create outsized returns in particular for smaller mining companies. Realistically mining companies will pursue a combination of acquisition-based and organic growth. The strategic degrees of freedom – namely commodities, geographies, financing options and of course strategy itself are reviewed in "Towards the 'DNA' of emerging mineral resources companies".

Market conditions dictate that equity-funded explorers seldom have the funds to pursue all the strategic growth options they would like. "Poker in the exploration boardroom" outlines the basic options facing exploration in which exploration assets to hold and which not. The options are straightforward, but the decisions are not.

Duly informed about the range of strategies available to mining companies, readers can then weigh the different options in "Another $200M mining strategy conundrum", considering whether a company should sell out to a buyer at a premium, conduct aggressive exploration, or acquire an asset at a discount. Potential answers to this conundrum are then given in "Three paths to mining industry growth – buy, sell, explore!".

Part Two finishes by considering the role of business model innovation in the mining sector. "Innovation strategies: beyond slow pizzas" cites royalty companies as a successful example of business model innovation in the mining sector, and drilling funds as one that did not (as yet) take off. With the ongoing strategic challenges facing the mining sector it is likely that some of the winners of the future will be those with innovative business models.

11. ROBIN HOOD MEETS THE RAPIDLY RECEDING MINING BOOM

12 Nov 2012 Strictly Boardroom writes from Sherwood Forest where he finds Robin Hood is facing similar pressures to those prevailing in the mining sector.

With the tougher (again) macroeconomic conditions of late around planet Earth, questions are being asked about the continuing health and fitness of the Australian mining boom. But challenges such as those facing the minerals sector now are not new. Indeed similar challenges befell a non-mining entrepreneur by the name of Robin Hood in the UK many centuries ago.

After a stellar debut in which Robin rose to fame with help from his faithful management team, including Little John and Friar Tuck, Robin's business environment gradually became ever more difficult – with his challenges akin to those faced by Australian miners now.

Firstly, Robin faced **declining business conditions** complete with both 'demand' and 'supply' problems.

That is, after years of plunder, rich people woke up to the fact that Sherwood Forest was something of a 'no go' area. Enter Sherwood Forest wearing your best silks and regalia and you stood a far higher than average chance of being robbed – so why go there at all?

The gentry of Nottingham started taking alternative routes and avoiding Robin's home patch. That made life tougher on Robin.

What's more is that there were now fewer and fewer rich people around the Nottinghamshire area anyway! Years of "Gillard-like"* higher taxes imposed by Prince John and the Sheriff of Nottingham had lightened the gentry's coffers.

But wait there was more. Robin's assistance to the poor had also taken effect, with the previous throngs of tramps and vagabonds now replaced by newly minted merchants thanks to Robin's assistance.

Next, Robin had always struggled with the **challenge of competing business objectives.**

It seems one day the focus was on Prince John and the Sheriff, while the next day Robin was off courting Maid Marian over dinner down at the newly opened Hog's Breath tavern.

Increased activism also required attention which originated from both Robin's shareholders and stakeholders – meaning the poor (who cried out for more) and also the Merry Men.

A **declining competitive advantage** was another challenge for Robin.

What was once a small, fast-moving technical team of Merry Men became bloated by the addition of bureaucracy as Robin's popularity swelled the ranks of his 'company'. With such a large contingent of Merry Men at his back, surprise ambushes were no longer the easy option they once were to lure in unsuspecting gentry.

The quality of his troop had also declined – as the fast-growing rob-from-the-rich 'business' had required rapid expansion of his 'workforce'.

What's more is that rivals had responded to his success. The Sheriff, for example, deployed reinforcements to counter Robin's insurgency.

Back in the forest, the Merry Men considered forming a union to lobby for more mead and venison. Union representative Will Scarlett had already promised a greater share for the Merry Men in the wealth being redistributed to the poor.

Lastly, there was a question mark over **the sustainability of past growth rates.**

Rabbits and deer were literally running low in number in the forest. A larger proportion of Robin's ill-gotten gains were required to balance the budget and to buy-in food and mead.

So like Australia's miners, the question hung over Robin as to whether the Merry Men's best days were already behind them. Ring any bells?
Australia's miners now face not dissimilar challenges.

- **Declining business conditions** are evident with the slowing of economic growth rates in China and ongoing economic travails of the Eurozone and US.
- **Competing business objectives** abound as many companies face multiple development opportunities across different commodities. Where then to focus key efforts?
- **Declining competitive advantage** is a major issue as Australia's costs have escalated both for construction and operating phases.
- **The sustainability of past growth rates** is also a challenge for those companies which have had early success in mining boom phase one. How can that momentum be maintained with the more challenging external environment prevailing now?

Robin Hood overcame his multiple challenges to become a world-wide folklore legend.
Can your company overcome the current business challenges too?

---

* Julia Gillard served as the 27th Prime Minister of Australia from 2010 to 2013. She attempted to introduce a Mineral Resource Rent Tax (MRRT) in Australia. The challenges of designing appropriate minerals taxation schemes are discussed in Part Nine: Of Mineral Policy and Mining Regulation.

12. TOP TEN STRATEGY ESSENTIALS

22 Sept 2014 Strictly Boardroom compiled a 'must know' list of business strategy concepts for the mineral resources sector and got as far as a Top Ten strategy hit parade. So what is missing?

Strictly Boardroom gets the opportunity on occasions to deliver lectures on business strategy as it applies to the minerals world. In a recent course, one bright student asked for a 'must know' crib sheet of concepts well ahead of the lead-up to the final exam. The result of that student request is the Top 10 strategy 'hit parade' list below comprising critically important strategic level concepts. Most are straightforward – at least in principle – but other concepts act to challenge companies as to whether their strategy is truly on-track towards their respective visions and missions.

Like a pop chart, Strictly Boardroom has aimed to order the list by popularity. This may be a very rough proxy (and we mean extremely rough) as to the relative importance of each of the concepts.

Here we go then. You are asked two questions. How right or wrong are the choices for inclusion on the list? Secondly, which critical concepts are missing?

1. **The Three Generic Business Strategies** – low-cost, differentiation and focus[1]. Outdated thinking yes but critical as a foundation for strategy deliberations nonetheless.
2. **Structured Problem-Solving and Issue Analysis** – meaning breaking down a challenge into its constituent parts in a regimented manner[2]. Pivotal to any business conundrum.
3. **Mineral Commodity Analysis** – the microeconomics of supply and demand but also the importance of industry structure, conduct and performance[3]. Do not pass go without this one in your back pocket. Porter's famous Five Forces[4] industry framework would sit within this strategy 'bucket'.
4. **Game Theory** – at least in a qualitative sense rather than the heavy mathematics of game theory[5]. The tricks of the trade here can mean the difference between business success and failure. The most important game theory mantra? Never create competition for free! Many companies do just that in the minerals world to the benefit of rival companies.
5. **Portfolio Analysis** – as Kenny Rogers sang, "Know when to hold them and when to fold them". The Boston Consulting Group said something similar a few years beforehand with their (in) famous Growth Share Matrix (or 'Boston Box')[6].

McKinsey's greatest hit is arguably the Three Horizons of Growth[7] in analysing a company asset portfolio.

6. **The Resource Based View of the Firm**[8] – distinctive capabilities and core/key competencies of a company sit here[9]: These are potential forms of competitive advantage, yet both are often misunderstood. Remember that some capabilities are worth more than others to a company. Those capabilities that can be scaled up and broadened in their application as the company grows are like gold dust. Having available cash is handy too, of course, and can confer strategic advantage, but cash is an asset rather than a capability.

7. **Benchmarking**[10] – many companies think they 'know what they don't know'. However, just as many companies 'don't know what they don't know'.

8. **Cluedo Strategy**[11] – Reverend Green with his lead-pipe in the bedroom is the analogy here – which translated into 'minerals-speak' means choosing the right commodity, in the right location and critically with the right entry point.

9. **Cost Curves are not equal** – knowing the shape and drivers of cost advantage in a mineral market makes the top ten[3]. The answer differs for each commodity. Stepped cost curves, along with steep and flat cost curves sit here.

10. **Value Chain Analysis**[12] – knowing who makes the money in a mineral market and where the value is added counts for a lot. So is upstream always the place to be? Is it downstream? Finally, when and where does it pay to be vertically integrated? The concepts of 'convex' versus 'concave' mineral commodities sit here[13], as does the concept of value-in-use for a mineral product.

That's it then. One immediate challenge lies in the fact that the current strategy lecture series runs over 12 consecutive weeks and not just ten. Country risk and resource nationalism sits just outside the top ten strategy themes so will certainly get a run. What else?

Any readers willing to deliver a guest lecture on a strategy topic not included on the above list are therefore very much encouraged to get in touch!

---

1 Porter, M.E. 2003. *Competitive Strategy*. Free Press, New York.

2 See short chapters 35 "Avoiding Keystone Cops Syndrome" and 36 "Mining Professional or Strategy Consultant?" in Part Four: At the Coal Face.

3 See short chapter 78 "Beyond China – Why some commodities are profitable (and others not)" in Part Eight: Of Mineral Economics and Finance.

4 Porter, M.E. 2008. *The Five Competitive Forces That Shape Strategy*, Harvard Business Review.

5 Nalebuff, B.J. and Brandenburger, A.M. 2003. *Co-opetition*. Profile Books, London.

6 Reeves, M., Moose, S. and Venema, T. 2014. *BCG Classics Revisited: The Growth Share Matrix*. Boston Consulting Group Perspectives, 4 June. (https://www.bcgperspectives.com/content/articles/corporate_strategy_portfolio_management_strategic_planning_growth_share_matrix_bcg_classics_revisited)

7 Baghai, M., Coley, S. and White, D. 2000. *The Alchemy of Growth: Practical Insights for Building the Enduring Enterprise*. Basic Books, New York.

8 Kay, J. 2007. *Foundations of Corporate Success: How Business Strategies Add Value*. Oxford Paperbacks, Oxford.

9 See short chapters 45 "From mediocrity to capability", 49 "Large mining companies: Capability lost?" and 51 "The best way is up: Crafting a winning strategy" in Part Five: On Competitiveness and Mining Strategy.

10 "Naked Benchmarking" in Trench, A., 2013, *Strictly (Mining) Boardroom – Management Insights from Inside the Resources Sector*, Major Street Publishing, Highett, Vic. p79-80.

11 "Mining industry growth strategies – Cluedo style" in Trench, A., 2013, *Strictly (Mining) Boardroom – Management Insights from Inside the Resources Sector*, Major Street Publishing, Highett, Vic. p118-119.

12 Porter, M.E. 2004. *Competitive Advantage: Creating and Sustaining Superior Performance*. Free Press, New York.

13 "Convex metals – smart commodity choices for mineral explorers" in Trench, A., 2013, *Strictly (Mining) Boardroom – Management Insights from Inside the Resources Sector*, Major Street Publishing, Highett, Vic. p160-162.

13. STRATEGY DELIBERATIONS – TAKE CARE

01 Sep 2014 Strictly Boardroom looks at mineral sector strategy and advises companies to take CARE.

Strictly Boardroom has been exposed to more than his fair share of strategy frameworks over the years – some better than others.

Whatever the chosen framework, however, in formulating and

executing a winning strategy, one aspect remains constant: companies should take CARE with all their deliberations.

So here is yet another strategy framework, where: C is for corporate-level strategy; A is for asset-level strategy; R is for risk considerations and E is for economics. Get that lot right and you're very much on the right track.

Corporate-level strategy is an overarching guiding light. All strategic actions must align with the corporate vision and mission.

The right commodities and geographies are two degrees of freedom that need to be considered carefully, along with the right value chain footprint, the right combination of exploration, investment, development, mining, processing and trading/marketing as principal activities.

Capabilities also loom large in respect of corporate-level deliberation. Doing what a company does best is the overarching factor to consider here. Companies need to know what their corporate capabilities are (most don't) and whether any of those skills are truly distinctive.

Capabilities are hard assets but sourced from softer, skill-based, origins. Cash is not a capability but rather an enabler of strategy.

Some capabilities are scalable while others are not. Consequently, some capabilities are worth far more than others.

Asset-level strategy is the next tier down from the corporate-level deliberations.

Getting portfolio decisions right is where strategy "hits the road", so to speak. Errors here take a long time to fix, whereas the right decisions are company-making decisions.

Right team, right approach but wrong asset is a very common error-type.

Risk is the most critical of filters applied to strategies.

Technical risks are generally well understood by minerals companies, even if they can still cause almighty problems. That is, even companies with strong skill-sets in geology, mining, metallurgy and marketing can still get it horribly wrong from a technical perspective.

Non-technical risks can arguably harbour even greater challenges for companies and are an area where the minerals sector is still building expertise*.

Social licence to operate is the current catch-cry. There are companies aiming to backfill capability in such disciplines as community consultation, environmental best practices, government liaison and achieving a fuller understanding of the impacts and risks of dynamic mineral policy and legislation the world over.

Economics is the final frontier of strategy. Nobody has yet developed 20:20 economic foresight but through tools such as scenario planning it becomes evident that some strategies are more robust to potential changes in both micro and macroeconomic factors than are others.

An understanding of future commodity prices and their drivers is only the starting point.

Good strategy is a tall ask indeed – and an exercise that should clearly be approached with great CARE.

---

* Trench, A., Packey, D. and Sykes, J.P. 2014. *Non-Technical Risks and Their Impact on the Mining Industry*. Australasian Institute of Mining & Metallurgy (AusIMM) – Mineral Resource and Ore Reserve Estimation, Monograph 30, Chapter 7, p605-617.

14. BEWARE NON-CORE ASSETS

14 Apr 2014 Strictly Boardroom looks at the question of acquiring non-core assets from other companies – and recounts some logical, if often neglected, clear warning signs.

Strictly Boardroom was recently contacted by an exploration company on the subject of a potential acquisition of a non-core asset held by a larger company. The asset was rumoured to be flagged for near-term divestment: did we have any thoughts on the matter?

To duly observe confidentiality, the following description has been sanitised as to the nub of the acquisition "opportunity":

- **Proximity:** the asset is half a planet away from the exploration company's current area of focus.
- **Commodity:** the project contains a material resource of a

commodity of which the exploration company has little prior experience.
- **Development:** the potential mine requires a little nation-building along the way to get it up and running. Start with "just a few hundred kilometres of rail – oh – and a port upgrade" and go on from there.
- **Risk:** the project sits in what most companies would consider a fairly risky jurisdiction. Our families would certainly not be keen to holiday there any time soon.
- **Capital:** the exploration company has scant funds available with which to buy the asset, and thereafter there's that rail line and port upgrade, and then permitting, and working capital, and in-country relationship-building, and far more, no doubt. Throw in business class airfares to get to and from the destination as an additional corporate overhead in coming years.
- **Inside running:** the exploration company did, however, have the scoop – of sorts – courtesy of a non-exclusive corporate adviser who had approached them on the deal and who would only require a fee if the company proceeded to the next stage.

Let's take a step back here. This is a pretty good exploration company by the way.

It is so good that it could (and probably should) continue to do just that – explore to the best of its ability – especially in those areas where it already has local in-depth knowledge of the geology and prevailing mineral policy that give the company an advantage over several of its peers.

So who should acquire the above non-core asset then?

That question is easy. The "natural owner" of the asset should. Natural ownership is a straightforward concept, championed by McKinsey & Company* among others.

Defining the concept is not quite as straightforward, however – but you know a natural owner when you see one (and the explorer is certainly not one with respect to the non-core asset in question).

At the risk of gross oversimplification, a natural owner can extract more value at less risk from an asset than anyone else who might develop the mine.

How exactly? The list is a long one. It took McKinsey 24 pages to explain but we would start with something like:

- **Proximity:** companies already active in the region, ideally capturing scale and scope economies.
- **Commodity:** an existing experienced operator.
- **Development:** a track record of delivery.
- **Risk:** the asset adds a level of value to the company portfolio that is consistent with the corporate risk appetite.
- **Capital:** a suitable balance sheet.
- **Inside running:** start with an exclusive track to achieve acquisition, add in existing in-country relationships and go from there.

The explorer in question has none of the above. Another party, however, will tick most, if not all, boxes.

It is the latter company and not the explorer that should be the one buying the asset – and it probably will unless another company decides to pay too much for it!

---

* Gerken, A., Hoffman, N., Kremer, A., Stegemann, U. and Vigo, G. 2010. *Getting risk ownership right*. McKinsey Working Papers on Risk, #23.

15. PROMOTING MINING HERESY – NOT ONCE BUT TWICE

04 Nov 2013 Strictly Boardroom challenges two of the 'core beliefs' of the mining sector – one being the misguided obsession over the threat of rising costs.

Costs, costs and then costs has been the mantra of the mining sector in recent months. Your scribe attended an industry conference last week and the focus was largely on – you guessed it – all-in costs.

In part as devil's advocate, therefore, Strictly Boardroom presents some countervailing views to the prevailing mining industry mantra – including a different slant on how the industry should look at its costs.

Not that costs aren't important – they clearly are – but they are not the only issue in the mining town.

Perhaps, if collectively we were better at managing mining operations than we presently are, then costs could be viewed more as strategic opportunity rather than perceived as the most major of threats to present and future business success?

So here are two 'heretical' points of view – first on mining costs and then on new mine investment – with brief explanations as to why such contrarian thinking may not be quite as crazy as it first appears.

Challenging belief #1: Low-cost mines are good, high-cost mines are bad

That must be right – yes?

Of course in the general case it is broadly right. Who would not want a low-cost mine versus a high-cost one? But miners need to be careful as to how low-cost mines enter a corporate portfolio. Pay too much and they are not really low-cost mines at all.

Full economic costing of acquisitions can reveal this. The major post acquisition write-downs of the most recent financial year are a clear line of evidence that we aren't quite there yet in optimising our decision-making to gain access to low-cost assets.

Consider this related question then. When would you purposely buy a high-cost mine?

Never ever? That may not be the correct answer.

Firstly, acquisition of a cheap high-cost asset might be perfectly rational if you anticipate the relevant commodity price to rise in future.

Secondly, you might acquire a high-cost asset if you were actually a better miner than your peers – a company capable of running the asset at a lower cost.

That very few companies buy high-cost mines for the latter

reason is a reflection of the current state of our industry. No one mining company is all that much better than its peers.

Therein lies the opportunity for any company able to become 'the Toyota of mining', so to speak.

Challenging belief #2: Commodity prices are falling – quick, cut back on new investment

This mantra has also pervaded 2013 in spades. Shareholders no longer trust management to spend money wisely on new mine developments, so they want their money back please. After all, commodity prices are falling. Actually, this thinking should be challenged too.

Many years ago your scribe did just that, with a financial model in nickel that showed companies would actually increase their chances of a strong financial return if they built new mines when prices were falling, not rising.

Why? By the time the mine built at the bottom of the cycle hit full production, nickel prices were inevitably higher.

Conversely, those nickel mines built when prices were at their highest suffered the opposite outcome – lower prices when production hit its straps.

Not easy I know. I can almost hear the feedback: "Just you try fronting up to a bank with the message that prices are going down so please loan us the funds to build a new mine please".

The irony is that this is actually the right thing to do – however crazy it might sound.

The difficulty of raising the equity side without excessive dilution is yet another challenge.

What's pertinent, however, is that the old financial model did not even factor in the fact it is cheaper to build a mine in the downturn – so the already positive outcome of "buying straw hats in winter" was actually underestimated.

Building a mine now is actually the right time to do it from an economically rational perspective. It is a pity the market and its participants are not always rational.

Makes you think, doesn't it?

16. A $200 MILLION BOARDROOM DILEMMA

01 Dec 2014 Strictly Boardroom poses a boardroom conundrum to you and wonders whether you will vote in favour of the proposal – or against it.

Strictly Boardroom has spent the last few months coordinating a course with the grand title of the "Strategic Management of Resource Companies". The class is now complete – so a sincere thanks to all those who helped make it a success*.

Of course strategic management is far easier to espouse in the lecture theatre than it is to execute within the boardroom. To close that gap between theory and practice, your scribe set up a conundrum during the course to which he expected opinion to be divided. It most certainly was.

The conundrum went something like this:

- You are an emerging A$150 million company by market capitalisation seeking to become a future Australian gold producer. At this stage however you are some years from first production. Your flagship asset is potential gold development at feasibility stage in Australia. To advance that gold asset you have sufficient cash reserves and no debt (other than trade creditors) to complete the feasibility study to a definitive standard.

- A large gold company has decided to sell out of a number of mines globally that no longer fit with its scale and mine life requirements. These mines have limited life and higher costs than the overall portfolio average for the large company. The divestment creates the possibility for you, as a would-be gold producer, to acquire one of the operating assets set to be divested by the large miner.

- Your chief financial officer (CFO), working closely with a corporate adviser, estimates the present value of future cash flow from one of the mines that is for sale at $150 million. Your technical team has a solid track record of operating experience of similar gold assets. Technical due diligence has

been satisfactorily completed. The asset is clearly not a lemon and as an operating asset it will generate cash from day one.
- You check the financial model and consider all the assumptions to be appropriate. You have independent financiers and engineers check the model without issue. Bank finance is available on what the board considers satisfactory terms. If the board recommends a deal it is anticipated that the required equity component can be raised from existing large (and small) shareholders without seeking out new investors.
- Now here comes the conundrum. You determine that to win the bid for the asset you will need to pay $200 million, some $50 million above what you consider to be fair value.
- The conundrum is simple: Do you make a $200 million bid to acquire the operating gold mine?

At this point in the exercise a large number of questions quickly appear.

People ask for further detail on the asset, the valuation and the bid process for example. Specific questions include whether the right discount rate has been applied (to reach the $150 million valuation), whether the real option value and exploration upside has been fully captured, the correct impact of the financial terms and advisory fees used to fund the acquisition, what the gold price assumption was, if sustaining capital has been accounted for and so on.

All these questions point to uncertainties in reaching the 'right' answer of course. But let us for the purposes of the exercise assume that all the above factors have all been correctly estimated (albeit that it is very difficult to value several factors with certainty) in arriving at the $150 million present value of future cash flows.

Similarly let us assume that the answer of $150 million represents the board's preference in terms of financing mix and any hedging contracts to be entered into. Whilst financial engineering could certainly change the answer, let us assume the financing terms and structure are considered the most appropriate and that the financiers are willing participants in the deal should it proceed.

Of course, as noted here, there is material uncertainty on any single point valuation number – so let's again for the sake of argument say that such uncertainty is understood. Let's call it plus or minus $50 million in present value terms. So while the base case valuation is $150 million, the upside valuation case is $200 million (the price tag required to win the asset) and the downside $100 million.

So there you have it. It is a simple conundrum really. Would you in these circumstances buy a $150 million asset for $200 million?

All those in favour of buying please vote YES. Similarly, all those against please vote NO. So what do you think?

---

* With thanks to guest speakers Erica Smyth (Toro Energy), Rich Krasnoff (Centre for Exploration Targeting), and Sally-Anne Layman (Macquarie Bank) for delivering lectures into the course.

17. $200 MILLION ACQUISITION VOTED DOWN

08 Dec 2014 Strictly Boardroom conveys the results from last week's boardroom conundrum – with a clear majority voting against buying a A$150 million gold asset for $200 million. So are the majority correct?

Thank you to all those who responded to last week's call for either a 'yes' or 'no' vote on the proposed acquisition of a $150 million gold mine for $200 million. First to the results. The split was around 80% voting no and 20% voting yes. One lateral-thinking colleague answered "neither" which is exactly why he is in the process of undertaking a PhD. But for the sake of argument here we will constrain the solution space to simply yes or no. That said, the answers are never quite as simple as they first appear.

By way of reminder, a short-form version of the conundrum is as follows:

- You are a A$150 million company seeking to become a gold producer. Your flagship asset is gold development at feasibility stage in Australia. You have sufficient cash reserves to complete feasibility.

- A large gold company has decided to sell a number of gold mines. These mines have limited life and higher costs than their overall portfolio average. You consider acquiring one of the operating assets.
- You estimate the present value of future cash flow from one of the mines at $150 million. Due diligence is sound. The asset will generate cash immediately.
- You check the financial model and consider all assumptions appropriate. Bank finance is available and if the board recommends a deal it is anticipated that the equity component can be raised from existing shareholders.
- Now the conundrum. To win the bid you will need to pay A$200 million, some $50 million above what you consider to be fair value.
- The conundrum is simple: Do you make a $200 million bid to acquire the operating gold mine?

The devil is always in the detail so the following information is critical. You can consider the discount rate correct (to reach the $150 million valuation), that real option value and exploration upside has been fully captured in the $150 million too, that the correct impact of the debt-equity mix, financial terms and advisory fees have been estimated, that the gold price assumption is correct, that sustaining capital is included and so on.

So what is the rationale for a yes vote? The case for no is simple of course. Buying something for $200 million that is correctly valued at $150 million makes no sense at face value, end of story. On that basis, especially as gold price upside and exploration upside had been ruled out, the majority response was a clear vote of no. The proposal is defeated.

The yes vote takes more explaining though, and it is worthy of investigation. The logical flow for a yes vote goes something like this.

1. The yes vote relies on the assumption of a degree of market inefficiency relating to the transaction. That is, the first

assumption for 'yes' is that the markets will not immediately mark down the acquirer for paying $50 million too much – indeed they may actually re-rate the company positively given it now has an operating cash flow.

2. The next assumption required to support a yes answer is to consider the 'standard' value accretion curve as a company progresses from discovery (an initial rise in value) through feasibility (declining value) to eventual production (re-rated value) at the company's existing flagship asset. If this plays out to the standard stylised form so often seen in investment banking presentations, then the company may well lose $50 million (or more) in value in coming months as the feasibility progresses at the existing asset should the board choose not to make the acquisition. That is, those voting yes saw the acquisition of a cash flow as mitigating the potential value loss as the flagship asset continued to progress through the 'feasibility malaise'.

3. Finally, one wag even suggested that the board of a company saying yes might then subsequently launch a takeover bid for any company saying no to the acquisition on the basis of the cash flow and larger market capitalisation. This bold move requires the assumption that an independent valuation would not reveal the value destruction of the acquisition. Of course if the board of a 'yes' company is willing to pay another premium then the board of the 'no' company may agree to the deal!

So there you have it. At a stretch, buying a $150 million asset for $200 million can be rational in such circumstances.

What do you think the probabilities are that assumptions 1 and 2 – or even assumption 3 – might hold in a continuing bear market? Is the vote still 80:20 for no?

Of course the management of any company has a strong vested interest in a yes vote here. Why? Executives of larger companies are paid more! Academics call this agency theory, resulting from a disparity in pay-offs between the principals (shareholders) and the agents (executive team). The same agency issue holds true for 'independent' directors too – although the decision bias is less marked in terms of the absolute size of non executive director fees.

Further thoughts are welcome.

18. CREATING VALUE IN EMERGING RESOURCES COMPANIES – THINK EXPLORATION

20 Jan 2014 In this chapter, Strictly Boardroom is joined by Graham Arvidson to look at how emerging resources companies create value through strategy*. The winning strategy? Exploration, of course.

Exploration has almost become a dirty word in financial markets. Nobody wants to support it – let alone put money into it – especially in greenfield environments that lie far from existing headframes.

That's a pit because a recent study reveals an exploration focus as the winner among a number of alternative strategies that small resources companies can deploy in order to reach critical mass.

Perhaps we always knew the answer but had somehow forgotten?

Faced with a choice of mergers and acquisitions, project development, buying an old mine and restarting production, seeking out a strategic cornerstone investor, or else exploration, small companies are leaning towards the 'ABE' (anything but exploration) strategies.

However, shareholder return data over five years from 80 emerging ASX-listed resources companies suggest that exploration is actually the biggest hitter in value terms – if it is successful of course.

Here is how the study was undertaken.

First a selection of 90 companies was chosen using size as the principal selection criteria. The largest 10 mining companies were omitted – as they were already established – leaving the next 80 to be analysed in more detail – the smallest having a market capitalisation of A$110 million.

The overarching research question was to ascertain what made the best 20 companies among the 80 so special, ranked by five-year shareholder return (2008 to 2013).

Of course such a brief research study has many limitations – not least among them that the dataset is biased towards successful outcomes (that is, omitting companies that 'failed' in their strategies and had yet to achieve the $110 million size cut-off).

Next a principal strategy was assigned to each company's activity over the five-year time horizon with the benefit of 20:20 hindsight.

The strategies were classified as one of the following:

- Exploration discovery
- Purchase and produce (restarting an old mine)
- Project development (of a new mine)
- M&A (growth by amalgamation)
- Strategic investor (attracting a 'big brother'); or
- Unclear!

Among the 80 companies studied – and remember they are all 'winners' by nature of having achieved reasonable scale – the most common strategies were project development (33%) and exploration discovery (30%) then followed purchase and produce (10%), M&A (7%) and strategic investor (1%).

For the 19% remainder, the strategy was not immediately clear.

The critical insight was then to look at the top 20 companies by shareholder return.

Here, the data jumps out at you.

Among these companies the strategies were led by exploration discovery at a whopping 65% (13 companies), then purchase and produce, and project development (both 15%, three companies each) and finally M&A (5% – one company).

So the data is pretty straightforward. Clearly exploration success unlocks the door to value creation – big time – beating out rival strategies on the winners list.

But then we always knew that exploration creates value for those companies that are successful didn't we?

Funny how the investment community across planet Earth seems to have forgotten!

---

* Arvidson, G. 2015. *The Case for Exploration as Strategy: An ASX Top 80 Mining and Metals Case Study.* Centre for Exploration Targeting Discovery Day, Fremantle, WA, 24 February.

19. TOWARDS THE 'DNA' OF EMERGING MINERAL RESOURCES COMPANIES

28 Jan 2014 Strictly Boardroom is again joined by Graham Arvidson to take a closer look at what makes emerging resources companies tick.

In the previous short chapter, Strictly Boardroom made some initial observations on what separates the best from the rest among emerging resources companies listed on the Australian Securities Exchange (ASX). Exploration success stood out as a key growth driver – with the value that comes from mineral discovery catapulting a number of companies towards the top of the pile.

Indeed, the majority of the 'Top 20' performers (by five-year shareholder return) from a study of a 'Top 80' emerging minerals companies had exploration success to thank for their market achievements.

Now Strictly Boardroom is looking a little closer at some other attributes of those same emerging resources companies, to build a form of corporate profile of what, how and where our next-generation minerals sector corporate success is coming from.

Data from the 80 emerging companies was assessed*, with each company having grown beyond a minimum A$110 million market value threshold.

Put simply, the aim was to reveal the DNA of our next generation successful mining companies? For example:

- What are they investing in?
- Where are they investing?

- What financing method is preferred?
- Is more than one strategy at play? (Just exploration – or far more than that?)

First to the **commodity markets of choice**: Here, it appears that size matters (of commodity market, that is). The larger global mineral markets of gold (31%), iron ore (16%), copper (14%) and coal (11%) are the most strongly represented across the 80-strong list of companies. Together those markets comprise over 70% of the focus. There are plenty of smaller markets represented too, including tin, uranium, lithium, nickel, mineral sands, platinum, manganese, graphite, rare earths and zinc. The results among the Top 20 companies (by five-year shareholder return) are not too different from the full dataset – with gold (40%), iron ore (20%), copper (10% and coal (10%) here comprising 80% of the corporate focus in total.

Next, to the **geographic focus for resources investment**: Australia is the clear winner across the full 80-strong ASX company dataset – with 50% having their principal assets close to home. Africa comes second – at 22% – with Southeast Asia (10%) and South America (8%) next in line. ASX emerging resources companies have a global focus – with representation for North America (Canada), Central America, Europe and Greenland. The results among the best-performing 20 companies by shareholder return are interesting, showing that success can be achieved globally from an Australian base. For the record, the stats (for geographic focus) came out at Australia (40%), Africa (20%), South America (20%), Southeast Asia (10%) and Canada (10%).

On principal **financing method**, equity is not surprisingly the dominant mode for emerging companies, but debt appears to punch above its weight among the better-performing 20 companies. For the full 80-strong company dataset, the 'financing split' sat around the 80:20 mark – equity (80%) debt (20%) – whereas 60:40 looks closer to the mark for the better performers. This debt–equity observation is likely a case of correlation not causation. That is, the financing contrast observed likely simply reflects that the more competitive projects within the dataset were able to attract suitable debt-financing terms that were executed by the project owners.

Finally to **strategy** – and to whether our emerging ASX resources companies have, as yet, moved beyond a single strategy horizon. In non-management-speak, that asks the question "are they just one-trick ponies?" The 80-strong dataset represents a moving target as each company continually evolves of course and most remain a work-in-progress. Suffice to say, that those companies having more than one string to their strategy bow are starting to look good. Those companies (still in the minority) with more than one clear strategic growth horizon all rank within the top half of the dataset, either by market capitalisation or shareholder return.

That in part answers the what, where and how of the key factors at play driving the next generation of successful ASX-listed mining companies. What remains to be answered is the why. That is, what distinctive capabilities make the better-performing emerging companies different from the others?

Hopefully, in the future there is an answer coming to that question too!

---

* Arvidson, G. 2015. *The Case for Exploration as Strategy: An ASX Top 80 Mining and Metals Case Study*. Centre for Exploration Targeting Discovery Day, Fremantle, WA, 24 February.

20. POKER IN THE EXPLORATION BOARDROOM

12 Aug 2013 Strictly Boardroom is playing cards again – but not poker in its usual form or any other well-known form of the game – mineral exploration boardroom poker is far simpler.

Exploration company boards face very difficult decisions in a market where traditional equity-side funding support has all but dried up.

Holding costs of exploration projects, usually just an annoyance in that those dollars paid out in rents and rates cannot be otherwise directed into the ground have become far more critical. Indeed, whether to continue to shell out tenement holding costs for properties can prompt make or break decisions as to whether to retain certain mineral titles or to surrender them.

For those explorers with cash, of course – and for those explorers with a greater risk appetite than their peers – it presents a great opportunity. That is, some prospective land that is usually tightly held is now becoming available.

In the world of mineral title, it is still the "fast who eat the slow" in the race to peg opportunities as they become available.

Back to the "hold or fold" property decisions themselves, however, in this short chapter your scribe pulled out a pack of cards to help with the decision-making at one explorer.

Exploration 'poker' in the boardroom goes like this: first deal a set of four cards to each company director – one card of each suit – hearts, clubs, spades and diamonds. The value on the card is not important, just the suit.

Now when it comes to decisions on each mineral property, each director gets to play their hand. Cards are placed faced down on the boardroom table.

- **Spades** – drill it – then decide.
- **Hearts** – hold onto 100% at the minimum possible cost: it's back to soil sampling.
- **Diamonds** – seek to joint-venture it out.
- **Clubs** – drop it, save the rents and rates.

There is a final card that can be played too – outside of the above standard four alternatives – this is the **Joker** card.

Playing the Joker means that a novel idea may trump all the above options: experienced exploration directors know the options that sit beneath the Joker card – but that would be telling.

Back to the main game though, where the rules of the game are up to the chairman. Either a unanimous decision is required for certain outcomes, or else the majority decision can prevail.

There are variations of course. One director quipped that his company could not afford to play with a full pack.

"We'd have to take out all the spades," was his response. "We just can't afford to drill – full stop."

21. ANOTHER $200M MINING STRATEGY CONUNDRUM

10 Aug 2015 Strictly Boardroom challenges you to make a decision – and a fairly large one at that.

Emerging mining companies bet the farm – well the company rather – on the first production asset. Whether the mine development of a new discovery or else an acquisition of a project or operating mine, the 'bet the farm' analogy still holds.

For the winners who emerge with a successful mine, the next strategic conundrum becomes the teasing question of a second asset. Carrying with it the tag of 'single asset risk', the strategic thinking around the boardroom table of the company turns to how to spread risk, whether to grow organically, or else to acquire a second asset (either a further operating mine or one primed for development).

The potential benefits of a second asset abound. Removal of the single-asset risk can potentially lower the company's cost of capital, can create purchasing power with suppliers and contractors, unlock operating and corporate synergies, offer potential scale/scope benefits, commodity diversification, career development opportunities for staff – and a great many more benefits too (including higher board fees by the way).

Finding the right second asset however is not easy. Let's imagine this scenario. As the managing director of a A$400 million market capitalisation single-asset mining company you hold the privileged position of managing a low-cost but modest-scale Australian mining asset, which generates strong cash flows even in times of mediocre commodity prices. The mine is 100% owned but the company holds no other material assets.

Analysts mostly have 'buy' recommendations on the company citing the low-cost position of the mine, the near-mine exploration potential and also the corporate appeal of the company as a takeover target.

The mine is recognised by the market as of high quality and you are lauded for achieving an ongoing high return on investment. The remaining mine life at the mine is finite however – let's call it around five years to instil a sense of urgency in strategy.

The specific mineral deposit style and the intricate geological, mining and mineral processing details are not critical, but let's say it is an underground mine with both base and precious metal revenues.

The exploration potential around the mine is universally viewed by both company and commentators as good. Near-mine potential exists but is as of yet unproven (not even as inferred resources). This is despite a concerted exploration effort for the last two years.

The company holds a strong ground position in the area around the mine and the potential for new discoveries within trucking distance to the existing plant also exists (although no satellite discoveries currently exist).

In the wider industry, the downturn in commodity prices means M&A activity has stepped up, as some companies look to stream line, others to bulk up, and others are just plain desperate for cash or cash flow. Of particular relevance are a number of diversified mid-tier miners using the downturn to pick up operating assets cheaply and to grow aggressively. Conversely, there are also a number of cash-starved junior explorers with modest sized projects they can no longer afford to develop.

Your (simplified) strategic choices* at this point are to:

1. **Sell the farm** – While the mine is not of a scale to interest the major miners, the asset is coveted by mid-tier miners globally. A cash sale to a diversified mid-tier miner is achievable (as would be a cash and scrip sale if preferred). Sale value is potentially up to A$200 million above current market capitalisation.

2. **Go organic** – The board has the choice to accept the single-asset risk at the mine and to seek to grow it organically through the exploration drill-bit to extend mine life and/or discovery satellite assets to feed the mill. The expected

monetary value of an extended exploration programme is around A$200 million, though of course the actual outcome is uncertain – including potential discoveries worth more than A$200 million, and also the prospect of finding absolutely nothing despite significant exploration expenditure.

3. **Bet the farm** – Your corporate advisers have proposed several deals for a second asset. The returns from second assets, mainly owned by struggling juniors, however are not as attractive as the returns from your mine continue to be, but still are estimated at above the company's cost of capital. Specifically, there are a number of appealing acquisitions around the A$200 million mark price-tag to choose from. Because of the depressed junior markets, your corporate advisers believe you can get one of these assets on the cheap and easily add at least A$200 million in value over time.

So, everything else being equal (which of course it never is) where does your preference lie?

You have a quarterly conference call due after the next board meeting where a number of influential analysts have signalled that they will ask pointed questions about the company's strategy going forward. Do you steer the board towards option 1, 2 or 3?

All votes are most welcome and will be counted. What do you think?

---

* There are variations on a theme, of course, including hybrids of the strategic options cited in this short chapter – plus several innovative commercial and financing strategies including joint ventures, alliances, partial-divestments or acquisitions, royalty streams, etc.

22. THREE PATHS TO MINING INDUSTRY GROWTH – BUY, SELL, EXPLORE!

29 Feb 2016 Strictly Boardroom uses some contemporary ASX mid-tier mining company case studies to try and answer that old strategy conundrum of how to grow a mining company.

In preparation for an MBA course on the 'Strategic Management of Resources Companies' last year, Strictly Boardroom set an 'unanswerable' strategy conundrum[1] – or at least if not totally unanswerable then a conundrum for which multiple valid answers exist.

By way of reminder, the case study saw a $400 million market capitalisation base and precious metals miner, with one very decent mine (but of limited mine life) facing the choice of what to do next – the so-called 'second asset conundrum'.

The simplified options made available were:

1. **Sell** – to sell the company (or asset) to a larger company for a profit.
2. **Explore** – to conduct an aggressive near-mine exploration program to find a second asset.
3. **Buy** – to purchase an additional second asset at a knock-down price – although without a guarantee that the quality of the new asset would match the existing one.

To add to the fun, all strategies were 'valued' about the same: $200 million of value could be added as a premium paid by the buyer, as the 'expected value' of the exploration program, or as the discount achieved on buying the second asset in a favourable market.

The exercise in class went well, though perhaps unsurprisingly participants remained divided over which was the best option, with different groups highlighting their various core capabilities as reasons to why one strategy would work for them over another. By the end, all groups were suggesting intricate and innovative strategy combinations – including leveraged buy-outs, complex hybrid financing, global domination and so on. Ivan Glasenberg would have blushed.

MBA students are however, particularly keen to hear of real-world case studies describing what happened to companies that chose the various strategic options. So in preparation for this year's course, Strictly Boardroom offers a number of case studies from ASX mid-tier base and precious metals miners that followed these different strategies on second[2] assets. The details are grossly over-simplified in order to highlight the strategic choices clearly. It should also be noted that the various case studies discussed are merely illustrative – and not of $200 million in terms of value-add equivalence. In practice, some examples are worth much, much more.

Contemporary ASX mid-tier miner strategies

Sirius Resources having discovered the Nova-Bollinger nickel-copper deposits, simply sold-up to Independence Group (Option 1).

Doray Minerals, having successfully brought the Andy Well gold mine on stream, then purchased the Deflector gold deposit, recently bringing that into production (Option 3).

Sandfire Resources discovered and developed the DeGrussa copper deposit, then conducted regional exploration around the new mine (Option 2). As this did not initially bring success, Sandfire bought into the Black Butte copper project in Montana via Tintina Resources (Option 3). Subsequently, regional exploration (Option 2) paid off, with the discovery of the Monty copper deposit.

PanAust, having successfully developed the Phu Kham copper and Ban Houayxai gold deposits, bought into projects in Thailand, Chile and Laos (Option 3) as its third-asset strategy. None were developed into a third asset. Eventually, however, the purchase of the Frieda River copper-gold project in Papua New Guinea (Option 3) led soon after to a takeover by Chinese group, Guangdong Rising, leading to a successful Option 1 outcome.

OZ Minerals developed the Prominent Hill copper mine and embarked on a combination of regional exploration (Option 2) and equity investments (Option 3), notably Sandfire Resources. The company then bought the Carrapateena copper project (Option 3). Eventually, most of the earlier purchases were sold off (a partial Option 1 strategy), with the company re-focusing on Carrapateena and regional exploration (Option 2).

Silver Lake Resources, having bought and successfully developed its Mount Monger gold operations, pursued regional exploration (Option 2) successfully. It then purchased gold exploration assets in the Murchison and North Monger regions (Option 3), followed by the takeover of Integra Mining (Option 3). Later, the Murchison and Great Southern assets were sold off or farmed out (partial Option 1 strategies); while the company re-focused on opportunities at its core Mount Monger operations (Option 2).

Exco Resources initially advanced the Cloncurry copper project, before jointly developing the White Dam gold project with Polymetals (Option 3) to gain a second asset. After bringing White Dam into production, Exco then sold its Cloncurry project to Xstrata (partial Option 1). Finally, as production from White Dam wound down, the company itself was sold – including the remaining Queensland copper assets (Option 1).

So what lessons can MBA students learn from all these case studies?

A one-line takeaway is simply that strategy is far more than just good decision-making process and outcome. Good data, the right capabilities and foresight, serendipity and outright luck – whether good and bad – all play their role too.

So, can you think of any case studies we've missed? The obvious ones are Northern Star Resources and Evolution Mining on the Australian gold scene which both have implemented Option 3, BUY, and then BUY again, and again, and again…

---

1 Chapter 21 – Another $200M mining strategy conundrum.
2 The real-world cases in some instances include third, fourth and even fifth assets.

23. INNOVATION STRATEGIES: BEYOND SLOW PIZZAS

13 Oct 2014 Strictly Boardroom looks at business model innovation in mining and exploration and cautions against the minerals equivalent of delivering slow pizzas.

Business model innovation is a great concept and something all mining professionals should be aware of. Basically it means doing things differently as a business in contrast to other companies that operate in the same sector. Remarkably it took management academics a long time to understand and describe this phenomenon.

The explosion in management literature on the subject area accompanied the 1990s technology boom as traditional ways of doing business were challenged by the new force of e-commerce.

Business model innovation is one name for it that does the rounds of academe and ivory towers, business *concept* innovation is another. To this scribe at least, the two labels are synonymous.

Outside the minerals sector there are many famous examples of business model innovation – as distinct, that is, from purely technical innovation.

As a mining business our whole industry is founded upon the latter – innovating technically to achieve good production economics. We should not forget the former, however – considering wholesale changes to the way we do business.

Michael Dell springs to mind as a poster child of business model innovation. Rather than place computers in a shop window, he chose to build them to client order. That was great business innovation indeed – even if very simple to understand after the fact – and came with the added benefits of lower inventory cost, a very limited requirement for computer stores and that the customer could better choose products that were customised to their requirements.

Some such business innovations work, as was the case with Dell computers. Others don't, of course.

So if Strictly Boardroom set up a pizza-making business promising to be far slower than all competitors in making home deliveries it is unlikely that such a business would succeed – albeit that the concept of 'slow pizzas' is indeed novel and innovative in the sector.

Slow pizzas would certainly qualify as innovative but not as business savvy.

While on the subject of pizzas, an insightful story from a management consultant friend is worth recounting here.

Commissioned to suggest ways to improve the economics of a pizza company some years ago, my colleague recommended, among other things, that cheaper but more voluminous product could be used as toppings for late evening special orders. The change made money, driving up order numbers after 10pm and also saved on costs due to lower quality toppings. It turned out from market research that late night pizza customers prefer volume to quality (all right, they were often drunk). Serving up pizzas that met that need required simple but effective innovation in the fast food pizza world.

Back to mining though. Are there examples of business model innovators in our midst? Of course there are.

Mining royalties companies are business model innovators and for the most part have been very successful ones too. They do no actual mining but have typically outperformed traditional mining companies in shareholder returns.

Mining investment companies also aim to innovate in their mode of business but have not generally been as successful as a group as their royalty-focused peers.

Mineral explorers always lay claim to using the latest technical innovation but few think about differentiating the way they position themselves to investors.

Business model innovation opportunities do exist in mineral exploration too.

As an example, at the bottom of the exploration cycle in the early 2000s there was talk of setting up special purpose commodity-focused drilling-funds to be available as an investment entity.

The aim was to beat the odds of exploration risk by earning project equity from specifically commissioned drill programs. Equity markets recovered too quickly for such novel concepts to come to market, with traditional explorers once again able to source capital. Drilling funds were quietly forgotten as a concept.

Whether any such entity would have been the equivalent of slow home pizza delivery or as successful as late night 'with the lot' pizza toppings is hard to say.

Perhaps one day we will find out.

Companies could do worse than put their thinking caps on as regards business model innovation in the minerals world.

There is no doubt a highly successful new business model staring us all in the face. The problem, of course, is that we can't see it.

KEY INSIGHTS: ON STRATEGIC MANAGEMENT

- The mining industry is currently facing decadal lows in commodity prices, increased minerals supply, and heightened challenges in balancing the interests of multiple stakeholders from shareholders to governments. Welcome to the wonderful world of strategic management!

- Mining industry executives should seek help from the wide range of strategic decision-making tools and concepts recounted in the management literature. Amongst the most useful are generic strategies, structured problem-solving, game theory, portfolio analysis, the resource-based view of the firm, and benchmarking.

- Additional frameworks that help address mining-industry specific risks and economics include: mineral market analysis, cost curves, value-chain analysis and the so-called "Cluedo strategy" (right commodity, right country and right entry-point).

- Mergers and acquisitions (M&A) can be a risky strategy in the mining sector, with the major miners taking multi-billion dollar write-downs following a series of poor acquisitions. As the majors now seek to divest non-core assets, smaller miners must seek to avoid the same strategic mistakes.

- Perhaps the single most important point about M&A strategy is that a low-cost asset acquired at a high-price is actually a high-cost asset.

- Beyond the 'right price' and the dangers of M&A noted above, there can, however, be legitimate reasons for paying a premium for an asset if it brings other strategic gains (corporate scale, lower borrowing rates, stability, etc.).

- Organic growth is the other major general strategic lever in the mining sector, usually consisting of exploration and development. Exploration has the potential to provide outsized returns for mining companies, especially emerging miners.

- There are a large number of degrees of freedom in the mining industry, not least – geography, commodity, financing-mix and strategy-mix. Case studies suggest that there is no single, one-size-fits-all 'winning' strategy. There are many ways to win – and to lose.

- In downturns, strategic decision-making tends to focus on divestment. The options available (pursue, hold, partner, drop) are simple, but the decisions in each case are not.

- Making strategic decisions in the mining sector is hard – even when armed with good information.

- To date, mining has seen relatively little business model innovation. The time may be right for more lateral thinking.

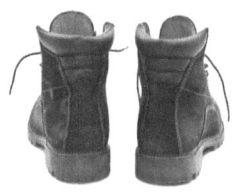

PART 3
Looking to the Future

The boards of minerals companies need to be forward-looking in their decision-making perspective, so Part Three is on "Looking into the Future". It opens with a review of how our current foresight capabilities are limited and how they might be improved in the future in "Beyond FUBAR forecasts".

Even minor improvements in the effectiveness of both macro-economic and sector-specific forecasting tools are likely to have a widespread pay-off across the industry.

In "Why equity analysts are always wrong" we highlight one common mining-industry forecasting 'error' – that of simplistic commodity price assumptions – and suggest that a simple adjustment to recognise commodity price cycles could improve equity analysts' accuracy. Seeking out and repeating such minor improvements across prevailing industry practices will give us all better foresight.

The next three short chapters look at the role of selected trends impacting on the future performance and practices of the mining sector. Industry trends can reflect underlying larger structural shifts that may impact on the whole minerals sector. "The future of mining 'GDP'" looks at the impact of declining ore grades, a rise in resource nationalism, and the need for a more educated, team-orientated workforce in the sector. "Women on mining boards hits all-time high" looks at an emergent trend in the mining sector, whereby the numbers of women on minerals company boards is increasing – a trend anticipated to accelerate in the near-future. Finally, "Return of the mid-tier miner?" makes the case that the entire structure of the industry is dynamic and that it may once again be due for a change.

Individual trends do not operate in isolation of course, and as such it is important that minerals sector boards think in an integrated, systems-based manner as to how the future may unfold. Boards should consider tools such as scenario planning which envisage multiple potential futures, and allow decision-makers to prepare strategically for a number of potential outcomes.

Scenario planning examples form the next four short chapters. Firstly, "Mining 2040: An industry under siege" plays out a scenario where a mining industry struggling to survive eventually cedes its future to other industries such as petroleum, logistics, technology and even to retail. Alternatively, "Mining 2040: The commodity crusades" considers a more positive scenario where the mining industry returns to boom times in the short term – and critically is then able to build on this advantage over the long term to adapt and prosper, embracing both long-term environmental and sustainability challenges. A third scenario – "Mining 2040: Major miners as counting houses" sees a present industry from which thriving major mining companies fail to adapt to the future – thus facing consequent self-inflicted difficulties over the long term. The final scenario – "Mining 2040: Peasants' revolt" – looks at how even an industry which is struggling can re-invent itself and adapt to the future. Unsurprisingly, the different scenarios lead to differing strategic winners and losers. Developing strategies and companies that are robust to a range of futures is therefore a great future challenge for industry boards.

Good foresight alone will not secure a company's future over the long term. Executives need to convert foresight into strategic insight. The final short chapter in Part Three therefore describes a fictional example of this in the exploration sector, utilising business model innovation: "Tales from the past: The reinvention of minerals exploration".

24. BEYOND FUBAR FORECASTS

04 Jan 2016 Strictly Boardroom makes a resolution to try and improve commodity price and minerals sector forecasting performance[1,2].

This New Year, Strictly Boardroom resolves not to contribute to the library of soon-to-be disproven forecasts for 2016 (at least until mid-January anyway) and instead reviews a number of ways in which forecasting methodologies applied to the mining industry could be materially improved.

Economic forecasters, whether of the broader economy or specifically of commodity prices, have a mixed track record. As the saying goes, "he who lives by the crystal ball soon learns to eat ground glass". Clearly much work remains to be done to improve forecasting methodology and accuracy. To extend the metaphor laid out by Donald Rumsfeld (former US Secretary of Defense) in reference to the unknown nature of the future, forecasters must consider and navigate three broad domains of uncertainty.

Known unknowns – the things you know you don't know

It has become clear that "what you do not know can hurt you…" and thus to deal with the uncertainty surrounding 'known unknowns' there has been a resurgence in the use of Bayesian statistical methods and real options techniques in forecasting. Nate Silver, author of the best-selling *The Signal and The Noise: The Art and Science of Prediction* is at the vanguard of this movement.

Bayesian forecasting is a probabilistic approach to forecasting that accepts in an uncertain environment many different futures could emerge. The aim of such forecasting is to be approximately correct, rather than precisely wrong. Forecasts that ultimately prove to be precisely wrong all too often result from detailed conventional forecasts that have failed to capture the uncertainty that arises from known unknowns.

Unknown unknowns – the things you don't know you don't know

'Unknown unknowns' by their very nature are difficult to understand, quantify and study objectively. That said, unknown unknowns cannot simply be ignored as being in the too-hard basket.

Inevitably such work is going to cross the line from objective to subjective; however, there are techniques available that aim to apply subjective forecasting more accurately than before. Whilst Bayesian techniques do have an element of subjectivity, in areas of wide uncertainty and when looking far into the future, methods such as scenario planning are now gaining greater prominence and acceptance.

Yet further advances in forecasting methods are advocated by Philip Tetlock, author of *Superforecasting*, who has identified measurably better techniques for subjective 'political science' type forecasting over a 12- to 24-month future timeframe. Tetlock's 'superforecasters' beat the best intelligence analysts consistently. To do so they deploy: teamwork, a mix of basic maths and probabilities; careful base rate selection; data and news search and regular forecast updating. They also carry out post-mortems on their own forecasts; seek out and balance a variety of perspectives; analyse key players, norms and protocols; and demonstrate an ability to know which forecasts to make and which ones to avoid.

Unknown knowns – we do not always know what we think we know

There is increasing understanding that we do not always know what we think we know – the so called 'unknown knowns'. Perhaps the most important area of work on this issue is in biases and heuristics where our unconscious mind misleads us in our understanding of an issue. Daniel Kahneman, author of *Thinking, Fast and Slow*, received a Nobel Memorial Prize in Economics for his work in this field.

Discussions of heuristics such as anchoring, availability and familiarity, which lead to bias in both analysis and outcomes, are now increasingly common across business and academia. Similarly, there is an increased recognition that 'expertise' itself can only be developed in 'high validity' environments, where we have repeated chances to learn from cycles of actions and consequences. Many of the things we wish to predict in the mining industry are in 'low validity' environments, including, for instance, long-term commodity prices, and thus the very nature of the role of the expertise in these areas is now evolving.

As well as 'unconscious' unknown knowns caused by heuristics, there are also more conscious forms of unknown knowns that can lead to forecasting bias and error. Amongst the sins here are those occasions where analysts refuse to recognise and assign value to critical new facts as they emerge which should result in updated forecasts. So why are such data ignored? Here personal pride can often play a role – whereby an analyst may irrationally 'stick to their guns' for example – as does the concept of 'paradigm-lock-in' which prevents a break from existing thinking. In such cases, external interventions led by consultants or again techniques such as scenario planning can break taboos and reframe ideas.

Forecasting resolutions

Strictly Boardroom's suggested New Year's Resolutions to help industry forecasters improve their game are as follows:

1. **Measure forecasting performance.** As the management mantra goes "what is not measured is not managed". This is also the key message of Philip Tetlock's work. Forecasting cannot improve until forecasting performance is routinely measured.

2. **Improve conventional practice.** The vast majority of forecasts are still sourced from conventional, often econometrics-based, numerical modelling. While other suggestions below such as

improved data and understanding of biases will help conventional forecasting too, effort still needs to go into improving existing practice. Since econometric techniques are so widely used, even slight improvements in conventional forecasting will have outsized impacts on our understanding of the future.

3. **Mine historical data.** Even where we already have the 'facts', we need to better study and understand them. That is, measuring economic history helps us to disaggregate previous industry and market developments and their impact on prices. Incumbent in this is an effort to improve the historical archive of information on the industry, including for example, the data on China and on minerals discovery and resource growth.

4. **Focus on drivers and assumptions.** Too much forecasting simply projects the top-line numbers into the future, without understanding why the numbers are as they are. More effort needs to go into understanding the drivers and key assumptions behind forecasts. This is the inherent problem with the current approach to 'big data'. Successful use of big data in the future will require an understanding of the underlying drivers shaping the data, as well as the development of smart 'search and model' algorithms.

5. **Adopt scenario planning and similar techniques.** Whilst one direction in forecasting improvement is taking us down an ever-heavier data route, some aspects of the future are going to remain highly subjective. In these cases, the techniques that best use subjectivity should be applied more frequently. Scenario planning is a key tool in this area alongside Tetlock's 'superforecasting' techniques.

6. **Recognise bias.** As understanding of the power of anchoring and other heuristics on human cognition develops, acceptance needs to also grow that forecasts contain bias and can always be improved. The next step is then to begin to develop

systematic sanity-check techniques that can counter the natural weaknesses of the human mind in making forecasts.

Making a start on that lot will make for a very busy year ahead.

---

1 "FUBAR" is defined here in the more polite form than is often used – namely "Fouled up beyond all repair".

2 Includes some text adapted from Trench, A., Sykes, J. & Robinson, P., *Edge of tomorrow: A tour of 2016-2020 mineral commodity markets*. AusIMM New Zealand Branch Annual Conference 2015, Dunedin.

3 Silver, N. 2015. *The Signal and the Noise: Why So Many Predictions Fail – But Some Don't*. Penguin Books, London.

4 Tetlock, P. & Gardner, D. 2006. *Superforecasting: The Art and Science of Prediction*. Crown, London.

5 Kahneman, D. 2013. *Thinking: Fast and Slow*. Farrar, Straus and Giroux, New York.

25. WHY EQUITY ANALYSTS ARE ALWAYS WRONG

19 Aug 2013 Strictly Boardroom looks at equity analysis – prompted by one colleague's exasperation at the valuation errors that proliferate across the resources sector.

A colleague recently complained to Strictly Boardroom that equity analysts should be locked up or at least held more accountable for getting their valuations so horribly wrong.

Without naming the specific investment bank that they were referring to, the email dialogue went something like this:

> "A year ago these guys have a 'buy' on the same stock valuing the company at around $2 with the share price not far below that level. A year previously they were saying 'buy' at $2.50 per share. Now they are advising a 'sell' at 50¢ – how can that be? These guys should have long since lost their jobs."

Our colleague's experience of following equity recommendations would not be uncommon. We suspect if there were a systematic study of recommendations across the emerging companies in the resources sector over the last two years it would reveal the example above to be more the norm rather than an outlier, so the numbers did not surprise us.

Why are analysts so often wrong then? And why your scribes' lack of surprise at the seemingly systemic valuation error?

The answer all lies in the numbers – and critically of course, in the various assumptions therein.

In the general case, most analysts (at least for producing or near-production assets) will do a net present value per share calculation using a sum-of-the-parts approach.

So say a gold company has a project with a net present value (NPV) of A$100 million (on a 2012 gold price assumption of A$1,600 per ounce) and an even 100 million shares then the NPV calculation would spit out a A$1 per share initial discounted cash flow value.

Next the fudge factors are added. These relate, among other things, to how analysts measure the value of early exploration properties and joint ventures.

In a hot market, exploration properties will attract premium (unsubstantiated) fudge factors, so say in the simple case above that A$20 million of extra value is attributed to exploration properties. Let's say the share price a year ago was 80¢ – the analysts say NPV of the mine is A$100 million and exploration of A$20 million, then their target price would be A$1.20 against 80¢ trading value and A$100 million 'visible NPV' (by discounted cash flow analysis) at an A$1,600/oz flat gold price assumption.

Analysts would say 'buy'.

Fast-forward a year: such a company's price would likely now be 30¢ (perhaps less).

The NPV at A$1,350/oz of future production, now nearing break-even, may only be A$30 million.

The company will have used up a year of reserves between drinks – and now faces lower flat gold price assumption from the analysts.

Indeed, to argue that they are prudent, the analysts may now choose to use A$1,250/oz to value the mine's cash flows, which are consequently deemed marginal.

The fudge factors would have changed too, of course – with a view that exploration is a 2013 liability more than a 2012 asset.

So exploration is now valued at zero, or even a negative figure (so as to account for tenement maintenance exploration that is required but attracts no revenue).

A particularly conservative equity analyst may now also 'remember' corporate costs – a further negative of perhaps A$1 to A$2 million per year.

Given the above it becomes easy to see how one could easily reach the situation where the analyst would say 'sell' at 30¢ versus 'buy' a year ago at 80¢.

Both pieces of analysis are short-sighted, but both work perfectly well on any spreadsheet.

So are they both wrong? Yes, of course they are.

Can the analyst justify why they are so wrong? The obvious excuse is that the facts have changed – and they have – but a good analyst would have tried to capture that likelihood in the first instance.

Some 20 years ago, it became possible to model mines on a full commodity cycle basis. Although back then, we used a steam-driven computer that needed a suitcase to carry it around.

Now it is far easier, of course.

Full commodity cycle valuation would have corrected both the overshoot errors in the simplified valuation examples described above (the first valuation being too high, the second too low).

Done correctly, full price cycle modelling does not just give you an impossibly wide range of possible future outcomes (which it will do if done wrongly) – but can make clear the valuation outcomes that are likely based upon where you currently sit in the commodity price cycle.

Perhaps one day full commodity price cycle valuation will become the norm rather than the exception (if the chorus of disquiet over incorrect valuations grows). For now we seem stuck with the equity valuation methods described above: analysis that will always be wrong.

26. THE FUTURE OF MINING 'GDP'

16 Sep 2013 Strictly Boardroom looks at the big picture that lies ahead for the mining sector if it is to make good on its full economic potential. One looming issue that is certainly not lost upon the industry's stakeholders is whether the mining sector can deliver upon its future global GDP potential.

Now GDP usually of course refers to the economic definition, gross domestic product – with the global contribution from mining and metals calculated as the sum of the parts from individual country contributions.

But perhaps another acronym of GDP sums up mining's present challenges quite well, too?

In this alternative definition of mining GDP, **G is for Grades** – which are falling. **D is for Distribution** – meaning who gets to share in mining's contribution to society and **P is for People** – starting with the mining workforce itself.

Grade: Both the challenge and the evidence here is clear. Recent work by CRU Group estimates that the global mined grade of copper, which sat at 0.81% back in 2002, will fall to just 0.61% by 2022 for existing mines. Selected copper projects offer some hope for reversal of this trend, but higher-grade copper opportunities are very much in the minority. The grade issue does not stop at copper. Commodities across the Periodic Table suffer from similar future grade challenges.

Local solutions to the grade decline exist at asset level – which will likely involve innovative pre-sorting and selection of ores, for example. But the industry needs a greater understanding of where the extra tonnage movements shift cost curves. For example, can mining and processing innovations offset the obvious cost impact of grade decline? That is a multi-billion dollar question. The default setting appears to be a case of 'bigger is better' for new projects – but can the 'right-sizing' of new developments find a sweet spot to capture scale and scope benefits?

Distribution: The challenge of distributing the benefits from mining is perhaps even tougher. Resource nationalism is on the rise, with governments the world over in the habit of reviewing royalties, for example (a very mild form of resource nationalism). The predominant approach is to tackle distribution issues bottom-up – flexing taxes, royalties and government interests to capture greater proportions of the economic rent for the host government. The more efficient method is actually to think top-down – starting with a pre-tax project NPV and dividing this between public and private interests in a transparent and equitable manner. Much work remains to be done on this issue and few participants in the sector can answer simple questions on where the split lies now in different jurisdictions and across different commodities and for Tier 1 through to Tier 3 assets.

Finally, there is the **People** challenge. The mining sector is in the process of transition away from viewing the labour force as marginal units of labour and as a cost. The future for mining is now through a lens that sees a highly valued, educated workforce capable of step-change improvement. One aspect of this is that the mining sector must focus less upon leadership (such as who sits at the head of which mining company) and more upon collective team performance – arming people with the necessary skills to make changes.

All the above transitions are slowly happening, but unfortunately only with plate tectonic velocities.

To deliver upon its full potential, the mining sector needs to make tangible progress on each letter of the alternative GDP acronym sooner rather than later.

27. WOMEN ON MINING BOARDS HITS ALL-TIME HIGH

18 Aug 2014 Strictly Boardroom and Morgan Trench update the latest numbers on gender diversity across ASX-listed mining boardrooms.

With the June 30, 2014 financial year close now behind us, Strictly Boardroom thinks it's timely to once again review the analysis of women on mining boards.

The news is good (or at least the news is a little better than it was may be a more appropriate tagline). Female participation in

Australia's minerals sector boardrooms has once again hit a new all-time high in the latest boardroom diversity analysis – but the rate of change still remains only incremental.

Using the Director Search[1] algorithm, Strictly Boardroom extracted and analysed director information from the 150 minerals companies listed as having the largest market capitalisation in the sector.[2]

To the results. Here are the headline numbers from that July 2014 dataset:

- 27% of companies had at least one female board member
- Women now occupy 6.3% of all positions
- That is, the data search revealed that 52 of 823 director roles are filled by women
- 11 companies have two women on their boards.

As with the previous gender balance analyses, the numbers of women on mining boards still remains modest – but the latest available data are nevertheless once again higher than for the all previous analyses reported in Strictly Boardroom.

By way of a direct comparison, the most recent comparable numbers from the end-2013 study were as follows:

- 24% of companies had at least one female board member
- Women occupied 5.4% of all positions in the (then) largest 150 minerals companies
- The December 2013 data search revealed 45 of 835 director roles were filled by women
- Nine companies (of the then largest 100) had two women on each of their boards.

Now to state the obvious. There is still plenty of scope here for these numbers to increase of course.

Clearly the underlying issue of under-representation of women on our sector's boards is not one that will be solved with repeated analysis of statistics alone. Our culture has to change too.

Unfortunately, culture is far more difficult to measure using a computer algorithm than are the actual gender balance numbers themselves.

Watch that space.

---

1 The Director Search algorithm is a custom-made web-search program that analyses key director information pertaining to each company as reported on ASX.com.au. The information reported here is current to July 24, 2014.

2 The largest 150 companies in the ASX minerals sector (excluding oil and gas) was identical to the list published by Gresham Advisory Partners in their July 2014 Gresham Group 150 market report. PCF Capital (http://www.pcfcapital.com.au/) now publishes a similar monthly publication to the Gresham 150 report that also tracks the ranking and relative performance of the largest 150 mining and exploration companies.

28. RETURN OF THE MID-TIER MINER?

18 Mar 2013 Having become an endangered species following the M&A activities of the majors over the past decade, mid-tier miners may now be set for a comeback. Strictly Boardroom outlines the path towards re-emergence.

The law of unintended consequences is always worthy of consideration when market disruption of one form or another enters the fray. Looking at this year's minerals sector landscape, the new-found austerity and cost-focus rhetoric emanating from the major miners is one such 'market disruption' that looks certain to play out in future. The majors are determined to lift margins and shareholder returns. In the absence of commodity price increases, this translates to a search for operating cost efficiencies accompanied by major capital project deferrals.

The intended winners from this renewed capital-efficiency drive are the respective shareholders of the likes of Barrick Gold, BHP Billiton and Rio Tinto. But the benefits from heightened capital discipline and project restraint could spread far wider than just the bottom line of the majors themselves. Arguably, the majors may even shift the leverage in the industry away from themselves towards their smaller counterparts. How is this so?

The first element is that a pull-back in the advancement of large new projects by the majors could open the door for smaller miners. How exactly?

The removal of a potential 'supply wave' originating from the majors into commodity markets as projects are deferred is good for commodity prices (while in the process it further strengthens the balance sheets of majors themselves of course as supply tightens). The former point is critical. Using copper as an example, surplus markets are already being forecast from 2014 – even with a number of major copper projects having already been held back. Projects held by majors comprise over half of the project pipeline in tonnage terms across copper. So any hesitation when it comes to future development timelines by the larger supply-side players is significant. Delays will nudge price expectations higher, making the financing of those projects held by companies willing to proceed easier.

Next, the project capital markets, including debt capacity, that would have potentially formed a part in facilitating large projects held by the majors now becomes available elsewhere – with the rider of course that the next tier of projects (those not held by the majors) must be bankable.

Who stands to gain? The smaller players once again.

Finally, the engineering, procurement and construction management (EPCM) 'A-Teams' become more available too – so delivery risk is lessened – as is the likelihood of capital cost overrun when the project development market loses heat.

All the above plays into the hands of smaller miners, being those seeking to develop projects of significant scale – but not quite of the scale of Tier 1 mega-projects. In the copper space this equates to projects in the 50,000 to 150,000 tonne per annum (tpa) range – where the output is material on a global scale – with a capital price-tag not beyond a well-supported mid-tier miner. Such projects are very significant to the next tier of miners and, once established, could also appeal to majors in the fullness of time.

So the likes of Sandfire Resources and OZ Minerals may be given a clear line of sight to grow, to develop new projects free from the attention of the majors in an M&A context. Smart boutique fund money is already placing bets on those development projects which they believe to be among the better assets held by emerging miners.

Eventually the capital restraint will abate and the coast clears for the majors to once again indulge in incremental M&A mopping up of the better-placed of the mid-tiers. Majors can afford to wait and see who does well, and who stumbles, and the whole cycle starts over again.

How long will this process take? Your scribe's guestimate is about five years – being the typical tenure for a major company MD. The clock has just started ticking.

The opportunity to become a true mid-tier is there. Will anyone take it?

29. MINING 2040: AN INDUSTRY UNDER SIEGE

02 Nov 2015 Strictly Boardroom discusses the first of four scenarios for the future of mining and exploration – including the likely winners and the losers across industry stakeholders.

With the recent tumbling commodity and mining share prices, it goes without saying that the future of the mining industry is uncertain. Anyone offering you a definitive clear vision of the future is either deceived or doing the deceiving.

Futures experts Philip Tetlock[1] and Clem Sunter[2] call these people hedgehogs. Such hedgehogs are tied to one idea of the future and will stick to it with impressive fortitude, even if the world brings contrary evidence – to metaphorically roll up in a ball and show their spikes. An iron will can be of great use in some situations, but not when there is a car hurtling down the road towards you.

In contrast, foxy strategists, such as Tetlock and Sunter, take the stance that there are many ways the future may work out. They're happy to use their fox-like cunning and adapt as they go along. It is of no surprise that foxes are equally happy rifling through hen cages in the countryside as they are scrounging from rubbish bins in the city.

So what might a foxy strategist have to say about the future of our mining industry?

In an attempt to try and answer this question, Strictly Boardroom over this and the next three short chapters, shares some preliminary results of a scenario planning exercise about the future of mining and exploration[3].

The scenarios follow the methodology of the Oxford Scenario Planning Approach[4] built upon the same forward-thinking foundations that has long formed the basis of strategic planning at oil giant, Shell.

The scenarios looked specifically at the copper industry, but they offer insights for all other mined commodities. They are written from the perspective of an analyst in 2040 looking back at how the industry has evolved since 2015.

For the avoidance of doubt, these scenarios are fictional and designed to provoke thinking on key issues, not predictions of what will happen. Real companies, organisations and countries are used to increase the impact of the scenarios, but this does not imply that these actors will behave as described, nor does it reflect the authors' opinions of the relative merits of the different actors mentioned.

Scenario 1: Under siege!

The Under Siege scenario describes an industry struggling with current profitability and with few future options for growth. The name suggests an industry defending its current operations (or castles), completely unable to go on any adventurous forays outside the castle walls.

How it started in 2015

In late 2015, a property bubble in China was already correcting – only to then reach all-out collapse in July and August 2016. The bad economic news spread across Asia. Renewed growth in the West stalled. The 2016 Chinese Financial Crisis (CFC) resulted – and then spread globally. Risk appetites were reduced. Western governments responded not with Keynesian-stimulus as for the GFC but instead they imposed ever greater austerity. Commodity prices reached new lows. All investment in mine projects, exploration and research and development (R&D) suddenly ground to a halt.

What had happened by 2025

The Chinese economy suffered a lost decade. It struggled to maintain social order as domestic income disparities grew but overall growth was anaemic. Economic and financial crises rumbled on around the world causing geo-political instability.

Populist governments introduced anti-immigrant and protectionist measures in an effort to insulate their countries from global woes. Trade agreements were rescinded. Foreign-owned mines were increasingly heavily taxed or in several cases nationalised. This started across several African states, but it eventually spread to South America, Asia and even Europe. Australia introduced the *Mining Revenues to the People Tax Act* of 2021 (MRPT) at federal level to counter ever increasing state royalties and charges. The increased prevalence of local employment and local content laws further reduced mine productivity.

International political co-operation was impeded by complex attempts to resolve the ongoing economic and financial issues. As a by-product, a lack of global co-ordination on environmental policy allowed national and local environmental legislation to be used increasingly as a protectionist measure. Environmental issues became conflated with the foreign exploitation of local people.

An increasing distrust of foreigners made access to foreign mine projects nearly impossible. Even domestic projects in remote regions became difficult to access as faith in 'the state' receded and rural residents increasingly distrusted 'urbanites'.

Anti-immigrant measures meant companies were increasingly restricted to domestic talent pools. This worsened a shortage of young engineers and scientists caused by demographic decline and further reduced interest in science and engineering degrees.

Where we are now in 2040

The lack of investment in mining has led to decreased productivity. The industry has fractured.

Former global mining companies have retreated back to safe 'home' locations and are now focused on local assets. Most countries have a quasi-state mining company running local mines, with governments using the funds to appease unhappy populations. Mining is a highly politicised industry.

Australia is a perfect example. The largest domestic mining company is now Big Australian Mining. The Australian government owns a golden share, using it to encourage the purchase and support of struggling mines, smelters and industrial facilities.

Codelco maintains its position as the world's leading copper miner, though it is state-subsidised. Chile chose to forcefully expand the state's interest in private-sector copper mines to grow Codelco's production. Globally, the next biggest copper miner is SinoCopper, a relatively new Chinese state miner, which has consolidated Chinese copper mining. Codelco, SinoCopper and the emergent state mining companies of Peru, DR Congo and Zambia recently attempted to form a cartel.

A combination of supply chain management improvements and tech-firm backed 'internet of things' companies means copper recycling has increased substantially. As much as 60% of copper is now recycled. Most copper in products is tagged with nanochips and flows around a circular economy constantly being re-used.

Both recycling and circular economy measures proved simpler to implement at a national level than at an international level, thus benefitting from the de-globalisation. The overall 'raw material intensity' of the world economy has shrunk.

The mining industry is widely seen as an 'old industry', a relic of the 20th century.

West Perth has become a bio-technology hub, thriving in proximity to large new hospitals and greater concerns about health and longevity from an aged population.

The winner and losers

In this 'declining sum' scenario, state mining companies backed by governments concerned about the limited number of profitable operating mines are the main long-term beneficiaries, along with environmental groups keen to restrict new horizons for the mining industry.

The major listed mining companies are barely hanging on. They have been forced to restructure, as they faced declining profits, closed mines and suffered repeated waves of asset-level 'incremental nationalisation'.

The listed junior exploration sector has all but disappeared due to a chronic lack of funding, although some privately-owned exploration syndicates with close government relationships remain active.

The shrinking nature of the traditional mining industry has meant that outside industries have taken over ever-larger parts of the role of copper supply.

PS. Don't worry; we outline a brighter future for the mining industry next!

---

1 Tetlock, P. 2006. *Expert Political Judgment: How Good Is It? How Can We Know?* Princeton University Press, Princeton, NJ.

2 Sunter, C. & Ilbury, C. 2011. *The Mind of the Fox: Scenario Planning in Action.* Human & Rousseau, Cape Town.

3 Sykes, J.P. & Trench, A. 2016. *Using Scenarios to Investigate the Long-Term Future of Copper Mining and Guide Exploration Targeting Strategies.* AusIMM International Mine Management Conference, Brisbane, 22-24 August, in press.

4 Ramirez, R. & Wilkinson, A. 2016. *Strategic Reframing: The Oxford Scenario Planning Approach.* Oxford University Press, Oxford.

30. MINING 2040: THE COMMODITY CRUSADES

09 Nov 2015 Next Strictly Boardroom introduces a 'good news' scenario for the future of mining and exploration – with opportunities for everyone from explorers to majors.

In the previous short chapter we presented Under Siege, the first of four scenarios for the future of mining and exploration[1] developed using the Oxford Scenario Planning Approach[2]. The second scenario sees the future industry in far better health – indeed with the mining sector undertaking a form of Commodity Crusade by 2040, opening up many new and exciting frontiers.

First some context as to how the various scenarios for the future differ in their derivation: the four Mining 2040 scenarios comprise a two-by-two matrix, with the matrix axes representing key strategic drivers for the minerals sector.

The X-axis comprises those factors that control the 'economic margins' earned by the industry: commodity prices, exchange rates and the cost of key inputs such as fuel and labour sit on this axis. However, this axis also includes a technical aspect – being all of the technological, scientific and engineering practices that influence the industry cost function.

All of these factors can act to increase or decrease the 'economic margin' of mining operations and therefore the forecast economic potential of mine projects, exploration and R&D programmes.

The Y-axis is best defined as the industry 'search space'. It is a representation of technical and business opportunities available to the industry[3] value chain. That is, the 'search space' as defined here is not restricted solely to minerals exploration. It includes new and improved mining and processing technologies to unlock value from critical metals for example; it seeks to measure economic and socio-political forces as they impact upon mining; the interaction of the industry with the natural environment and so on. All of these areas contain issues, opportunities and challenges that may radically transform the future mining industry – either for better or worse.

In the Under Siege scenario, the economic margin' by 2040 was under severe pressure and the search space' was becoming ever more constrained over time. By contrast, in this scenario, we find a 2040 mining industry in which the economic margin is substantial and the search space has materially grown.

Scenario 2: Commodity crusades

The Crusades scenario envisages a highly profitable mining industry investing in a range of new ideas and projects, able to successfully transition into the future. The name suggests sturdy foundations (or castles) with ambitious leaders (or crusaders) looking for great adventure and conquest beyond the confines of their respective castles.

How it started in 2015

This year proved the humble beginnings of a sustained resurgence of economic growth in the US and Europe. The economic wobbles in China proved to be just that with a return to accelerating GDP growth from 2016 onwards. 'Abenomics' finally helped re-start the Japanese growth engine. Narendra Modi's economic reform plan in India began to take shape. Locally, Malcolm Turnbull's elevation to the Prime Ministership of Australia saw the instigation of a strong push into the commercialisation of technology and innovation outcomes.

With economic and financial problems receding, governments began to focus on global issues. The first indication of this was the success of the Paris Climate Summit and renewed global resolve towards reduced carbon emissions. Investment in shale gas in both Europe and China over the subsequent decade maintained a trend towards lower prices for cleaner energy that had started with the US shale gas revolution. Improved off-grid energy solutions opened up new frontiers for mine development in remote areas.

Miners saw a dual benefit from higher commodity prices and lower energy costs and a return to strong profitability. Australia's innovative push into mining equipment automation gathered momentum. Australian Geographic Information Systems (GIS) and minerals/agricultural sector software companies led the world.

What had happened by 2025

By 2025, it had become clear that the Paris Climate Summit of 2015 marked the beginning of a decade of multinational agreements on environmental, indigenous peoples, sustainable development, free trade and foreign investment issues.

The proliferation of multinational rules and frameworks made new technologies and ideas more readily accessible, opening up numerous areas for new development including several advancements in the extraction and processing of minor and previously critical metals.

Sustained profitability attracted scientific and engineering talent to the minerals sector, keen to adopt the challenge of re-designing the industry in a less environmental and socially intrusive manner.

Where we are now in 2040

A number of significant but ageing large copper mines have now closed but long before they ran out of lower-grade open pit resources amenable to truck and shovel extraction. Traditional large-scale open pits now only make up around a quarter of the industry.

New copper mines are now predominantly underground operations in previously politically risky countries across Africa. They employ new generation, remotely-operated mining equipment. Companies with long-term experience in Africa, such as Anglo American and Glencore, enjoyed first-mover advantage in the now rapidly growing mining sectors of the developing world.

A new type of mine is emerging and is rapidly evolving: that is, highly targeted, automated underground operations are opening up in remote, covered regions of Australia, Canada, Scandinavia and also in South America's 'copper capitals' of Chile and Peru. The drift of talent from the deep offshore petroleum sector has greatly contributed to the technological advances required to facilitate this 'real-time mining' (RTM) within months from initial discovery.

Rio Tinto, a long-time leader in underground and automated mining technology, has been amongst those companies forging the new generation of mines. Mining services companies and start-ups thrive, most based in one of the industry's global technology hubs of Perth, Vancouver, Houston or Stavanger.

A number of new in-situ leaching mining technologies, variously utilising acid, polymers, bacteria and nanobots are also gaining broader adoption globally.

The winner and losers

The mining industry saw two main winners in this scenario. Both groups were 'first movers'.

The major miners that most aggressively partnered with governments, NGOs and aid bodies in developing world locations gained preferential access to the best mineral deposits. Similarly, major miners who rapidly embraced dramatic technological change also benefitted.

Beyond the majors, the technology focus also provided countless opportunities for a number of new start-ups, many utilising skills and methodologies adapted from other industries such as petroleum. Explorers too underwent successful transition – with renewed strong investor support for frontier exploration accompanying the widespread profitability of the sector.

The thriving mining sector afforded little scope for disruption from industry outsiders – with the 2040 technology-based mining industry of the future almost unrecognisable from the truck and shovel era of the past.

---

1 Sykes, J.P. & Trench, A. 2016. *Using Scenarios to Investigate the Long-Term Future of Copper Mining and Guide Exploration Targeting Strategies*. AusIMM International Mine Management Conference, Brisbane, 22-24 August, in press.

2 Ramirez, R. & Wilkinson, A. 2016. *Strategic Reframing: The Oxford Scenario Planning Approach*. Oxford University Press, Oxford.

3 Hronsky, J. 2009. *The Exploration Search Space Concept: Key to a Successful Exploration Strategy*, Centre for Exploration Targeting Quarterly Newsletter, June, p14-15.

31. MINING 2040: MAJOR MINERS AS COUNTING HOUSES

16 Nov 2015 Strictly Boardroom discusses a new scenario for the future of mining and exploration – with some good news for the major miners.

In this short chapter, we envisage an alternative scenario for the mining industry in 2040 – that of an industry counting out its money – a form of 'Counting House'. Unfortunately however, the mining sector of 2040 is not doing a great deal else. So rather than an industry 'Under Siege' or else a sector embarking on an expansive global 'Commodity Crusade', the Counting House scenario sets out an entirely new future.

Counting House is the third of four scenarios[1] developed using the Oxford Scenario Planning Approach[2] where the future is broadly defined on two key axes: 'economic margin' and 'search space'. The Counting House future is one of strong economic margins for large incumbents (the good news) but with only limited new growth horizons for new projects (the bad news).

Scenario 3: The rise of The Counting House

The Counting House scenario is named after the nursery rhyme 'Sing a Song of Sixpence' where "The King is in his counting house, counting out his money." It is a metaphor for an industry collecting rents from current operations (or castles), but uninterested in the world beyond the castle walls.

How it started in 2015

In late 2015, to help re-energise its economy, China committed to a major shale gas development programme. Over the next few years, the domestic cost of energy fell dramatically, triggering a broad-based economic boom. Demand for raw materials increased sharply, leading to higher non-energy commodity prices.

Combined with the US shale gas boom, both the world's major economies now had abundant, cheap sources of energy. Europe, Japan and other economies, facing increased competition, also commenced large-scale investment in new gas and nuclear power facilities. Australia's shale gas and off-shore liquid natural gas (LNG) investments began to come on-stream.

Mining companies returned record profits, benefitting from elevated commodity prices and cheaper global fuel sources. A major wave of M&As occurred over the following two years, with mid-tier companies in Australia amongst the most prized of targets. For example, each of Iluka Resources, Independence Group, Northern Star Resources, OZ Minerals, Sandfire Resources and Western Areas were absorbed by larger global miners in this period, all for significant premiums.

The gap between large and small companies grew, with exploration companies left on the sidelines.

What had happened by 2025

Responding to rapid commodity market growth, mining companies focused on capacity expansions and brownfields projects. Investors demanded dividends and discouraged wasteful greenfields exploration and R&D. One prominent CEO was ousted by activist shareholders when proposing a vote to support the exploration budget at an annual general meeting.

Generally, greenfields exploration projects and R&D programmes have been divested, returned to governments or simply shut down and abandoned. No minerals related IPOs have occurred on the ASX, Toronto Venture Exchange (TSX-V), London Alternative Investment Market (AIM), Beijing or Santiago exchanges since 2021.

For operating assets, however, cheap energy meant that mines were increasingly able to capture economies of scale. The additional energy intensity required to process lower grade ores was more than offset by the advantages of scale. Major desalination plants were developed to feed water to the giant copper mines of South America and the southern United States.

Mining fleet automation circumvented an emerging shortage of frontline labour. By contrast, professional workers were in relative abundance, attracted to mining by stable employment and exciting mega-engineering projects.

However, despite the major investments in clean coal, shale gas and nuclear power, these were increasingly seen as stop-gap solutions. Thus concerns over climate change continued to mount, combining with a multitude of other environmental and local community issues which remained largely unaddressed.

Some developing countries also began to complain about the colonial attitudes of American, Asian, European and Australian-based companies operating abroad. The few small, usually private companies attempting to explore and develop new mines in foreign locations found that it was easier to already have a social licence to operate (such as for the mega miners) rather than to try and gain one.

Where we are now in 2040

To head-off international governmental pressure to mitigate carbon emissions most mines have now built extraordinarily expensive carbon capture and mini-nuclear power facilities. The capital cost of carbon mitigation has however reinforced the advantage of currently operating, energy intensive mines.

The premium on operating assets over development assets has never been greater. Few new mines, unless heavily government backed, have been developed in the last decade, though most mines have undergone substantial expansions and upgrades.

With few new assets under development, growth efforts have focused on M&A and after a number of heavily leveraged takeovers the big three mining companies are now American-Australian Mining (AAM), Commodities Inc. (COMI) and Mining & Global Metals (MGM) – all far bigger than their early 21st century predecessors.

2040 has, however, not been a good year for the mining industry. First a major anti-trust enquiry into the mining sector was launched in the US. A few months later, AAM and MGM announced a write down of 25 to 35% of their reserves, due to incorrect cost inflation assumptions. Their dividend policies are now under pressure due to their heavy debt loads.

Later in the year, there was an accident at a mini-nuclear power plant on one of COMI's mines in China. Several local executives were arrested. Protests ensued. COMI has put aside $50 billion to meet the expected damages to be levied by the Chinese Ministry of the Environment. It is likely dividends will be suspended for several years and assets will have to be divested to meet the damages claims.

A powerful group of international environmental and civil rights non-governmental organisations (NGOs), backed by a number of Asian, African and South American governments, have formed a coalition vowing to block the development of any new mine; encouraging investors to boycott mining shares; and campaigning for rich-world governments to provide subsidies for the recycling industry.

The winner and losers

In this scenario, the incumbent major miners are the main beneficiaries initially. Mid-tier companies also win – albeit by selling themselves to the highest bidder. Exploration and other smaller mining companies on the other hand wither and in most cases die.

However, over the longer term, the major miners are found guilty of perpetually living in the short term and seeking to engineer their way out of social, political and environmental problems. Whilst major technological successes have been achieved at operating assets, the development of new search space has been abandoned and room for manoeuvre has shrunk. The industry is profitable but has limited social licence to operate beyond the confines of the existing mine gates. When problems have finally arisen, the industry has found it has few allies.

"My name is Ozymandias…"[3]

---

1 Sykes, J.P. & Trench, A. 2016. *Using Scenarios to Investigate the Long-Term Future of Copper Mining and Guide Exploration Targeting Strategies*, AusIMM International Mine Management Conference, Brisbane, 22-24 August, in press.

2 Ramirez, R. & Wilkinson, A. 2016. *Strategic Reframing: The Oxford Scenario Planning Approach*. Oxford University Press, Oxford.

3 "…'My name is Ozymandias, king of kings: Look on my works, ye Mighty, and despair!' Nothing beside remains. Round the decay, Of that colossal wreck, boundless and bare, The lone and level sands stretch far away." – Percy Shelley, 1818, "Ozymandias".

32. MINING 2040: PEASANTS' REVOLT

23 Nov 2015 Strictly Boardroom presents a scenario for mining and exploration in 2040 where new entrants from other industries are well placed to capture future opportunities.

In this short chapter, we envisage a further alternative scenario for the mining industry in 2040 – that of an industry with something of an identity problem. It is an industry under stress from low margins at existing operations but with widespread opportunities for resource developments nonetheless. The potential strategic outcome may be described as a form of 'Peasants' Revolt' – where the current mining company 'rulers' are under threat of being ousted by new entrants.

Peasants' Revolt is the last of four scenarios[1] developed using the Oxford Scenario Planning Approach[2] where the future is broadly defined on two key axes: 'economic margin' and 'search space'. The Peasants' Revolt future is one of strained economic margins for large incumbents (the bad news) but with significant new industry growth horizons available for those entities willing and able to attempt them (the good news).

This scenario may resonate with stakeholders. It describes a struggling industry that re-invents itself (again all scenarios are fictional).[3]

Scenario 4: Peasants' Revolt

The Peasants' Revolt scenario describes a mining industry experiencing low margins, but one in which many future options remain available. Such a scenario describes a sector that is extremely vulnerable to disruptive outsiders. This leads to a re-making of the established order. So is the mining sector setting itself up for a future Peasant's Revolt?

How it started in 2015

China's 13th five-year plan proposed a marked switch away from a polluting, industrial economy, towards a digital economy.

As part of the plan, copyright and intellectual property rights protection were strengthened in the country. These provisions, combined with fewer restrictions on foreign investment, triggered a major technology boom in China.

The Chinese economy began its reorientation towards digital services far more quickly than most analysts expected, leading to a significant stall in demand for most industrial commodities.

Surprisingly, the only large commodity market to benefit was thermal coal as the rapidly growing Chinese economy consumed ever more energy. However, increasing media attention turned to the pollution from coal power plants that used poor quality domestic brown coal.

In a landmark agreement, at the 2016 Marrakesh Climate Summit, China agreed to end its use of domestic brown coal and import higher quality coals, particularly from the US and Australia. China's hunger for energy raised the price of coal, oil and gas.

Globally, miners (with the exception of thermal coal miners) were hit by lower commodity prices but by higher energy costs. Investment in new mines and exploration was severely curtailed.

What had happened by 2025

At an OECD summit in 2025 it was agreed to implement carbon taxes and trading across all member countries. In the short term this led to even higher global energy costs.

The carbon trading schemes had a severe impact on the copper mining industry of Chile. The Chilean government was forced to undertake a bail-out of several large domestic copper mines.

A decade of low profits meant the industry had suffered a talent drain. Mining was now universally seen as an "old industry".

Fast-growing technology firms continued re-locating to Asia, seeking access to its large talent pools and young populations. As these companies sought new sectors for growth they began to target the supply of raw materials as a sector ripe for next generation innovation. Technology firms started to combine with major manufacturers to take control of supply chains and accelerate recycling rates.

Meanwhile, Chinese oil companies conducted major investigations into undersea metalliferous mining, utilising deep sea oil technology.

Where we are now in 2040

The copper mining industry in both the Atacama and Southwest USA has shrunk. It has been a victim of water shortages, high energy costs, low commodity prices and declining asset quality.

Metals are now increasingly sourced from undersea mining, particularly focused on Asia, with China, Malaysia and Japan all major producers.

In Europe and North America recycling rates have increased enormously as the circular economy finally starts to become a reality.

After years of divestments, the 'major miner' has now all but disappeared with former 'Tier 1' mining assets acquired cheaply by major oil companies and emerging China-based technology companies. The former mining majors have themselves transformed too – into an investment bank, a global commodities trading platform and an African-focused heavy industrial firm.

A 12-year minerals IPO drought ended this year, with the $25 billion float of Ivanplanets, a Silicon-valley firm looking to mine asteroids. Former astronaut, space entrepreneur and friend of Robert Friedland, Anousheh Ansari is the chairwoman.

The winner and losers

Although the major miners survive in the short term, over the long term, without credible new plans they reduce their focus on mining and re-invent themselves in other sectors.

Outsiders are able to make significant advances into the mining industry. Some reform the metals supply chain into a circular economy. Others apply oil industry technology to deep-sea mining.

A few entrepreneurial mining companies have success via the new types of mining and raw materials provision. The mining universe of 2040 looks vastly different to that of 2015. So keep your strategic options open and build carefully selected new capabilities.

---

1 Sykes, J.P. & Trench, A. 2016. *Using Scenarios to Investigate the Long-Term Future of Copper Mining and Guide Exploration Targeting Strategies.* AusIMM International Mine Management Conference, Brisbane, 22-24 August, in press.

2 Ramirez, R. & Wilkinson, A. 2016. *Strategic Reframing: The Oxford Scenario Planning Approach.* Oxford University Press, Oxford.

33. TALES FROM THE PAST: THE REINVENTION OF MINERAL EXPLORATION

19 Oct 2015 Strictly Boardroom is in 2035 – and describing a new global exploration giant that has turned the traditional exploration business model on its head.

One-time problem gambler and maths student dropout, David Cruikshank today became Australia's richest person under 40. Dave, as he prefers to be called, is a co-founder and current CEO of BetExploration.com; the 2035 international mineral resources company of the year and global exploration/gambling interactive web portal listed in New York, Toronto, London and Sydney and headquartered in the Cayman Islands. For the past two decades BetExploration.com has been one of the fastest-growing and highest-performing companies in the world.

Founded in 2015, by a group of University of Western Australia (UWA) maths students adept at online poker and some recently graduated geology students looking for work, BetExploration.com now has a global turnover measured in billions, not millions, of dollars.

The company has also been credited with five 'Tier 1' mineral deposit discoveries over the last 15 years – a feat that surpasses the exploration performance of all the world's largest mining companies combined. After on-selling these discoveries to traditional mining houses, BetExploration.com also enjoys the benefits of multiple royalty streams.

The rapid emergence of BetExploration.com on to the global resources scene hailed from an unlikely starting point. Back in 2015, the mineral exploration sector globally was in dire straits, albeit still populated by literally hundreds of listed mineral explorers, mostly based in Australia and Canada. At the time however, many of these companies were becoming known as 'zombie explorers'. They had insufficient capital to undertake any meaningful field activities.

Competing forms of speculative investment to exploration,

including the lure of high-tech business models, had left listed junior mineral exploration companies totally starved of risk capital and all-but-dead.

To add to the challenges for the sector at that time, there was also an emergence of shareholder activism. This was led by concern that the directors of small exploration companies had long been more interested in mining the financial market itself rather than making new mineral discoveries. Share price performances had been abysmal. Typical investors saw their investments decimated, returning only a few cents in the dollar.

In parallel, ever tighter listing and regulatory controls meant higher administrative and compliance costs were being placed on junior exploration companies. The consequence was growing investor disinterest in buying mineral exploration company shares – where their funds were more often than not withered away.

Large mining companies for the most part chose to sit out the challenges and opportunities of mineral exploration. They opted instead to focus upon their mining assets with the aim of maintaining high dividend payout ratios. However, in the end they were forced into bidding wars for new growth projects. This resulted in criticism from industry analysts for paying top-dollar to acquire discoveries (many of which were made by BetExploration.com). After a series of asset write-downs, analysts questioned the majors' long-term growth plans and the absence of exploration programs.

So how did Bet Exploration.com enter such a depressed market for exploration stocks and succeed so spectacularly? The clue is in the company tagline: "A rock-solid bet".

The company saw the opportunity that in hindsight now seems obvious. Investors in exploration stocks were essentially seeking to gamble on drill program outcomes – but seldom saw any demonstrable benefits from funding junior exploration companies in a meaningful short-term timeframe offered by other competing speculative 'investments'.

The BetExploration.com business model in contrast guaranteed that a drilling program would be undertaken within two weeks of the closing of any capital raising – with significant cash prizes available to those investors correctly selecting the right drill holes and depths for which the highest metals assays were identified from the program. So regardless of whether an actual mineral discovery was made, there was always a highest assay value – and thus for BetExploration.com investors consequently every drill program created the repeated opportunity to win big – the so called "rock-solid bet".

By guaranteeing not only continuous drilling activity, but also a series of cash prizes from each drilling program, BetExploration.com as a new company thus set itself apart from the hundreds of other established exploration companies in the sector. Investors liked the new offering. The benefits of scale allowed the company to negotiate and achieve far lower drilling costs than its more traditional exploration competitors.

New risk capital provided to the company rocketed to unprecedented levels for the exploration sector. Investors not only received shares in the company but also of course entered the betting pool on exploration outcomes from specific drilling programs with the chance to win big.

Dave Cruikshank was recently interviewed for the *Harvard Business Review*, by authors of *Blue Ocean Strategy* Renée Mauborgne and W. Chan Kim*. The business gurus were impressed with BetExploration.com as a "blue ocean strategy" and wanted to know how Dave and his mates came up with the idea:

> "*We were knocking on lots of doors in West Perth looking for work at the time, and we noticed everyone was doing the same thing and failing. We just thought we'd have to do something different if we wanted to make it in the industry. It's surprising really, you'd think exploration companies would know that in business, just like in exploration, you have to do something different to everyone else to get anywhere.*"

---

* Mauborgne, R. & Kim, W.C. 2015. *Blue Ocean Strategy: How to Create Uncontested Market Space and Make the Competition Irrelevant*, Expanded Edition. Harvard Business School Press, Watertown, MA.

KEY INSIGHTS: LOOKING TO THE FUTURE

- Foresight is critical for good decision-making in the mining sector. However, as of yet the track-record of future-gazing in the industry has not been good.
- Efforts need to be made to improve conventional economic and financial forecasting techniques. Industry executives and minerals sector boards need to be aware of the flaws (in particular, various heuristics and biases) in these techniques before making decisions.
- Attempts need to be made to understand key underlying trends in the sector, rather than just the high-level numbers, potentially by more fruitfully mining 'big data' and the copious historical information available about the industry.
- Some key trends include declining orebody quality, a rise in resource nationalism, a shifting demographic within the workforce, and potentially even a change in the overall corporate structure of the industry – with a potential return of additional mid-size companies.
- Because individual trends do not act in isolation, industry participants should consider utilising systems-based, team-based and scenarios-based decision-making tools to create more integrated and holistic views of the future.
- To be of use, foresight needs to be converted into strategic insight.
- Executives should aim to create companies and strategies that are robust across a number of potential futures and outcomes.
- A likely very different future for the industry presents good strategic opportunities in business model innovation.

PART 4
At the Coal Face

Part Four is penned "At the Coal Face", looking at some of the day-to-day critical issues that companies need to deliver upon in order to achieve operational success.

Mine sites are complex operations with many parts. They demand a range of skills and qualities from the modern mining industry manager – a subject we view through the words of Mark Twain in "Mark Twain on mine management". It is easy to become overwhelmed by the sheer numbers of problems and solutions that are possible – a situation we address in "Avoiding Keystone Cops syndrome". In order to avoid clueless running around like the metaphorical police officers it helps to adopt a management consultant's mindset – quickly focusing in on the most critical issues and highest value options. The management consultant's mindset is discussed further in "Mining professional or strategy consultant?" – the most critical of the tools employed being strict logic in breaking down problems and building up solutions.

In general, getting production costs 'right' remains perhaps the most obvious way of laying a foundation for operational improvement, however the challenge is more nuanced than it first appears. "Mining costs demystified" begins to tackle the flaws with common industry costing systems, and highlights alternative systems which may be useful for different professionals in the industry. For example, the CEO and mine manager – and ultimately the frontline workforce – need different types of operating cost measurements to make their decisions. In the present industry climate there is an increased focus on cost-cutting (though it is fair to argue such a focus should be omnipresent). That said "Cost focus – be careful what you wish for" carries a warning to implement cost efficiencies carefully, not to the detriment of overall optimal performance. Finally, "Mining cost escalation – lest we forget" discusses the mining cost cycle, which follows the commodity price cycle. Thus when looking to the future, decision-makers should be thorough in their modelling. Higher commodity prices beget higher operating and capital costs.

Another key element of improving operations is building a high-performance culture with an engaged workforce. This is an area that receives insufficient attention from the companies in our sector. We may say that "people are our best asset" but do our deeds always align to that mantra? It should go without saying that "High morale fosters high achievers", though obviously it frequently needs repeating. A common theme in fostering strong morale in the workforce is effective communication, which can be as simple as a well-considered email from the top as discussed in "A little more conversation…" or even a personal letter of thanks to an employee delivering good results, as described in "Ask not what your company can do for you…" Workforce morale can however be destroyed very easily, with one of the common culprits being inappropriate performance measures, as addressed in "The undercover KPI". This short chapter also serves as somewhat of a warning to industry leaders to make you understand how your performance is measured too!

"Managing through the downturn" presents particular challenges, however, there are some basic activities that can help you, your company and its workforce increase the chances of making it through to the next upturn – remaining proud of your company and professional institutions, continuing to help other professionals along, and keeping your eyes open for unforeseen opportunities (and risks).

34. MARK TWAIN ON MINE MANAGEMENT

29 June 2015 Strictly Boardroom seeks inspiration from Mark Twain – and finds Samuel Langhorne Clemens had many things to say of relevance to contemporary mineral industry managers.

Surviving and thriving in the 2015 mineral sector is proving something of a challenge to all but the lowest cost amongst miners and the well-funded amongst explorers and developers.

It is time for some much needed inspiration. So who better then to provide uplifting and thought-provoking counsel than legendary American author Mark Twain? Indeed, Samuel Langhorne Clemens attempted a brief if unsuccessful mining career himself, reportedly mining silver from Virginia City, Nevada. It was whilst in Nevada that Clemens adopted his famous pen-name and proved his far greater talent for prose than with pick. Here are selected quotable quotes attributed to Mark Twain on 'mineral sector management' (well kind of):

On mine finance:

"A banker is a fellow who lends you his umbrella when the sun is shining, but wants it back the minute it begins to rain."

"The lack of money is the root of all evil."

On mineral exploration:

"Don't part with your illusions. When they are gone you may still exist, but you have ceased to live."

"There is something fascinating about science. One gets such wholesale returns of conjecture out of such a trifling investment of fact."

"Reality can be beaten with enough imagination."

On project feasibility, reserves and resources:
"Facts are stubborn things, but statistics are more pliable."
"Get your facts first, and then you can distort them as much as you please."

On operations management:
"I have spent most of my life worrying about things that have never happened."
"History doesn't repeat itself, but it does rhyme."

On innovation management:
"Name the greatest of all inventors: Accident."

On joint ventures:
"Never allow someone to be your priority while allowing yourself to be their option."

On responding to ASX queries:
"I was gratified to be able to answer promptly, and I did. I said I didn't know."

On business development:
"I was seldom able to see an opportunity until it had ceased to be one."

On boardroom debate:
"Whenever you find that you are on the side of the majority, it is time to pause and reflect."
"That is just the way with some people. They get down on a thing when they don't know nothing about it."
"The man who is a pessimist before 48 knows too much; if he is an optimist after it he knows too little."
"There is nothing so annoying as having two people talking when you're busy interrupting."
"Action speaks louder than words but not nearly as often."

On career development:
- "He who asks is a fool for five minutes, but he who does not ask remains a fool forever."
- "Always acknowledge a fault. This will throw those in authority off their guard and give you an opportunity to commit more."
- "Anyone who stops learning is old, whether 20 or 80. Anyone who keeps learning stays young. The greatest thing you can do is keep your mind young."
- "I have never let my schooling interfere with my education."
- "Education: the path from cocky ignorance to miserable uncertainty."
- "Keep away from people who try to belittle your ambitions. Small people always do that, but the really great make you feel that you, too, can become great."
- "Don't go around saying the world owes you a living. The world owes you nothing. It was here first."

On time management:
- "The secret to getting ahead is getting started. The secret of getting started is breaking your complex overwhelming tasks into small manageable tasks, and starting on the first one."
- "Never put off until tomorrow what you can do the day after tomorrow."

On company presentations, reports and announcements:
- "The right word may be effective, but no word was ever as effective as a rightly timed pause."
- "Many a small thing has been made large by the right kind of advertising."
- "I didn't have time to write a short letter, so I wrote a long one instead."
- "Writing is easy. All you have to do is cross out the wrong words."

"It usually takes me two or three days to prepare an impromptu speech."

On company road-shows:

"I have found out that there is no surer way to find out whether you like people or hate them than to travel with them."

Finally, Twain also had something to say about shareholder resolutions at company meetings:

"If voting made any difference they wouldn't let us do it."

35. AVOIDING KEYSTONE COPS SYNDROME

09 Sep 2013 Strictly Boardroom looks at corporate effectiveness and worries that companies risk resembling the Keystone Cops in their approach to capturing opportunities.

Silent movie stars the Keystone Cops are celebrating their centenary – with the hapless crew at the height of their Hollywood popularity approaching 100 years ago. As a child, I remember clips of their black and white silent films being replayed on occasions on TV. The cops were running around randomly as a pack, first one way and then the other and in the process making multiple failed attempts to apprehend a criminal.

You certainly could not fault the Keystone Cops for their effort – or for their intent either. The squad seemed clearly aligned to their apparent 'corporate' goal. However, when it came to results they were sadly lacking of course, which in part was the butt of the joke. Never once can I recall the squad of 30-plus policemen chasing a robber and actually 'getting their man'.

Mining sector managers would do well to watch the old film clips again and reflect upon whether they are not in danger of a similar fate (to the Keystone Cops, not to the uncatchable criminal).

That is, nobody comes to work each day to be purposely slack

– at least not at senior management level – but managers are, however, always under constant risk of being woefully ineffective.

Let me cite one simple example. Many years ago I had opportunity to visit a rather large gold mine as a consultant with the "I'm here to help" message being sent in from head office. The mining manager proudly communicated the excellent level of engagement between the senior staff and the frontline. Indeed, looking through the results of various frontline engagement sessions, the manager had accumulated more than 1,000 action items to improve in-pit performance.

That is a tall order. There are only 8,760 hours in the year – so that meant one solution every shift continuing 24/7.

The problem? The 1,000 action items were reminiscent of the Keystone Cops – nobody can handle that level of white noise around improvement potential. There was no focus. The mining managers were essentially chasing the criminal (read improvement opportunity) all over the place without actually knowing where the real opportunity lay (which was actually in the mill).

A more successful approach would have been to focus – that all-important F-word. If, for example, the drill and blast area was the bottleneck to smoother operations, then the focus should lie there.

However, even that level of insight is not sufficient. Knowing that, again for illustration, hose failures on drill-rigs were the number one cause of downtime would entirely change the way in which the pit was managed.

Once you know where to focus the answers soon emerge. Even though there still may be 1,000 ways to solve the issue, at least implementing a selection of the 1,000 ideas will make a material difference.

Try looking up Keystone Cops on YouTube and you will get the idea of what not to do.

Unfortunately, actually approaching the issue in the right manner doesn't make for quite such good movie footage.

36. MINING PROFESSIONAL OR STRATEGY CONSULTANT?

28 Sep 2015 Strictly Boardroom sets you an age-old logical challenge of how to put a giraffe into a refrigerator. Get the answer right and you could have missed your professional calling as a highly-paid business strategy consultant.

Over-promising and under-delivering is not a way to make it to the top of any organisation. In your scribe's lowly profession of university teaching, the most obvious place to make big promises (and subsequently fall short thereof) is in the brief outline for a new course unit. In the more heady roles of leading sizeable minerals and energy sector companies the cardinal sin is to promise financial outcomes that do not eventuate – whether through lack of production, through lack of operating margin or in the worst-case through the combined impact of falling short on both counts.

Keen to attract students to the "Strategic Management of Resources Companies" course, some months back your scribe made the promise in the respective course unit outline to communicate what is known as the 'management consultant's toolkit'. This was a series of tips and techniques to solve the most challenging of board-level strategy assignments.

In Strictly Boardroom's view, knowing the various tools and techniques of the strategy consultant does indeed help with solving board-level conundrums and challenges. It also then helps with communicating the recommended steps to implement solutions.

Confessions of a Management Consultant[1] aimed to give a short-form guide to the consultant's toolkit – where each of 10 'confessions' suggested a best practice for consultants as follows:

1. Communication must be short and to the point
2. Ask the 'so what' question quickly
3. Run a ballpark answer in the first five minutes
4. Start on a storyline at the outset
5. Use two-by-two matrices to rank outcomes
6. Look at the revenue side early
7. Structure a problem

8. Say it in slides
9. Be hypothesis-driven – and last but not least…
10. Use networks.

The above list had an important omission, number 11 – which is also to maintain a ceaseless 'end-product focus' – working towards the recommended strategic outcome (and importantly nothing else) from the start to finish of the engagement.

The skill in moving towards implementation solutions is then to commence by stating the obvious but to do so at a granular level.

So for example, if the strategic recommendation to the board is that a company must endeavour to become a "best practice operator" then there needs to be a clear and granular roadmap to that end. The same would apply to a recommendation that a company build "excellence at mergers and acquisitions" too – including for the sake of completeness a detailed guide the delicate art of post-merger management.

So to the aforementioned logical challenge then: "How do you put a giraffe in a refrigerator?"[2]

For those who have a succinct answer to that question, the next question is pretty similar. It is: "How do you put an elephant in a refrigerator?"

If you have good answers to both of those questions then there are just two questions to get correct now and you can sign yourself up as a strategy consultant. The penultimate question is as follows: "There is an animal conference being held by the Lion King – which animal does not attend?"

Finally, perhaps on the way to the said conference: "There is a river you must cross inhabited by crocodiles – how do you cross it?"

How did you do? Did you answer correctly?

The takeaway is that successful strategy is an accumulation of a large number of granular but logical small steps on the pathway towards a targeted goal. As for the ability to deliver on a strategy, now that's another matter altogether. In the perfect world, strategy and capability go hand in hand. In the real world, finding a big refrigerator and a willing giraffe is not easy.

1 "Confessions of a Management Consultant" in Trench, A., 2013. *Strictly (Mining) Boardroom – Management Insights from Inside the Resources Sector*. Major Street Publishing, Highett, Vic. p140-144.

2 A quick internet search on "putting giraffes in refrigerators" will reveal all the 'correct' answers. Around 90% of professionals tested get all answers wrong. Many pre-school children get several answers correct.

37. MINING COSTS DEMYSTIFIED

04 Aug 2014 Strictly Boardroom laments the misrepresentation of production costs across the minerals sector and tries to keep definitions simple in suggesting that costs are best recognised with reference to mineral production value-chain.

Strictly Boardroom is a student of mining costs and a long suffering one at that. Multiple cost definitions abound in the minerals sector, most of which do not help investors or managers a great deal at all.

What are known in the industry as C1, C2 and C3 production costs are quite popular with some miners but as an experienced mining colleague recently suggested, "the C system of costs should really be called 'see-nothing' as the derived costs are of little use in decision-making".

All-In Sustaining Costs (AISC) have gained traction in gold but are less useful in base metals and bulk commodities. Why? Gold has no substantial logistical costs – but most other commodities do – so cost systems beyond gold need to fully describe the value chain.

The question of by-product credits reveals an even worse situation. Current normal practice (termed "normal" costing) is to offset the full revenue of by-products against the main product revenue in order to report (artificially) lower main product costs.

This works for small fractions of by-product production in revenue-terms but is also widely used (and largely abused) in reporting costs from co-product mines. Copper-gold mines are the worst culprits – with the AISC system not designed to address such cost complexity. Few managers that report such "normal" costs realise that the underlying assumption is that the co-product production cost equals the full co-product revenue. Implicit in normal cost reporting is the fact that no margin exists for the co-product.

Few realise this. Try asking an executive who reports an artificially low gold cost at a combined copper-gold mining operation what their copper production costs are as a brief experiment. The mathematically correct answer is that the copper production cost must, by definition, be actually the price that has been assumed for copper revenue, but few will answer that way.

It is time for a back-to-basics approach. Managers need cost information in order to manage and investors need it to assess where the true margins lie (or the lack thereof).

The approach that CRU Group takes to mining costs, termed value based costing (VBC), is based on a production system from mine through to customer. For any given production operation, VBC identifies four basic levels of cost along the value chain:

- **Site costs,** primarily of relevance to the operating management team of a specific facility or group of related facilities.
- **Business costs,** primarily of relevance to managers taking key marketing, business development, and investment appraisal activities.
- **Corporate costs,** primarily of relevance to the financial management team.
- **Full economic costs,** primarily relevant to the CEO, board and stakeholders.

Why this approach? Simple really – it allows the different managers along the chain the ability to actually manage their costs.

Staff at a mine or plant site are primarily responsible for production volumes and cost control. Staff at a business unit or divisional level take the short and medium-term planning, purchasing and marketing decisions and are responsible for the free cash flow and return on investment of a group of mines or plants producing a specific range of commodities. A central corporate staff are responsible for longer-term strategy and the interface with the shareholders and the broader financial community.

Naturally, in smaller companies the business and corporate levels may be merged and a company with a single operation will have all of these levels consolidated. However, even in these cases there will normally be identifiable individuals whose responsibilities can be classified.

Site costs, as the name implies, are all the costs incurred at the specific production site. This is the relevant concept for such activities as benchmarking, Six Sigma programs, and other forms of technically focused performance improvement. For downstream plants, site costs can be usually subdivided into raw material costs and conversion costs.

Business costs include the additional costs associated with the transportation, sales and marketing of the commodity. It is here that VBC introduces the important concept of 'realisation cost' so that business costs can be directly compared with the commodity's benchmark price, thus yielding an estimate of the free cash flow associated with the production unit. This is the relevant concept for asset valuations and also for most cyclical price forecasting applications.

Corporate costs include the additional costs associated with corporate activities and responsibilities, including where appropriate recognition of the changes in the value of various corporate assets and liabilities. Unfunded mine closures and other environmental liabilities are also a potential cost at this level. This is the relevant concept for corporate finance and equity investment analysis applications.

Finally, **economic costs** include a capital charge that reflects the market value of the asset, amortised over its remaining production life at the weighted average cost of capital. This is the relevant concept for value based management applications and strategic investment decisions.

Cost clarity still has a long way to go in mining and metals. Watch that space.

38. COST FOCUS – BE CAREFUL WHAT YOU WISH FOR

04 Feb 2013 Strictly Boardroom has some words of warning about the unintended negative consequences of cost discipline.

Media reporting – and the industry's response to that reporting – has followed a predictable pattern over recent weeks.

The story goes something like this. Firstly, the end of calendar year financial press carried its usual annual focus upon the relative equity returns across the various industry sectors, the performance of superannuation funds, initial public offerings, bonds, cash deposit rates and the like.

Share prices in the mining sector, along with profits and operating margins, were correctly reported as having underperformed against previous benchmarks. In the case of the gold sector in particular, it also underperformed against the rise in commodity price over time.

The transparency of industry cost reporting was next questioned (rightly so) with cost pressures highlighted by miners as the root cause of margin pressure. Those miners outside the gold sector were also able to highlight China's slower than trend growth last year and its influence upon bulk commodities and base metals prices.

All that is now history. What comes next across our industry by way of a response is now critically important to future performance.

Faced with growing shareholder pressure to take action against rising costs, and having already weathered the storm of shareholder backlash against executive salaries during AGM season, boards are now turning their attention to cost control far beyond the annual remuneration report.

But there are unintended pitfalls to additional cost control initiatives unless they are implemented very carefully and well communicated upon roll-out.

Let's take a closer look at one simple example. One typical response aimed at cost containment is to lower the authority levels for frontline supervisors, site-based and middle managers. So, while a site manager might previously have been able to approve up to

A$100,000 of unbudgeted expenditure, requests for, say, A$25,000 and above will now go to head office for assessment – and sometimes for far lower thresholds than that.

As an aside, this reminds your scribe of an amusing anecdote from veteran management guru Charles Handy in his book, *The Empty Raincoat: Making Sense of the Future.**

> "One of my early jobs had the fine-sounding title of regional co-coordinator (oil), Mediterranean region. My friends were certainly impressed, but they did not know the reality. The reality was a three-page job description outlining my duties, but the hard truth was contained in the final paragraph: 'Authority to initiate expenditure up to a maximum of 10 pounds'."

Handy's warning here is obvious – curtailing the responsibility of down-the-line management and frontline supervisors may have negative repercussions in terms of staff morale.

But Handy's story misses another point of equal, if not greater, importance. Faced with lower authority levels, the default response of those in the chain of command is to immediately think that the changes are intended to curtail expenditure – why else would they be instigated?

This is the reason that such revisions generally work, after all – but the problem can actually be that they work far too well. The danger is that a line manager does not then send all the requests up the chain of command that he or she should do – seeking to please in the process – but creating false economies with significant risks attached to them.

What happens next can be catastrophic.

For example, stocks of essential maintenance spares can be depleted under such 'capital efficiency' measures, to the point where breakdowns result in far greater downtime and economic loss to the company. These losses are not trivial either – running to billions of lost revenue in the oil sector when one major global company systemically made this error across its operations.

So the modified Handy message to those now seeking to

manage costs in this way is not only to carefully manage staff morale throughout the roll-out process but also, beware the latent unintended consequences of such cost efficiencies. Those future consequences will be far harder to see and also carry far greater risk.

---

* Handy, C. 1995. *The Empty Raincoat: Making Sense of the Future.* Random House Business Books, New York.

39. MINING COST ESCALATION – LEST WE FORGET

31 Aug 2015 Strictly Boardroom issues a timely reminder not to forget the cost pressures of the past when looking to the future.

The conference season is again upon us – and for those needing more frequent flyer points to keep airline privileges there are certainly a lot on offer to attend. The largest number of industry gatherings occur from September through to early December each year.

The perennial bar-talk at such events typically includes the outlook for commodity prices. When will price relief finally filter through? Is the outlook really that bad? Surely renewed Chinese demand will see prices pick up once again, won't it? New mining projects cannot be justified at these low prices…and so forth and so on.

Unfortunately the industry outlook as it applies to forecasting costs receives generally far less attention. This is somewhat surprising. Only some three years after cost pressures in the sector reached their peak, our collective memory of runaway costs is already fading fast. Ideally, cost forecasts should sit alongside price forecasts in terms of their level of market interest.

Indeed if we are not very careful, our sector could make a monumental stuff-up in the assessment of the cost and competitiveness of next generation minerals projects. That is, whilst 2015 still sees cost efficiencies continuing to filter through to the bottom line of companies, the abatement of industry cost pressures will not last forever.

A general recovery of commodity prices as we approach 2020 is a common industry outlook. As such, future higher commodity prices are now being used to model attractive project economics (on a spreadsheet at least) for would-be next generation mine developments. We need to be very careful here.

Let us explain further. In some instances, the lowered costs of 2015 are being matched with future higher price commodity forecasts in project financial models, thus making the (often unwritten) assumption that costs in the likes of 2018 to 2020 will resemble those of 2015. This practice is becoming ever more common of late: your scribe has read a number of published feasibility outcomes over the last six months which consistently repeat this error.

The intended message of such feasibility announcements is simple. It is to say to shareholders: *"just look at how good our project could perform when commodity prices eventually recover. We have a great NPV now costs have fallen – and a far lower capital cost than in the boom years too."*

The lower construction cost is certainly admissible and it presents an opportunity to any company with the financial capacity to push ahead in terms of 2015 project investments.

The assumed perennial lower operating costs (sometimes also matched with an ever lower Australian exchange rate), yet with far higher US-denominated commodity prices, are all dangerous assumptions however. Indeed, Strictly Boardroom would rule them as inadmissible for project feasibility work.

That is, industry sector costs follow industry sector prices through the cycle*. So costs follow commodity prices down just as we are seeing now. Costs also follow prices upwards too of course – as we all enjoyed in our pay-packets during the heady days of the mining boom years.

Boom-time cost escalation is indeed now a thing of the past, but costs will not stay entirely benign forever. As both readers and writers of our next generation mining project feasibility studies, we must all be on our toes. As for the memory of mining cost escalation – lest we forget.

---

* See for example: Trench, A. & Sykes, J.P. 2014. *Perspectives on Mineral Commodity Market Cycles and Their Relevance to Underground Mining*. AusIMM 12th Underground Operators Conference Proceedings, Adelaide, 24-26 March, p19-31.

40. HIGH MORALE FOSTERS HIGH ACHIEVERS

17 Dec 2012 Strictly Boardroom revisits a case study into the year-on-year performance of three departments within the one mining operation – with one a clear standout.

Your scribe had the pleasure of giving a presentation on the minerals sector and the global economy to a group of senior mining types at an end-of-year corporate function last week. Being keen to keep everyone entertained between drinks, the presentation included audience participation by way of a number of impromptu quiz questions. So thank you to all who played along and for knowing – among other things – how to put a giraffe in a refrigerator (the first warm-up question – see Chapter 36).

Most of the question-and-answer-style parts of the presentation went closely to script. So in the 'Spot the International Economy' round of questions, a photo from the climax of the 'Thelma and Louise' Hollywood film was instantly recognised as being analogous to the state of the US-economy and the looming 'fiscal cliff'.

Further, in the 'Know Your Mining Industry Remuneration' round of quiz questions, your scribe was highly impressed by the ability of the group to select the correct remuneration package for various senior mining industry roles to well within a A$50,000 range.

But one question did not quite go to the script. However, this fills your scribe with confidence for the future of the mining sector. Let us explain further by trying the same question here to see which of three possible answers you believe to be the correct one. Here is the business case.

Some years ago, I was engaged to conduct an operational excellence 'audit' across a number of operations for a large mining company. One mine site stood out, in that morale among the frontline troops differed markedly between departments, as did operational performance.

In the mining department the morale was bleak, as was performance. In the engineering department, things were somewhat better. In the processing part of the operation, morale was very strong, as were the operating results.

The following pithy quotes summed up the situation from the frontline, which my consultant colleague summed up with a green, amber and red traffic light ranking system.

The processing department received a 'green light', with the frontline comments paraphrased as, *"I really love my job. We already generate lots of ideas, but more feedback (from management) will really accelerate things."*

The engineering department scored an amber traffic light on the informal ranking system, with paraphrased frontline feedback along the lines, *"Morale is OK. We need to see action on implementing improvement ideas. We're not sure our supervisors are really prepared for frontline engagement."*

Finally, the mining department was flagged with a red traffic light: Why? Feedback towards the line management was not particularly good. It went something like the following, *"We don't trust 'em. With all the favouritism and politics, I don't think anything is going to happen by way of improvement."*

So which department do you think improved most over the next year? That's right. The processing department lifted even further (from an already strong performance level).

The engineering department nudged its performance higher too, but the mining department continued to struggle.

When I have told this story in the past and asked an audience which department would improve the most in the year following the initial assessment, the most common answer was the mining department.

Why? One presumes that either people are anticipating some form of stellar turnaround case study to be recounted, or that from such a low performance base things could only get better.

This time around, the audience picked out the processing department as the one most likely to further lift performance from an already high level. That's good.

It shows the message that high morale drives even higher performance is hopefully being heard.

It's simple really!

41. A LITTLE MORE CONVERSATION…

02 Jun 2014 Strictly Boardroom looks at communication from the top down within organisations and highlights one simple practical tool that works wonders.

Strictly Boardroom attended a full-day corporate strategy 'love-in' last week and has another one in the diary for the coming week too. Whoever the manufacturers are of butcher paper will be doing very nicely thank you as a result of such gatherings. The makers of marker pens should have a liking for regular strategy sessions too.

The strategy event last week proved a timely reminder of the power and also the challenges of good communication within an organisation.

Inevitably, after such events people feel happier, if for no other reason than such get-togethers give everyone a chance to be heard. They also offer the opportunity to listen and to learn exactly where the company is at in terms of the competitive landscape.

This brings us around to the subject of this chapter – internal communication. In over 25 years of such corporate naval-gazing events, 'communication' always comes up as an area that could be improved when the inevitable question as to what we can do better is posed.

In fact, never once in more than 100 of such events has the word communication not appeared at least once on butcher paper at some point during the day. There should be a prize for the first person to mention it.

The focus upon improved communication is not misplaced. Internal communication is critical to both morale and to the business effectiveness of organisations. So how can it be improved then?

The answer, you will be pleased to hear, is not simply to schedule more frequent corporate get-togethers – pressing work commitments and the tyranny of distance usually defeat that potential solution to improving the effectiveness of communication.

In Strictly Boardroom's experience the satisfaction level regarding internal communications at a company can be materially improved with just one email per week. That is not a bad return when the daily email count can reach more than 100 a day for staff.

So how can just one email each week make such a difference? The answer is that the email comes directly from the boss to all staff. It speaks to the issues of his or her choice that week.

A regular weekly message from the boss helps staff a great deal in building engagement with an organisation. If heartfelt and sincere then such an email can have a near-infinite return on investment.

For example, it can energise people towards key short-term deliverables, critical to making budget; it can celebrate the collective and individual achievements of staff in the many varied outposts of a multi-site company or business unit; and it can even cut short staff grumbles about the latest economy class corporate travel policy.

Why does such a simple communication tool achieve so much in just a few lines?

A regular weekly email from the top sends out an important message between the lines. Indeed, the between-the-lines message may be even more important than the email content itself.

Between the lines, regular communication says that the boss considers keeping the staff informed as critically important. It also says that people do matter to the organisation. They are far more than economists would label 'units of labour'.

Elvis Presley's call for "a little less conversation, a little more action please"* may have been off the mark. A little more conversation please (from the top) can result in a lot more action.

---

* 'A Little Less Conversation' was originally recorded in 1968 by Elvis Presley. A remix and re-release of the song by Junkie XL in 2002 became a worldwide hit.

42. ASK NOT WHAT YOUR COMPANY CAN DO FOR YOU…

24 Aug 2015 Strictly Boardroom looks backwards to some tough times from a decade long past and finds some inspiration there for the current downturn.

The early 1970s was a pretty tough time globally – and in particular for the UK. In early 1972, the UK's coal miners were on an extended strike, unemployment rose above a million people for the first time since the 1930s depression and Northern Ireland witnessed the infamous 'Bloody Sunday' events with the deaths of unarmed protesters shot by the British Army. Things certainly weren't all that flash to make something of an under-statement.

On a brighter note however – in literal terms at least – glam rock was commencing its heyday. David Bowie was leading a pack of new performers that included T-Rex, Slade, Sweet and Roxy Music. Incidentally, your scribe last saw Slade when they included Kalgoorlie on a global tour over 20 years later: they were exceptional.

On the cricket front, Australia played England for the Ashes in the UK that year, winning the fifth test at the Oval to tie the series 2-2. However, the drawn series meant that England retained the urn.

Back on the frontline of the 1972 UK manufacturing workplace, things were indeed pretty bleak. Productivity improvement was very much needed but was far from easily enacted. Time and motion men existed, sometimes hidden within the workforce, and were universally reviled. "Workforce engagement" had not yet even been invented in 'management-speak' amongst academics, let alone on the shopfloor. Workforce engagement back then was simply an oxymoron.

But the right attitude to work is hard to quell entirely. Whilst searching through family archives last week, your scribe found a faded, stained, original type-set letter dated from January 1972. The letter was kept for over 40 years by its recipient, a frontline worker at a car-parts plant in Wales. That letter reads as follows and came from the company's managing director:

> "Dear Bill,
>
> This morning whilst walking around the workshop my attention was drawn by Mr Stan Ellis to Machine No. 114, BSA 6 x 20 Profile Lathe on the Ball Pin Section.
>
> It was pointed out to me the work you had done in completely redesigning the method of automatic feed.
>
> I think this is a first class effort Bill, and you are to be complimented most highly for your initiative.
>
> Please accept my sincere thanks and appreciation.
>
> Your attitude is of the highest order."

Let's pause here for a second. To all the managers and directors out there who are reading this, please ask yourself a simple question: When was the last time that you credited a frontline worker for their good work and wrote to them personally about it? Last month? Last year? Can't remember? A collective 'well done' email does not count here; neither does a chat to the shift supervisor for general frontline dissemination. Indeed, have you ever written a personal one-to-one letter commending one of your workers?

The opportunity here is obvious. Let's recognise the right attitude and innovation when it is evident – and do it personally. The opposite challenge exists for the frontline of course.

Your scribe recalls vividly a number of frontline interactions in the 'mining boom' years. At the very mention of an improvement focus, the mentality of the mine-site workers immediately turned to what was in it for them. The more innovative (or should that read cheeky) amongst workers, for example, asked on more than one occasion whether they could negotiate a royalty agreement for any benefits from their work that improved the economics of the mining operation.

Times do change. The Australian mining industry of 2015 may not yet be in the terminal decline that was UK manufacturing of the 1970s but our response to the current downturn is critical to our future. It can start from the top by recognising incremental innovation, just as it did over 40 years ago in the example above.

The right working attitude can make a comeback – both from the perspective of managers and also from frontline workers. In a nutshell, managers need to take a personal interest – and to mentor and reward those employees focused on adding value (but likely stopping short of signing royalty agreements!). Similarly, all workers from the mine site frontline to the corporate office need to know who and what they are working for – and realise it is not entirely themselves. Shareholders expect returns and management has a responsibility to deliver them.

The comparisons between 1972 and 2015 are not exact of course. Glam rock has yet to make a comeback. However, the latest Ashes result from the Oval has not changed.

Workforce engagement is of course a lot healthier now than it was back then but that does not mean there are not latent lessons lying hidden in the past.

The time is now, to misquote John F. Kennedy* (from 1961), "Ask not what your company can do for you…"

---

* "And so, my fellow Americans: ask not what your country can do for you, ask what you can do for your country." John F. Kennedy, US Presidential Inauguration Address, 20 January 1961.

43. THE UNDERCOVER KPI

19 Nov 2012 Strictly Boardroom looks at performance management and recounts first-hand an example of being on the wrong end of an 'undercover' KPI.

With the end of the calendar year fast-approaching, the subject of 2013 KPIs is now approaching top of mind at many companies. KPIs are shorthand for Key Performance Indicators – for any readers who are residents of Mars that is – with the KPI 'bug' having long since gone viral across the four corners of planet Earth. Before the ubiquitous acronym took precedence, a grab-bag of other labels applied to what are now more often termed KPIs. Among others, the use of the term KPI has in part replaced vernacular such as 'management incentives', 'business performance measures' and 'management accounting metrics'. In practice, KPIs form a continuum with these and with other general management measures. KPIs in the broader sense can relate to everything from individuals to the department, the division, the entire company, safety performance and also remuneration parameters such as bonuses and piece work.

Unintended consequences are the things to watch out for when setting KPIs. Here is a personal example from my WMC Resources days of an 'undercover' KPI – on which I think the statute of limitations has now well and truly expired.

The early '90s found your scribe move into a company-owned fibro-duplex in East Kambalda. The previous occupant had let the garden, if it could be called that, run to native bush, but the home itself was in good shape. As no previous employer had ever provided cheap accommodation as part of a salary package I was more than happy with the new abode. It was only 50 metres from the bottle shop in one direction and 100 metres from the town swimming pool in the other direction.

Kambalda in those days was buzzing – with 13 nickel mines, five gold mines and also a major exploration budget that required geophysical input of various types. Having been hired as one of only two mine-based geophysicists, there was certainly no shortage of work on offer. As a consequence, weekends were for the most part spent at work, especially given that my wife was at that time mostly living and working some 700km away in Perth.

Now, for anyone who has not lived in a mining town, a contextual point here is useful by way of background explanation. The head of a mining town is not in fact the operations manager or even the general manager. It is actually whoever manages the housing allocation across the town. So, for example, upon receiving the news that the Trench family was set to increase in number by 50%, who do you think got to know that wonderful family news first? The mother-in-law? My parents? Neither found out first actually. You guessed it, the housing co-ordinator was the first person to be told – closely followed by my boss. Why? With so many operating mines around the place, accommodation in

Kambalda was in very short supply indeed and the gestation period (no pun intended) to move to a property with an extra bedroom could be up to six months. The idea was to get into that housing queue as quickly as possible.

Now, this is where the undercover KPI part comes in.

Your scribe's application to move to a property with an extra bedroom was turned down, despite having satisfied the overt corporate KPI to achieve an accommodation upgrade – that being a pregnancy! So what was the problem then? Your scribe was quietly advised that there was a second, implicit, 'undercover' KPI also – and one on which I had failed miserably. What was that KPI exactly? I had failed to achieve a pass mark on the unwritten KPI of gardening. That is, the continued lack of anything vaguely green, currently alive, or demonstrating even the remotest potential to grow outside my Larkin Street duplex was my downfall.

The answer? Stopping short of quickly calling in a team of gardeners, I chose to pen a letter to senior management instead. In it I asked whether a housing policy that rewarded couples who spent their weekends in bed together (with the greater potential for pregnancies), while also nurturing a well-kept garden on weekends, was really in the best interests of the company. Surely someone who at least on occasions put work ahead of gardening – and ahead of other forms of cross-fertilisation too – should not be denied a bedroom for a new baby. It worked. Soon afterwards, a property with an extra bedroom was made available to me.

So that's it. The clear lesson to all is to beware those 'undercover' KPIs in corporations – and for managers to avoid the unintended consequences of 'wrong' KPIs too. This lesson applies whether you are on the receiving end of the undercover KPI – or else are involved in its conception!

44. MANAGING THROUGH THE DOWNTURN

20 Jul 2015 Strictly Boardroom has some tips – only three actually – for managing your career through the downturn.

Last week Strictly Boardroom had the privilege of briefly addressing a charity dinner of mining professionals held in aid of cancer research*; a personal and poignant milestone as both my parents passed away from cancers. The occasion provided opportunity to discuss dealing with difficult times – not least those that beset much of the exploration and mining sector at the time.

So here are three thoughts by way of counsel for managing through the current tough times.

1. Be proud of your affiliations

Like it or not we tend to be measured by the company we keep. There are some excellent resources sector organisations currently experiencing very tough times; some as a result of low commodity prices and weak sentiment and others as the fallout from past decisions that, with hindsight, added more risk than value to the company.

At a trivial level, tough times mean the loss of some of the perks enjoyed in better days – be that a company mobile phone account, premium economy travel (alright business class too), or the funds to attend a conference or short course that would provide a great learning opportunity.

The challenge is to put aside these small personal sacrifices and maintain pride in the organisation itself. All organisations and individuals face tough times. Learning from adversity is often the making of those same companies and people down the track. So aim to enjoy the challenge, in the knowledge that the situation is only cyclical. It will not persist forever!

2. Pay it forward

Part of the collective benefit from charity events comes from the joy of giving. Leaving charity aside though, the same general thinking applies to everyday work. One way to create impact is to use your skill-set for the benefit of others – even before they ask (as they often will not).

Put simply, all of us can do some things better and easier than can others. Adam Smith worked out the economics of this simple concept close to 250 years ago – and humans have applied the same thinking since the days of hunter-gathering.

So something you can do easily, at negligible personal cost, can have far greater value to others who can only achieve it at far higher personal cost (if indeed at all). The opportunity is then obvious: help others. It may be as simple as making a key introduction for someone to open doors for them. Doing that costs you very little but can create great value for them.

3. Neither opportunity nor risk announces itself by those names

Nobody lines up to promote you when times are tough. The idea of walking into your manager's office to ask for a pay-rise went out the door with boom-time commodity prices.

Often the greatest opportunities to shine – and to stuff up too by the way – do not announce themselves in your email inbox.

Sure, we all have to do the tasks in the budget and business plan but watch out for those unseen opportunities to create value that are less than obvious.

Similarly, the errors of omission at work that can put your very job in peril do not typically announce themselves either.

Risks need to be looked for – because the greatest risks are just that (the greatest) because they lie hidden. Opportunity can knock unexpectedly too. By way of personal experience it is well over 20 years ago now, with nickel prices less than $US2 a pound, that I asked WMC Resources if I could attend a conference on metals markets to understand exactly why things were so dire.

The response was that I could attend if I paid my own way. That conference ended up changing my career – for the better I believe – yet it would have been easier to miss it.

Better times will inevitably return to the minerals sector. Those who take great pride in their work, make choices to help others wherever possible and continue to seek out new opportunities will be in pretty good shape come the next up-turn.

---

* Ride to Conquer Cancer – Perth – Harry Perkins Institute of Medical Research: http://pr15.conquercancer.org.au/site/PageServer?pagename=pr15_homepage

KEY INSIGHTS: AT THE COAL FACE

- Mining operations are complex and thus demand a range of knowledge, skills and qualities from the modern mining industry manager.

- Embedding a structured approach to problem-solving as the management mantra at production sites will pay dividends. That is, deploying the 'management consultant's toolkit at operations can enhance performance.

- Never forget to deploy the F-word – Focus. Having less than 10 action items as the focus for improvement is a far better situation than having closer to 1,000 action items.

- Be especially wary of taking the reported production costs in the minerals sector at face value. Definitions vary between companies – as do the processes of cost allocation and calculation. Put simply, there are "lies, damn lies – and reported mining costs."

- Directors through to the frontline workforce need to be made aware of the true costs of production – and the key site-based revenue drivers – as a baseline and catalyst for performance enhancement.

- Directors should also approach cost-discipline, which is a good thing, carefully. Inappropriate cost-cutting over the short term can cause performance problems over the longer term.

- Minerals companies are always interested in forecast commodity prices – for good reason – but place less emphasis on the flow-on effects from revenue-side changes into costs. Costs follow prices – both up and down.

- The creative power of an engaged frontline workforce can be awesome – teams with high morale perform better.

- High morale and front-line engagement requires that mutual trust is established between line management and workforce as a prerequisite. Effective communication, which can be as simple as a well-meant email or letter, is critical in building trust.

- Morale and trust can however be easily destroyed. Onerous restrictions of decision-rights, miserly equipment purchase-limits and inappropriate performance measures are all common culprits.

- Managing your team through a downturn is particularly tough. However, organisational pride, a Samaritan's attitude and a mind open to unexpected risks and opportunities are helpful in getting to the other side.

PART 5
On Competitiveness and Mining Excellence

Part Five moves to the engine room of minerals companies and is focused "On Competitiveness and Mining Excellence". It remains a frustration that no mining company has yet attained the informal title of 'The Toyota of Mining' – being able to extract consistently more value from any given mining asset than can its peers, as "From mediocrity to capability" suggests. There is no 'Google of mining' nor 'Apple of mining' either – with a reputation for industry-leadership in mining innovation. "Mining emperors wear few clothes" looks at some of the excuses for collective underperformance – with price volatility chief amongst them. However at least some of the performance gap transpires from simply not measuring the long-term economic potential of the industry, and indeed even if we did, would the industry seek to close the gap – or choose instead the short-term benefits of riding the up-cycle rather than delivering long-term excellent performance?

This lack of overall industry excellence is founded upon a lack of razor-sharp focus on competitiveness, both at a corporate level and at the national level too. Taking an example near to Strictly Boardroom, Australia, the 'lucky country'[1] in terms of mineral wealth has begun to fall behind in many of its key mineral sectors, including gold, uranium and nickel as described in "Mining World Cup 2014 – Australia thrashed". Again, excuses will abound – and the fortunes of sectors will ebb and flow – but a deeper look at the gold sector in "All is not well with gold" reveals an industry that is reliant on a series of ageing assets and brownfield developments (with of course the rare exception).

The iron ore industry in Australia remains robust – despite a severe price downturn. But in iron ore Australia is blessed with amongst the 'best' assets globally, so our competitiveness may to a large extent simply reflect asset quality. The industry is asset-focused rather than capability-focused as highlighted in "Large mining companies: Capability lost?" A change in mindset towards capability-driven competitiveness would benefit all.

Beyond the trials and tribulations of major mining companies, it is only fair to say that the junior sector also faces its fair share of challenges on the way to excellence too, as listed in "On mining juniors: A view from the city".

The road to operating excellence starts with a better understanding of corporate capabilities, and developing strategies that leverage distinctive capabilities, as described in "The best way is up: Crafting a winning strategy".

Developing capability-led strategies will not be easy, such that lateral thinking in dealing with old problems in new ways will always be required. We discuss this in "Lateral thinking – there is always a way".

Industry assumptions that underlie current industry strategies require testing, as exemplified by, "Grade: The King – or serf – of gold orebodies". We will have to do things differently too, for example in tackling bureaucracy, refer to "Struggling with bureaucracy? Introduce adhocracy".

A further problem is that the mining sector still presents

impediments to half the world's talent pool, as discussed in "The Real Housewives of Mining".

Perhaps in a future book we can trumpet the successes of emerging or established minerals companies in achieving pre-eminence amongst competitors through capability-led success?

---

1 This is a reference to: Horne, D. 2008. *The Lucky Country*. Penguin Australia, Docklands, Vic. 300pp, first published in 1964. The term 'Lucky Country' nowadays is often used in a positive context referring to Australia's abundant mineral resources, weather, natural history, blessed isolation and high levels of prosperity. However, in the context of his book, Donald Horne meant that Australia was simply 'lucky' in rising to prosperity despite what he perceived as weak economic and political systems.

45. FROM MEDIOCRITY TO CAPABILITY

10 Dec 2012 Strictly Boardroom reports the results of three spot polls conducted with mineral industry participants in recent weeks, with the result that few of us really seem to know which companies stand out from their peers based upon their exploration and mining capability.

Your scribe has been fortunate enough to deliver presentations on mineral exploration research on behalf of the Centre for Exploration Targeting to a number of industry groups.

Always keen to promote audience participation and feedback, a quick-fire set of questions on exploration and mining capability were raised in each of three separate talks. The questions were pretty straightforward. Knowing the answers is more challenging.

So here goes.

The first question asks: *"Which of the following companies is the best mine operator?"*

The options were Newmont Mining, BHP Billiton, AngloGold Ashanti or 'don't know'.

One of the audiences sought to clarify what was meant by the word "best" – to which my answer was that the term implied an ability to produce more mine product, at lower cost than peers would achieve given the same assets.

So what is your answer?

Without embarrassing the individual companies noted above, the outright winner from all three audiences was 'don't know'!

This may come as no surprise as in some cases it is contract miners and not the principal owners of an asset that 'do' the actual mining. But then does not the 'best mine operator' tag implicitly include a capability to also be the 'best' mine contract manager too?

So did your view align with that of the audience's in issuing a resounding 'don't know' answer?

The second question asks: *"Which of the following companies is the best mineral explorer?"*

To keep things simple, the potential answers are the same, being Newmont, BHP Billiton, AngloGold or 'don't know'.

Again, one audience sought clarification on what was meant by "best" in mineral exploration terms.

The answer I gave here was that it meant discovering economic deposits more often and at lower cost than peers deploying best practice exploration techniques and management.

So what is your answer to question two then?

Again, so as not to embarrass the individual companies listed I will advise only that the winner was – you guessed it, 'don't know' once again, by a very clear majority.

Next to the third and final question: *"Which of the following companies is the best car manufacturer?"*

The options were Ford, Mitsubishi, Toyota and 'don't know'.

Your answer? This time 'don't know' actually lost out – with the clear winner being Toyota, and nobody questioned what was meant by "best" in the context of car manufacturer.

There you have it, we have a clear winner – but not among minerals companies.

So how is it that in the minerals sector we don't even know which are the best companies in our own sector but we seem to be aware of excellence elsewhere?

Therein lies our clear challenge. In order to know who is best among miners and explorers – and then to manage towards it – we first need to be able to measure excellence in our sector.

That is a subject for another time. Right now I'm off to a meeting – driving my '89 Toyota Kamikaze.

46. MINING EMPERORS WEAR FEW CLOTHES

24 Mar 2014 Strictly Boardroom looks at the prevailing investment mantra in the mining sector and questions whether it borders on silliness, hopelessness, or even insanity.

Strictly Boardroom suspects that deep down we all really know the truth that the mining industry never quite delivers on its true economic potential, but for various reasons we all choose to accept that the gap in performance is just the way things work in a cyclical industry.

When pressed, we can blame the performance gap on external factors – most often on commodity prices, which have a habit of not being quite where we expect them to be.

Far less often we challenge our own collective conduct as an industry in making the right decisions to maximise return.

Let's take a step back though. The actual economic potential of our industry is not actually routinely measured. We have few numbers to play with. The full-cycle performance gap of the mining sector no doubt exists but there are no estimates of its magnitude that have any rigour.

It is a big job to measure the gap – and beyond the scope of Strictly Boardroom in this short chapter – but just why is it that we do not measure it?

Partly this is because it would be too embarrassing to do so and partly because it is not in the short-term interests of major companies to complete such analyses, let alone make the outcomes public.

Ask yourself whether BHP Billiton or Rio Tinto would wish to publicise not just their material achievements but also their lack of performance against a technical limit of what is possible in economic returns across the investment mining cycle if the right decisions had been made? It will not happen anytime soon.

Why? There is no grand conspiracy here. Arguably, neither executive management nor shareholders would benefit from making the results public.

Respective governments of resource-rich countries have a far greater incentive to know the performance gap but do not have the ready data with which to do the maths.

Right now the owners of BHP Billiton and Rio Tinto, meaning the shareholders, certainly don't actually want to see the truth of the matter, because capturing the economic opportunity requires counter-cyclical investment.

Shareholders would much prefer to have cash back now please, in as tax-effective a manner as possible too – not an optimal investment strategy that actually maximises economic returns for the future.

Here are four reasons why we are collectively 'hopeless' as a mining sector in this respect. The underlying reasons for our quandary are linked and generally fall into the realm of the 'unwritten rules' that govern the mineral sector's collective strategy. Unfortunately these unwritten rules are seldom challenged. Put another way, the emperor that is the collective mining sector may be wearing very few clothes!

1. We don't know the upside

As stated above, there is no accepted estimate of the economic return that would eventuate if production capacity increases (particularly in the larger commodity markets) were linked more closely to actual global mineral demand requirements.

2. Even if we knew the numbers we would ignore them

Shareholders and executives prefer an industry where they can make choices of when to hold or fold. If a shareholder can enter an industry just as returns are taking off and make a timely departure before the hard times, then timing the market pays more handsomely than a steady but higher overall return.

A common throwaway line is that volatility is bad but both shareholders and management quite like it.

3. Short-termism prevails – and will continue to do so

If the market shows that it will reward cutting not only fat but muscle too, at least in the short-term, then the temptation is too hard to ignore for companies. Short-termism has a positive feedback loop. If wrong decisions are rewarded by the market then they will perpetuate. Employment patterns add further fuel to the fire.

4. CEOs typically have short shelf-lives – let's say five years as a ball-park figure

So a minimum decade-long development plan for a new greenfields mining project is materially longer than the tenure of your typical CEO. As a result, long-term investment must overcome a decision-bias in the boardroom. What a funny industry we live in: a fascinating one but clearly flawed.

47. MINING WORLD CUP 2014 – AUSTRALIA THRASHED

07 Jul 2014 Strictly Boardroom looks at Australia's surprise early exit from the Mining World Cup following defeats by Kazakhstan (uranium) and Indonesia (nickel).

After successive high-scoring wins over Brazil, India and ultimately a group of China's high-cost iron ore producers in the steel materials 'group of death' at the 2014 Mining World Cup, Australia was widely expected to also be competitive in the higher-priced commodities rounds of the global mineral production tournament.

Unfortunately for late-night Australian mining fans closely watching the mine-supply numbers, the Australian mining team, affectionately known as the 'Diggeroos', suffered an early exit from the tournament in the critical high-value commodities second-round qualifiers.

Losses to both Indonesia and to Kazakhstan in the nickel and uranium rounds of the tournament were both characterised by heavy defeats.

The precious metals gold-plate play-off round also saw defeat for Australia. Despite reaching the final, this time at the hands of China's gold miners, the Diggeroos finished as runners-up in the gold-plate competition.

Diggeroo coach Ange Macfarlane[1] was at a loss to explain the lack of growth in Australia's key export numbers, particularly in established industries such as nickel and uranium over the last decade.

"Perhaps we focused too much on the iron ore sector where we have blitzed all-comers," Macfarlane said.

"The nickel and uranium numbers don't lie and they don't look all that good for Australia either.

"As for gold, we have been hearing from exploration pundits for a while that the golden generation of Australian operating mines has now reached a mature stage. We desperately need new gold discoveries there to compete with China's continually emerging assets."

Strictly Boardroom looked back at some key historical results achieved by the Australian mining sector in the glory days of the past in order to place the latest defeats in context.

Nickel

In 2003, Australia posted some 186,000 tonnes (t) of annual nickel production, easily beating Indonesia's 144,000t of production that year and also eclipsing a young team from the Philippines that managed only a modest 23,000t of nickel production.

In the latest 2013 annual production round, however, while Australia posted a material gain to reach 238,000t nickel, the Diggeroos lost out to their Asian group competitors.

Despite a creditable 28% production gain over the last decade, Australian miners did not bank on a phenomenal performance from both Indonesian and Philippines nickel producers. Indeed, it was Indonesia first, daylight second. In 2013, Indonesia notched up

750,000t of contained nickel production. For the record, the Philippines also beat Australia in 2013 posting more than 300,000t for the year.

Suddenly Australia's scoreline looks less impressive. Coach Ange Macfarlane commented that the Diggeroos were keenly awaiting the age qualification of a talented new nickel player from Western Australia – currently undergoing late-stage trials (feasibility) with the highly successful Sirius Resources' management team.[2]

Uranium

In 2003, Australia posted a credible 8,900t annual uranium production, recording a handsome margin over Namibia at 2,400t and also over Kazakhstan at 3,470t that year.

Fast-forward to 2013, however, and Australia's production had not increased – indeed had retreated to only around 7,900t.

In contrast both Namibia and Kazakhstan have both made strong gains bringing on new uranium production. Namibia is emerging as a serious competitor to Australia, now breaching the 5,000t production threshold in 2013.

As for Kazakhstan, the country's success story as a uranium producer is second to none in recent years. Kazakhstan's 27,000t of uranium production handsomely won the most recent global mine-supply tournament.

Coach Ange Macfarlane remains hopeful of resurgence in Australia's uranium discovery and production track record. With larger uranium production from Olympic Dam currently ruled out through price-induced injury in the near-term, Macfarlane is hoping for new generation uranium discoveries elsewhere across Australia.

Good luck to the Diggeroos in the 2018 Mining World Cup: the preparation starts now.

---

1 Angelos "Ange" Postecoglou is an Australian former soccer player and head coach of the Australian national soccer team, nicknamed the 'Socceroos'. Ian Macfarlane is a former Australian federal politician who has held ministerial accountability for both energy and resources and industry portfolios.

2 This reference is to the Nova-Bollinger nickel sulphide deposit in the Fraser Range area of Western Australia discovered by Sirius Resources NL and now undergoing mine development by Independence Group (ASX Code: IGO).

48. ALL IS NOT WELL WITH GOLD

03 Nov 2014 Matthew Kanakis joins with Strictly Boardroom to look at Australian gold – with a focus on the domestic industry's vital statistics.

The Australian gold industry is a cornerstone of the domestic mining sector. That about 50 mines operate across the country is a credit to the local industry – as is the fact that Australia ranks second only to China in global production at around eight million ounces a year. Australia also sits atop of the global list of producer countries when ranked by audited resource inventory.

For the record, the world rankings in gold production are China, Australia, the US and Russia. By resource inventory, however, Australia is first, followed by South Africa, Russia and Chile.

Australia is certainly a global force in gold. Those close to the Australian gold industry know, however, that all is not as well as these headline rankings suggest.

The bulk of the resource-build in recent years locally has come from established assets, such as the likes of copper-gold assets at Olympic Dam and Cadia/Ridgeway, rather than from new gold discoveries and new camps. That gold production itself in Australia has stalled now at around eight million ounces for a decade, despite the rise in gold prices this century, also signals the difficulties the local industry is facing. The overall lack of new quality in the Australian gold mine portfolio, with a few notable exceptions, is of growing concern to gold's domestic stakeholders. Australia's costs are among the highest globally – substantially higher for example than emerging African producing nations (excluding South Africa).

Australian gold may not quite be in crisis mode just yet, but that label is not too far away unless things start to improve. Accepting that there is a looming problem (and many still do not as yet) will go some way towards fixing it. The precipitous fall of South Africa's gold production is the analogy to the downside future scenario that Australia needs to work very hard to avoid.

Whether Australian gold will just survive or else will once again thrive in margin terms has thus far not been the subject of any serious study. Thriving will mean adding new high-margin gold discoveries to the existing portfolio of mines. Where are they?

Building a great future for Australian gold first requires an understanding of the present industry of course. To that end, here are some vital statistics of Australia's gold sector*.

1. Approximately 56% of Australia's gold production is mined from underground versus 44% from open pit.

2. Around 72% of annualised Australian gold output is produced from gold-only mines versus the remaining 28% from gold-copper and other mines where gold is produced alongside other metals as either co-product or by-product.

3. The 'first quartile' threshold of production costs in Australian terms, i.e. the 25th percentile of Australian production costs, sits around A$700 per ounce on a cash-cost basis or A$925 on an all-in-sustaining-cost (AISC) basis.

4. Conversely, production costs in Australia above around A$950 per ounce on a cash-cost basis, or A$1,205 per ounce AISC, would be considered to lie in the fourth, highest-cost, quartile of local production (i.e. beyond the 75th percentile of production in cost terms).

5. The average production-weighted grade of Australian gold mines is 3.26 g/t gold.

6. The highest and lowest grade gold mines are Andy Well (> 12 g/t) and Cadia Hill (< 0.4 g/t gold).

There you have it. Australian gold described in less than 750 words. Unfortunately solving the industry's future is not as easy as synthesising the state of play at present.

---

* Kanakis, M. 2014. Grade Expectations: Exploring the Cost-Grade Hypothesis in Australian Gold Production, *CET Quarterly Newsletter*, September, p14-17.

49. LARGE MINING COMPANIES: CAPABILITY LOST?

18 Nov 2013 Strictly Boardroom looks at competitive advantage across the mining sector and asks whether distinctive capability has disappeared as a driver of shareholder returns for larger resources companies.

Students have a knack for answering the wrong question in exam scripts year after year. An alternative explanation may be that it is actually the examiner at fault – for continually asking the wrong questions. In marking exams this time, it was *deja vu* all over again. However, on this occasion, it was very much the examiner who had asked the wrong question. The test question was:

> "Suggest sources of competitive advantage for large diversified mining companies over smaller, less diversified mining companies."

The answers were excellent but the question was pretty average.

A far more interesting question – and a correspondingly tougher one to answer – would have been to ask for suggestions as to sources of distinctive capability in larger mining companies versus smaller counterparts. Answers to the first question produced a list as long as your arm. Here is a quick selection of the competitive advantages for larger miners described in exam scripts.

In no particular order, large miners were attributed the following potential advantages:

- Greater access to capital
- Lower cost of capital
- Economies of scale and scope
- Tier 1 assets within portfolio
- Infrastructure ownership
- Ability to fund counter-cyclical investment
- Stronger balance sheets
- Factor mobility between operating assets (labour, equipment, capital)

- Diversification of risk by commodity
- Diversification of risk by country
- Strength-in-depth of in-house technical expertise
- Market share influence on supply-side volume
- Bargaining power with mining services suppliers
- Ability to optimise saleable product specifications from multiple operations to capture value-in-use pricing benefits
- Greater access to governments and regulators
- Negotiating power with developing country governments (at least more so than smaller companies)
- Ability to 'hibernate' resource projects to advantage
- A strong 'hand' in the game theory analogy of mining sector business strategies
- Financial capacity to undertake M&A
- Preferential access to M&A deal-flow 'at the top-end' of the market
- Local monopoly and/or oligopoly advantages in key markets
- Price leadership power in non-exchange-traded markets
- Greater capacity to assume exploration risk – including long-term greenfields exploration.

Do you see the obvious omissions from the list? No doubt there are many gaps but one stands out.

Critically, very few if any of the above attributes refer to any form of distinctive capability within larger mining companies. That is, distinctive capabilities are notable by their complete absence from the 'big is better' list of business advantages.

So what exactly are distinctive capabilities again?

Just like the list above, they form potential sources of competitive advantage – but those that originate principally from a skill, or set of skills, that are superior to competing entities. Importantly, distinctive capabilities are not linked directly to a company's financial accounts or physical resource assets.

So why do they not appear on the list? Two possible explanations spring to mind. Either large resources companies do not have many capabilities that can be regarded as distinctive, or distinctive capabilities in the resources sector are not typically scalable? After all, a scalable distinctive capability is akin to the Holy Grail of business strategy – so they are not common.

Which of these answers do you prefer? Any which way, next year's exam scripts will read very differently. Why? The examiner will change the question.

50. ON MINING JUNIORS: A VIEW FROM THE CITY

11 Nov 2013 Strictly Boardroom relays the views on the mining sector's junior companies hot from the city of London and the overall verdict is none too good.

It is easier to comment upon than it is to actually play sport – just as it is easier to analyse mining companies than it is to run them. The key difference between sports commentators and industry analysts and their close cousins the fund managers, however, is that commentators do not buy and sell the players on the sports field. The latter, however, often do have access to the purse strings of the investment community.

So while your scribe has great empathy with the actual 'doers' of the minerals sector over those simply willing to offer their opinions in hindsight, it would be foolhardy to ignore the views of influential analysts and fund managers.

Recently, colleagues at CRU Group relayed some timely messages for the junior mining sector originating from analysts and funds in the financial capital that is London*.

Here are some key excerpts:

- Management has tended to factor in 20 to 30% contingency for projects but cost overruns have often exhausted the contingency funds well before commissioning.

- There has been a systemic over-reliance on engineers and contractors with a lack of a 'point person' with ultimate company responsibility for a project.
- Junior companies are unlikely to get the 'A-Team' of engineering expertise, making it critical that the company takes a very active role in overseeing project management.
- Financing plans should factor in likely project delays – they will arise.
- Allow for delays in receiving finance, especially when dealing with Asian partners.
- Do not forget full working capital requirements in structuring a financing package – many do.
- Aim to secure a back-up debt facility or bridging facility.
- Consider modular staged capital expenditure project building over the 'big bang'.
- Most juniors are 'options' on commodity prices and shares have behaved as such.
- Prioritising investor relations over actual resource management can lead to disaster.
- That juniors are often 'one project ponies' concentrates risk.
- The best form of finance can be from people who want your product – the off-takers.
- Big was beautiful, but no longer – these days companies are seeking nimble operating bases.
- Many junior explorers and project generators base their business model on being bought out once exploration success has been achieved. Buyers have not been forthcoming – as yet anyway.
- Small deals continue but often only at a level that 'keeps the lights on' at junior companies.
- The industry awaits the catalyst for the next bull-run but when and how will it come? Renewed M&A interest is seen as one possible trigger.

Finally, a word of comfort – at least of sorts – for the juniors from the analysts:

> *"It is worth bearing in mind that the majors have written off more value than the entire market capitalisation of the junior mining sector."*

---

* Presentation extracts from Olivia Ker (Blackrock), Mark Wellsley-Wood and Christopher Welch (Ocean Equities).

51. THE BEST WAY IS UP: CRAFTING A WINNING STRATEGY

14 Dec 2015 Strictly Boardroom takes the view that determining your company's strategic capability and advantage is a key step towards a great future.

Strictly Boardroom is itching to start the end-of-year annual reading season with the holiday reading pile already including books on business strategy this year. Indeed, even if your scribe lived to be over 100 there would still be no way to find enough time to have read and digested all of the strategy books now available – let alone all the strategy books yet to be written.

But do such strategy tomes take a relatively simple concept and make it overly complex? Strictly Boardroom has some considerable sympathy with that viewpoint on the existing strategy literature. So why read hundreds of pages when just a few words can convey the nub of strategy and act as a call-to-arms?

Here is an attempt at that call-to-arms in a nutshell then. The world of business strategy comes in two basic parts – the internal and the external. That is, 'Strategy Part One' is all about what your company is actually capable of now and in the future. This is a form of self-help improvement text but for corporates rather than for individuals. Without capability, company strategy depends more upon luck than substance.

In contrast, 'Strategy Part Two' is all about the external business and economic environment in which a company operates. For minerals and energy companies this requires an assessment of the pros and cons of the relevant commodities markets in order to seek and judge opportunity.

So how do you short-circuit a lengthy analysis of corporate capability, meaning 'Strategy Part One', into a short-form manageable exercise? We'll leave 'Strategy Part Two' of the formulation for another day. Achieving a first-pass answer to 'Strategy Part One' is actually fairly simple. Unfortunately, most strategy texts fail to get there despite hundreds of pages dedicated to the subject.

The first milestone is to arrive at an informed perspective on your company's distinctive capabilities – if it indeed has any such capabilities at all that stand out from the crowd. To achieve such a perspective, just have the key personnel within your company answer the simple question below:

"What do you consider the three foremost distinctive capabilities that set your company apart from others?"

Some coaching is needed to avoid 'wrong' answers here. So, in setting the above question it is important to also communicate to the recipients that a distinctive capability originates from a skill or set of skills that are superior to those of your competitors and does NOT mean simply referencing physical assets or a company cash balance. That restriction makes answering the question a whole lot tougher.

As a rider to the question, each respondent is also required to provide evidence to support each of their answers. That makes the question even tougher once again. So whilst it is a very simple question, it is inevitably a very hard one to provide well-supported answers to.

The second milestone is then to look beyond capability towards strategic competitive advantage for the company. Once again, some informative context is required here to help avoid 'wrong' answers to this second and final question. Advantage can indeed accrue from the financial and physical assets of a company – and also from the aforementioned capabilities too. So the second question goes like this:

"What do you consider the current strategic advantages, if any, that will enhance future profitability and growth?"

This question requires an answer in two parts – where the first part of the answer is simply a yes or no response. If the answer is no, in that there are presently no strategic advantages, then the respondent need go no further. If the answer is yes however, then a follow-up question is for the recipient to allocate (from a total 100%) the proportion of the company's competitive advantage that has its root cause in each of capabilities (i.e. the answers to the first question). Then how much comes from the physical assets and consequent market power of the company – and finally how much of the advantage is due to liquid assets such as cash?

Get good answers to these questions and you have the foundation from which to construct a capability-led strategy that is closely linked to the company's existing strategic advantages.

What's more is that you just saved yourself several weeks of background reading to work out how to 'do' strategy. Armed with the results of this exercise you can then tackle the Periodic Table and the macroeconomic environment – but those questions can await the New Year.

52. LATERAL THINKING – THERE IS ALWAYS A WAY

26 May 2014 Strictly Boardroom recounts a brief brainstorming story of an inspirational left-field solution to a near-term production challenge.

Finding ways to make budgeted tonnes is one of the thrills of production challenges.

Admittedly, a well-run operation needs no heroes. Good management processes trump the need to continually bail out production with unforeseen impressive deeds. Nevertheless, when times must, a resort to some lateral thinking is often a welcome reprieve.

Recently, Strictly Boardroom had time to read through some old chestnuts from the management bookshelf and found an inspirational anecdote from a 1998 book entitled *The Guru Guide*

– *The Best Ideas of the Top Management Thinkers.** Somehow I missed this one when first reading the text many years ago but it is a gem. It is symptomatic of the backs-to-the-wall culture that pervades many operations during hard times.

No doubt readers will have their own experiences of overcoming similar challenges at mine sites right now.

The author of the piece, Jack Stack, writes that:

> *"It is amazing what you can come up with when you have no money, zero outside resources and a payroll of people all depending on a solution for their jobs, their homes, even their prospects of dinner for the foreseeable future."*

The story hails from a tractor plant in the US faced with tough economic times and an industrial relations climate of frequent strikes and disruptions.

The future of the production plant was already on a knife-edge when there was a strike among local truckers supplying the facility. Closure seemed the inevitable outcome.

The local truckers were up for a fight – even closing down the roads to cut off the supply lines in the region. For the tractor plant, this meant that getting steel feedstock delivered from which to manufacture tractor parts looked impossible. The strike was so acrimonious that truckers were literally sniping at any trucks still running. So how then to transport steel without risking getting shot? A brainstorming session threw up an answer – from very far left-field:

> *"Someone said: 'School buses. They wouldn't shoot at school buses would they?' Another guy said: 'It depends who's driving the buses'. Someone else said: 'They wouldn't shoot at nuns driving school buses'."*

It turned out that the 'guys dressed as nuns' solution was exactly what took place. The plant rented a school bus and volunteers dressed up as nuns. The nuns duly drove to the steel plant, loaded the steel bars into the school bus and safely made the return journey to the tractor plant. Love it. The 'nuns in a bus' story is a brilliant example of a left-field solution.

Now back to the present day. Strictly Boardroom has a course to teach in July to Master of Business Administration (MBA) students on resource sector management. Operations management will be covered in double quick time – and I suspect that I cannot do it the justice it deserves (although the students have other operations research courses that will fill the gaps).

If Strictly Boardroom readers could advise of stories along similar lines to the above it will no doubt lighten the load of what can be a dry subject area. Your anecdotal contributions would be most welcome.

---

* Boyett, J. & Boyett, J. 2000. *The Guru Guide: The Best Ideas of the Top Management Thinkers*. Wiley, Hoboken, NJ.

53. GRADE: THE KING – OR SERF – OF GOLD OREBODIES

15 Sep 2014 Matthew Kanakis joins with Strictly Boardroom to look at geological factors that influence production costs in Australian gold. What matters may surprise you.

'Grade is King' has become the accepted industry mantra as a proxy for deposit quality in gold.

When everything else is equal, of course, a higher-grade deposit should clearly have a competitive advantage over a lower-grade asset in cost terms, but the relationship appears far from simple in reality.

A study of 2013 public-domain cost information from gold mines in Australia and New Zealand attests to the real world complexity of the cost function in gold.[1] Instead of costs falling as mine grade increased, there was no easily discernible relationship between costs and grade in the Australian data. The X-Y plot of costs versus grade resembles a shotgun blast in its pattern.

Grade aside, the broader geology of a gold deposit should also influence the cost of production at gold mines. Geometry of the ore zone is an obvious factor. Large dimension, easily accessible near-surface gold accumulations should lend themselves to far lower costs of mining than small deposits that require intricate underground development in order to access and mine. This hypothesis appears to be supported by the latest available data. Elsewhere, while previous studies have shown scant difference, at least on average, between open pit and underground developments in Australia, hybrid operations that combine pit and underground mining typically incur a cost penalty for doing so.[2]

The style of gold mineralisation is a further factor that should have some relevance to realised costs. Broad zones of mineralisation with gold throughout should prove a lower cost target than tighter discrete mineralisation structures (again when grade is considered to be equal). The former mineralization style allows more flexibility in mining and may also allow higher production rates to capture scale and scope economies. The evidence for such scale and scope economies does indeed exist in the 2014 (and 2013) data at high level. Put simply, larger gold mines do typically have lower costs than their smaller peers.

Let's look a little deeper though. The prevailing 'grade is king' logic would suggest that if the grade-to-cost relationship at gold mines is hard to see, then the likelihood of unravelling a relationship between mine cost and mineralisation style would be remote indeed.

Certainly mineralisation style, as a qualitative parameter, requires pre-classification to give the search for cost impact any chance. So what of the case for mineralisation style as a factor of relevance to costs? The predominant mineralisation style at Australian mines was first classified into different styles:

- Quartz reef/lode/lens
- Quartz tension veins
- Laminated quartz veins
- Ladder quartz veins
- Breccia-hosted
- Stockwork veins
- Thicker veins in broad shear zones.

Of the above, the first four styles were then grouped as discrete mineralisation styles – with the latter three styles considered to be dispersed mineralisation.

Which style wins? Dispersed mineralisation is associated with statistically lower mining costs. Scale of production may be the intermediate factor at work in the dataset, but the finding is nonetheless impressive given that more 'obvious' factors such as grade failed the same statistical tests.

The story does not stop there. It appears that host rock also has a discernible relationship with costs of production although that relationship is still under investigation.

Grade was the obvious favourite as having an inverse relationship to costs going into the analysis, but as every punter knows, favourites do not always finish first.

Like the broader industry we had 'grade expectations' in looking for the drivers of lower costs in gold mining. Those expectations were left unrealised.[3]

---

1 Kanakis, M. 2014. Grade Expectations: Exploring the Cost-Grade Hypothesis in Australian Gold Production. *CET Quarterly Newsletter*, September, p14-17.

2 De Assuncoa, J.C. 2013. *Economic Insights from a Cost Analysis of Gold Production in Australia from 2008 to 2012*. Capstone Individual Research Project, MSc in Mineral and Energy Economics Programme, Curtin University.

3 Matt Kanakis expresses thanks to Professor Steffen Hagemann and Emeritus Professor David Groves of the CET for guidance on this project.

54. STRUGGLING WITH BUREAUCRACY? INTRODUCE ADHOCRACY

25 Mar 2013 The 'new way' of cost-containment and capital discipline across the mining sector as a means of delivering increased margins and shareholder returns faces a massive challenge from within that should not be under-estimated: bureaucracy. Strictly Boardroom suggests one solution: adhocracy.

Recently, your scribe has been on the wrong end of a massive chain of bureaucracy, trying to make small directional changes to a university administration system that has a turning circle several times that of the *Titanic*. The mining sector also faces bureaucratic challenge, but that will only grow as companies seek the responsiveness to lift margins without relying upon rising commodity prices. How can bureaucracy be overcome? The management literature may be one source of assistance to those seeking to 'just get things done'.

When it comes to under-rated business books, *Adhocracy* by Robert Waterman[1], published in the 1990s, takes some beating. Waterman presents just over 100 pages of evidence showing we are our own worst enemy as organisations when it comes to actually getting things done. Waterman defined adhocracy as:

> "*Any form of organisation that cuts across normal bureaucratic lines to capture opportunities, solve problems and get results.*"

Critically, adhocracy should not be confused with business anarchy. Systems and process are critical and, indeed, can differentiate good companies from bad, but getting things done is critical too. Systems and processes need to be streamlined, rather than built up and extended as an end in themselves. This is a point that is often forgotten, particularly by those in charge of the said processes. Such people unwittingly see their value in building process to administrative perfection over and above achieving any actual results.

Leaving aside the book, to which reference is given below, let's look at some pertinent examples. But first, please excuse me for citing one example that I can never forget and that I hope will resonate with you, too.[2]

The story relates to the manager of Royal Dutch Shell's Malaysian activities. Frustrated with excessive paperwork, the manager gathered up a vast stock of requests sent from headquarters. Knowing that a board meeting was taking place, he then jumped on a plane at Kuala Lumpur and went to The Hague unannounced, highly irregular behaviour in itself. He arrived at the board meeting and for all practical purposes barged in. He opened the suitcase on the spotless boardroom table and dumped out 30 pounds of forms, asking:

> "*Do you want me to fill these out or hunt for oil?*"

The immediate response is not recorded, but the manager went on to head the Shell Group through a profitable overhaul.

The above story reminds me of working at a large oil and gas company. The managing director (MD) was an early riser and was in the habit of leaving notes on people's desks well before the freeway had hit peak traffic and most staff had arrived for work. These notes provided excellent direction to all who received them and could be used as 'virtual currency' to cut through layers of bureaucracy in real time in order to actually get things done.

I also remember vividly the MD's mantra that an organisation should aim to minimise the time it spends doing business with itself, which aligns with the adhocracy theme espoused by Waterman. Let me repeat that statement. Large organisations can descend into bureaucracy such that they spend an inordinate amount of time on unproductive administrative process – not actually advancing a business initiative externally at all.

What lessons lie in the above dialogue? For the major miners, the challenge is very clear. Implementing a new regime of cost control could easily degenerate into a new (and expanded) regime of bureaucracy. That is to be avoided. The challenge is greater than it may at first appear. Why? Those who stand to gain from bureaucracy in terms of power and influence will resist and use the bureaucratic system to do so.

For smaller resources companies and emerging miners, the challenge is to maintain the character of a smaller organisation as growth eventuates, where decisions do not get unduly held up by administrative process.

As for the likes of universities, perhaps the vice chancellor, like the oil and gas company MD, will take up the habit of writing individual notes to staff in order to assist in getting things done?

---

1 Waterman Jr., R.H. 1993. *Adhocracy*. W.W. Norton & Co., London.
2 The Royal Dutch Shell case study is from: Peters, T. and Austin, N. 1989. *A Passion for Excellence: The Leadership Difference*. Grand Central Publishing, New York, first published in 1985.

55. THE REAL HOUSEWIVES OF MINING

17 Nov 2014 Vikki Lauritsen joins with Strictly Boardroom to look at some of the challenges to increasing female participation in the mining sector workforce.[1]

TV series have introduced us to the Real Housewives of Orange County, New York, Atlanta, Washington DC, New Jersey, Beverley Hills and Miami across the US. The real housewives concept also reached Australia in 2014 with the release of the Real Housewives of Melbourne. As yet however, the 'Real Housewives of Mining' has not appeared on our screens, although the experiences of women in the minerals sector are no doubt worthy of such focus.

When compared with an all-industry average, female participation in the mining industry remains very low, at around 15% compared to 46% across all industries. Why? Here are a few ongoing challenges to increasing female participation in the mining sector:

- **Men's work:** The mining industry has a long history of male dominance and as a result has gained a reputation, perhaps outdated but still relevant, as a 'masculine' industry not suitable for women. The sex segregation of many roles in the industry as 'men's work' has discouraged women participating in the sector. Many traditionally male-dominated roles continue to be so. Managerial, technical and trades, frontline labour and machine operator positions continue to be male dominated in the mining sector statistics.

- **Employment type:** Although more women are participating in the Australian workforce, a large proportion of female workers across all industries are employed on a part-time basis. That is, recent statistics show nearly an even number of women working part-time as working full-time. Furthermore, the part-time employment status of females is much higher than that of their male counterparts. Contrast this general situation with that in mining where most mining workers are full-time employees (more than 96%). Part-time work in mining is only around one-tenth of that of the all-industry average (3% compared to 30%).

- **Age distribution and family status:** Workforce participation and employment status for women varies according to age and parental status. The age distribution of the 2014 female workforce shows a distinct fall in the full-time status of female workers between the ages of 35 to 44 years, coinciding with an increasing maternal age in recent years. Such an age distribution for female workforce participation aligns poorly with the current mining sector age demographic. That is, the mining industry workforce has a median age of 40 years compared to an all-industries average of 37 years. As such, the mining industry employs a higher proportion of workers aged 25 to 44 years with 58% of workers falling into this age group, compared with only 45% for all industries. Consequently, the proportion of workers aged 15 to 19 years is lower in mining than across all industries, reflecting the industry's preference for mature, qualified and experienced workers.

- **Education and skills:** Younger women in the workforce today are the most highly educated, with more women having university degrees than men. However, most women are enrolled in fields of study such as health, education, commerce, society and culture rather than mathematics and physical science. This could reflect the 'traditional' nurturing character of the female stereotype. Recent figures from Graduate Careers Australia show that women make up only around 18% of Bachelor of Mining Engineering graduates. Furthermore, only a small percentage of women are involved in apprenticeship or trainee programs when compared to males, reflecting that trade occupations are conventionally male-dominated, physically labour-intensive roles. Statistics show that women are still inclined to undertake training and seek employment in 'traditionally' female roles such as administration, finance, education and health.

- **Concentration in regional areas:** Close to 88% of mining industry employment is concentrated in Western Australia, Queensland and New South Wales, with 59% of the workforce being located outside of state capital cities. The fly-in, fly-out nature of employment in many mining operations inhibits the industry's ability to offer flexibility in employment and thus creates a further barrier for women entering or remaining in the industry.

Overall, it's tough out there, with the many factors above all conspiring to make change difficult and slow. How can we speed up the process of normalising the mining workforce? Perhaps reality TV beckons after all for the 'Real Housewives of Mining?

---

1 Lauritsen, V. 2014. *Gender diversity in the Australian minerals sector: Key insights from a labour force statistical review.* Capstone Individual Research Project, MSc in Mineral and Energy Economics Programme, Curtin University.

KEY INSIGHTS:
ON COMPETITIVENESS AND MINING EXCELLENCE

- The mining industry is still not collectively aware of who are the best mine operators in the business (net of asset-linked natural competitive advantage). Without such knowledge the industry will struggle to instil a performance culture that strives to achieve operational excellence.

- The industry is 'asset-centric' with the best companies synonymous with the highest quality assets.

- Mining companies would benefit from a greater focus towards developing distinctive capabilities – over and above an asset-centric focus.

- To develop new such capabilities and strategies a certain amount of lateral thinking, re-thinking about old problems and challenging of long-held industry assumptions will be required.

- Unlocking the full potential of the workforce is a clear opportunity, with an increased future role for women in the minerals sector a priority area.

PART 6
On Exploration Strategy

Part Six starts out by looking at the business case for exploration. "Why big companies should explore" highlights that the strategic aim of exploration is to find better mineral resources rather than merely more resources. "Is exploration really high risk?" challenges the accepted maxim that exploration is a strategically high-risk endeavour, pointing out that whilst exploration involves high technical risk, with a consequent expectation of failure on a hole-by-hole basis, overall corporate financial exposure is low, so strategically it is a low corporate risk endeavour. The technical challenge of exploration is highlighted in the chapter: "Where are the mines of tomorrow? Hiding in plain sight", with case studies of significant mineral discoveries demonstrating just how many nearly were not discoveries at all – picking and following the occasional positive lead amongst the many inevitable false leads that is the business of exploration.

"Towards big exploration" looks at the wider role of exploration in developing social licence and instigating technological innovation. Expanding upon the idea of big exploration, "The

X-Files on mineral exploration: Building a perfect team" considers the blend of creative and scientific cognitive abilities required to deliver exploration effectively – one focused on exploration efficiency and one focused on making entirely new discoveries. "The X-Files on new exploration search space" looks at this latter type of exploration in more detail and suggests a number of ways explorers can open up new search space and increase the odds of making major new mineral discoveries.

"Corporate excellence in exploration" is the first of two short chapters looking at how to wire a company for success in exploration – both in conducting efficient exploration and in making major new mineral discoveries. The chapter highlights the importance of a clear corporate vision for exploration, backed by executive level support for the enterprise. Such a structure maximises the chances of undertaking the higher (technical) risk exploration for major new discoveries, and maintaining the funding required to be constantly drilling and exploring. "Large company volunteer required: Exploration champion" re-iterates these points in the context of major companies, where exploration is something of a forgotten strategy. Excellent exploration that delivers major new mineral discoveries can make an existential impact to a major miner's sustainability in the long-run – thus the stakes are very high.

"Mystery in the exploration boardroom" concludes with some thoughts on what we do not know about the business of exploration – which alas is still quite a lot. Exploration strategy and management is still a research backwater for both academics and industry consultants. As an example, little is known empirically about the ideal structure for an exploration company board – what is the optimum blend of skills and experience?

56. WHY BIG COMPANIES SHOULD EXPLORE

23 Feb 2015 This week Strictly Boardroom looks to that age-old but most challenging question: why should big companies explore?

Explorers in large companies will no doubt have been asked to defend a proposed budget for exploration or research and development in their careers – all the more often in recent years. Their bosses typically take the following stance:

> *"Why should we maintain exploration expenditure 'through the cycle'? Why would we want to find more supply when markets are weak?*

The next time you are asked you might try this.

True greenfields exploration is not about finding 'more' supply or meeting short-term market needs, it is about finding 'better' supply of long-term strategic value, i.e. new deposits that can be mined at lower cost than those already being mined. Such industry-changing, world-class deposits are found in places we have not looked in before, and using techniques we have not mastered as yet. Exploration and discovery is about looking for something new and finding it against all odds. Greenfields exploration finds the next generation of mines and thus does not add more supply instantaneously to accentuate the current business cycle.

The situation is analogous to research and development (R&D) in other industries. R&D is not undertaken to find 'more' technology, it is done to find 'better' technology – technology that will replace what went before by doing things cheaper and better. You discover this new better technology by once again doing things you have not done before and going places (metaphorically in this case) you have not been before. So researchers are explorers too; they are just exploring the boundaries of science and technology, rather than the boundaries of the mapped earth.

Look at another famously R&D focused industry. In the hi-tech world it is all about inventing the next disruptive technology. Mobile phones for example replaced landlines, search engines and websites replaced encyclopaedias and newspapers and e-commerce replaced bricks and mortar stores. All these innovations do things better and cheaper than the previous way things were done and, in the process, offer more choice at better prices. This can be illustrated using the example of a current disruptive high technology: 3D printing. The potential of 3D printing is not in making incremental improvements to the low-cost manufacturing of sprockets in China (a 'more' tactic), it is in completely eliminating production line manufacturing and introducing a new type of manufacturing which is much more bespoke, but still retains the economies of scale. It is about replacing mass production with mass customisation. In this case, you get 'more of what you want' (i.e. better), rather than just 'more'.

Hi-tech companies do not stop investing in these highly disruptive potential technologies just because of a downturn in the business cycle. Instead, they keep plugging away, knowing that inventing the next disruptive technology beats the cycle and it changes the game. For example, Apple launched a new iPhone each year through the 2007-09 financial crisis and grabbed market share off Blackberry, setting Apple on the way to being the world's biggest company. Apple's iPhone changed the game in two ways:

1. Phones are now smart with intuitive touchscreens (i.e. better)
2. Smart phones are for everyone, not just businessmen (i.e. more).

The dual lessons here are that you keep investing in long-term disruptive technologies because if you invent it, you change the industry and dominate (Apple), whereas if someone else invents it and you cannot respond then you're fruit toast (Blackberry).

Similarly, true high-risk minerals exploration and mining R&D is about disruption – replacing what went before and gaining a new competitive edge that takes over the market. An example of an industry-changing discovery is Australia's very own Pilbara, which replaced low-quality iron ore mines in North America and Europe (thus it was better), whilst simultaneously materially increasing the supply of cheap iron ore to the market, allowing both traditional Western economies and fast-growing Asian economies to build and to consume more.

A technology-focused mining example is the package of exploration and production technologies that re-invigorated the Chilean copper mining industry in the latter half of the 20th century, leading both to major new discoveries (such as Escondida) and the development of previously uneconomic deposits. The technologies and innovations included the development of the porphyry geological model, greater understanding of residual terrain, lower-cost drilling techniques, better helicopter access and geophysical imaging on the exploration side; and solvent-extraction-electrowinning (SXEW) processing technology and computer-aided resource modelling and mine scheduling on the production side.* This technology package grew the Chilean copper mining industry at the expense of the less efficient US and Central African copper mining industries, but again also increased the supply of cheap copper to the global market allowing for greater consumption of economic goods (usually electrical and electronic) in the Western World and Asia.

The same logic applies to investing in the high-risk, high-reward exploration and mining R&D over the long term and thus throughout the cycle, because if you discover something genuinely disruptive (lots of new low-cost supply) the business cycle is largely irrelevant.

The prize is for Australia's mining industry to grow faster than everyone else's industry (and provide more, cheaper minerals for all of us to consume, including in iPhones). However, be warned that if we do not do it, then someone else will discover the great new deposits and inventions elsewhere. That is, in the absence of next generation exploration discoveries locally, Australia's mining industry will fail to remain competitive. Such a future will make the current situation in the industry look positively rosy. Think of the UK coal industry in the 1980s or the current print news industry.

Let us know whether your exploration budget is approved.

---

* Sykes, J.P. & Trench, A. 2014. *Finding the Copper Mine of the 21st Century: Conceptual Exploration Targeting for Hypothetical Copper Reserves*, Society of Economic Geologists (SEG) Special Publication 18: Building Exploration Capability for the 21st Century, Chapter 11, p273-300.

57. IS EXPLORATION TRULY HIGH RISK?

11 May 2015 Strictly Boardroom is joined by Graham Arvidson to discuss an analytical perspective of prevailing business growth strategies in the minerals sector, including a focus upon exploration.

Most BHP Billiton and Rio Tinto shareholders couldn't care less about this year's exploration budget at either company. Why? The pay-off from exploration success will not move the corporate profit & loss (P&L) dial for these mining giants anytime soon. In the accounts of these companies, exploration appears principally as a year-on-year cost. Indeed, for the majors of the mining world, exploration is actually far more about ensuring long-term company sustainability than it is about influencing the foreseeable profit outlook and growth.

The converse is true for the other 99% of minerals companies. For all but the majors, exploration is a powerful growth lever. The key question for the boards of these companies then becomes a simple one: do the returns from exploration stack-up?

Surprisingly little data exists to evidence the degree to which exploration strategies pay off. A recent study* has, however, shed some light on the high returns that exploration can bring compared to alternative business strategies in the minerals sector.

Using a group of 80 companies that sit below the majors in terms of market value, the study attributed the following prevailing strategies to each of the companies based on a qualitative analysis of their five-year corporate history:

1. **Exploration discovery:** Significant exploration discovery to realise shareholder returns.
2. **Purchase and produce:** Investment(s) in either operational or previously operational assets to achieve near-term production (typically less than 12 months).
3. **Project development:** Investment of typically more than $100 million over a period of more than 12 months by taking a project through the development cycle and into first production.

4. **Mergers and acquisitions:** Growing scale by combining with another company at a corporate level.
5. **Strategic investor:** Attraction of a strategic investor in order to drive shareholder returns.

So which strategy accreted by far the most value to shareholders? Overall, the most successful strategy proved to be exploration discovery.

The five-year compounded annual shareholder returns, inclusive of dividends by each strategy, were as follows:

- Exploration discovery: 20%
- Purchase and produce: 4%
- Project development: -12%
- Mergers and acquisitions: -20%
- Strategic investor/alliance: -17%.

A closer look at those 20 companies among the 80 companies in the study that yielded the highest returns supports the shareholder impact that exploration can deliver. That is, 12 of the top 20 companies have exploration to thank for the exceptional value accrued for their shareholders. Indeed, some 59% of the entire value accreted to firms in the top 20 was attributable to exploration discovery.

The catch? The Top 80 study considered only successful strategy outcomes, of course. That is, the impact of those companies who failed at each of the strategies, including failed explorers, is not taken into consideration.

Unsurprisingly, delegates at a recent industry conference were sceptical of the findings with comments typically linked to a common theme. Most feedback went something like this:

> "OK, exploration is great when it is successful, but what about failure? Exploration is high risk, surely?"

But is exploration truly 'high risk'? When it comes to technical risk the answer is undoubtedly yes. More than 99% of exploration programs fail. With exploration, however, you can only lose the amount invested in the exploration program.

Conversely, most other corporate strategies risk the whole company. So while the technical risk of something like 'purchase and produce' may be lower, the corporate risk (the likelihood of losing the entire company) is demonstrably higher.

A synthesis of the exploration outcomes in strategy terms might be along the following lines:

> *"Exploration-led growth as a strategy offers a unique opportunity to maximise shareholder return within a risk framework that is entirely quantifiable, being that of principally technical risk rather than corporate-level risk and, where the downside is likewise quantifiable, is small in magnitude – and where management decision-making can control the level of risk exposure."*

Can the same be said of the other strategies? Our view is certainly not.

Unfortunately the drought of exploration funding indicates that the capital markets have either not realised this risk–reward relationship as yet, or else have long-since forgotten it.

What do you think?

---

* Arvidson, G. 2015. *The Case for Exploration as Strategy: An ASX Top 80 Mining and Metals Case Study*. Centre for Exploration Targeting Discovery Day, Fremantle, WA, 24 February.

58. WHERE ARE THE MINES OF TOMORROW? HIDING IN PLAIN SIGHT

18 Feb 2013 Strictly Boardroom has been on a voyage of mineral discovery* – everywhere from Abydos in the Pilbara region of Western Australia, to Gosowong in Indonesia, to Ernest Henry in Queensland, to Jacinth/Ambrosia in South Australia and across regional Western Australia to Telfer, Rocky's Reward, Harmony, Spotted Quoll, Flying Fox – and finally to DeGrussa and Nova. All these mineral discoveries had one thing in common: they were all hiding in plain sight.

ON EXPLORATION STRATEGY

Last week your scribe had the pleasure of hosting the Discovery Day forum at The University of Western Australia, with case studies describing company-making discoveries from the length and breadth of Western Australia, and from well beyond, too.

So it is appropriate to open with sincere thanks to David Flanagan (Atlas Iron), Shannan Bamforth (Sandfire Resources), Mark Bennett (Sirius Resources), Tim Craske (Iluka Resources), Charles Wilkinson (Western Areas), David Tyrwhitt (ex-Newmont Mining), Rocky Osborne (Emmerson Resources) and Dan Wood (ex-Newcrest Mining).

Finding world-scale mineral deposits is not easy. Each exploration case study overcame many challenges that could have resulted in failure. Those challenges varied from deposit to deposit.

It might be insensitive to carefully match the challenges to each of the individual company case studies – but by way of illustration, the non-technical challenges included the likes of funding (or more appropriately the lack of it); through to maintaining corporate focus; belief and trust; through to meddling governments and corporate hierarchies; and to what seems the simple task (but it is not, of course) of keeping experienced mineral explorers in the front line of the exploration effort itself, away from the corporate, legislative and administrative paperwork.

Get all that lot right and there's still the ever so slight problem that orebodies don't quite fit with their textbook role-models – lying tantalisingly close to historical drilling (DeGrussa, Rocky's Reward) or surface sampling (Telfer) – yet sometimes leaving Agatha Christie-like technical clues that were either not identified at all or else not followed up on for years.

One takeaway from the day – and there were many others – was that orebodies 'hide in plain sight'. They are actually present in the technical data but often are not revealed by the most obvious of anomalies.

Let me repeat that statement. We have likely already discovered clues to many of the mines of tomorrow in our exploration campaigns to date. We just don't realise it yet.

So, for example, a deposit can leave clues, such as a 500

nanoTesla magnetic anomaly (Rocky's Reward), but not the adjacent 10,000 nanoTesla 'obvious' target. It can be a near insignificant 'bump' on a ground electromagnetic profile that is dominated by nearby sulphidic shale responses (Spotted Quoll), else the highest grades of a copper discovery can hide just over 20 metres from historical drilling that is anomalous for gold (the chalcocite at DeGrussa).

Orebodies are not where you expect them to be, yet may be closer than you think.

They can sit virtually under the exploration access track (Spotted Quoll), within a nine-iron of the exploration camp (Gosowong) or within clear sight of the mine head-frame beneath a popular lunch spot (Rocky's Reward). They may even be on the map already (as for some of the 'undiscovered' iron ore deposits in the Abydos region). Others lie far in the outback, where one more (unplanned) hole on a traverse can make all the difference (Jacinth/Ambrosia).

The clues are there before us but we seldom see them. Sometimes ground geophysics reveals the orebody secrets quite quickly (Nova, Ernest Henry) where even basic technology (not necessarily 21st century high technology equipment) would have located a good anomaly.

The skill is to be smart enough (and gutsy enough) to actually do the ground survey in the first place, before other less-than-perfect 'red herring-type' clues weaken the corporate hunger to press on.

The lesson here is to pull out the exploration data again and look ever more closely at it. Then get out there to acquire more primary exploration data.

Agatha Christie may not have discovered any mineral deposits but the likes of Poirot and Miss Marple would have made pretty good exploration directors.

---

* The following names all refer to significant mineral deposit discoveries – with the relevant mineral commodities in brackets for each deposit name: Abydos (iron ore), DeGrussa (copper), Ernest Henry (copper-gold), Flying Fox (nickel), Gosowong (gold), Jacinth/Ambrosia (mineral sands containing payable zircon, ilmenite and rutile) Nova (nickel-copper), Rocky's Reward (nickel), Spotted Quoll (nickel) and Telfer (copper-gold).

59. TOWARDS 'BIG EXPLORATION'

11 Jan 2016 Strictly Boardroom draws inspiration from business strategists Richard Whittington and Richard Rumelt, and takes the view that the multipurpose role of exploration in adding-value to the minerals sector is neither understood nor valued – and that the future lies in 'Big Exploration'.*

As an industry we have yet to recognise the full impact of exploration in adding value to the minerals sector. That is, collectively we have thus far fallen into the trap of thinking 'Small Exploration' – not only in terms of the quantum of annual exploration spend but more critically in underestimating the vanguard role of exploration in potentially even shaping the very future of the minerals sector itself. Future success requires effective 'Big Exploration', and with it a radical broadening of our industry mindset from contemporary thinking.

Let's define terms. Small Exploration is the consequence of viewing exploration merely as a peripheral function to the entire business that is mining, where the exploration goal is solely to replenish mineable reserves in a cost-effective manner. As such, Small Exploration is all about the process for setting and managing exploration budgets and outcomes, measuring discovery costs, calculating reserve replenishment and then auditing the carrying value of capitalised exploration.

Small Exploration includes new minerals discoveries too. It is not merely the administration of the exploration process. Small Exploration is what we have done as a sector for decades now. It has become routine to the point that we tend to view exploration itself as just a technical sub-discipline, servicing a far bigger business – 'The Business of Mining'.

We may have all become Small Exploration thinkers without even realising it. In Small Exploration, explorers are responsible for finding brownfields resources and reserves that extend the life of mining assets. Occasionally (thankfully) explorers also turn attentions to exciting new greenfields discoveries too that add to the corporate development portfolio and value.

So what's the problem then? The Small Exploration mindset does not capture the full value of exploration activity.

Big Exploration by contrast is a new and broader way of thinking. Big Exploration certainly does not stop at the administration of the exploration function and does not stop either when new discoveries are made. Big Exploration seeks to recognise and embed the broader societal and corporate impact into the scope and true significance of mineral exploration activity.

So what are the additional areas that make Big Exploration distinct from what we have done for decades?

As the initial point of community contact in the mining value-chain, Big Exploration has a critical role to play in establishing, advancing and maintaining the social licence to operate for mining companies that ensures their very existence. That is, by definition any threat to the social licence to operate represents an existential threat to the industry itself. The value of exploration as the first point of community and government contact and relationships is certainly not captured within a Small Exploration mindset. By contrast, a Big Exploration perspective sees both community and government interactions as important, value-adding opportunities in themselves. Both hold latent value to be valued and managed.

But there is more. Exploration technology innovation and the corporate learnings that come from the success of exploration 'skunk works' are important too. Similarly, the 'big-data' opportunity that arises from the 'mining' of historical exploration data sits at the forefront of the many factors required for 21st-century miners to succeed.

In Small Exploration, the innovation management lessons from exploration teams have little chance to make it back into the corporate memory. In Big Exploration achieving that aim is very much part of the mindset in capturing the true influence and value of the exploration function.

Thus the impacts of Big Exploration stretch well beyond exploration performance itself as we traditionally measure it. The Small Exploration approach has neither the tools nor the attention span to grasp such larger effects.

We can choose Big Exploration. We can also choose the continuation of Small Exploration that carries with it an existential threat to our industry.

Which do you think we should choose?

---

* Some credit is due here to Richard Whittington of Oxford University whose dichotomic essay: "Big Strategy / Small Strategy" acted as a source of inspiration for this article which in turn drew inspiration from Richard Rumelt's: "Good Strategy / Bad Strategy".

Whittington, R. 2012. Big Strategy / Small Strategy, Strategic Organization, 10, (3), p263-268.

Rumelt, R.P. 2011. *Good Strategy / Bad Strategy: The Difference and Why It Matters*. Crown Business, New York.

60. THE X-FILES ON MINERAL EXPLORATION: BUILDING A PERFECT TEAM

25 Jan 2016 Strictly Boardroom and Jon Hronsky look to '90s sci-fi TV heroes Mulder and Scully for some guidance on how to build the perfect mineral exploration team.

The current state of the mining industry perhaps has many readers feeling suspiciously like they are back in the 1990s reliving the last nadir in the industry. With the release of a new series of The X-Files after a 14-year hiatus, fans of the '90s science fiction conspiracy drama may also be forgiven for thinking they are back in the '90s too.

As such this gives us tenuous cause to link The X-Files and minerals exploration. The X-Files is of course all about exploration and discovery, hence the show's tagline "The truth is out there". Whether chasing down the 'monster of the week' or evidence supporting the series-long alien conspiracy theory, Mulder and Scully were searching for and hoping to discover the truth, albeit with very different approaches. The odd-couple pairing of their two epistemological characters was at the heart of the show's success and made David Duchovny and Gillian Anderson into TV icons.

Dr Dana Scully represented the rational scientist, testing

hypotheses about the known world with data and facts. Fox Mulder was more interested in the unknown, inventing new hypotheses, theories and sometimes conspiracies. As individuals they were vulnerable to their weaknesses; Scully to the unexpected, unpredicted, the previously unobserved and the ascent of the minority view. Conversely Mulder had a tendency to believe everything, ask too few discriminating questions, see links where there were none and lean towards conspiracy rather than theory. But together they complemented each other in their search for the truth. Mulder generated lots of ideas, Scully worked out which represented the truth and which (i.e. most) did not. Much patience was required from Scully in the process.

Minerals explorers will recognise this kind of knowledge-balanced dichotomy as the ideal sort of exploration team. Exploration itself merges two types of thinking task, best undertaken by two different types of epistemological character. Although exploration is often classified into greenfields and brownfields the real difference lies in conceptually what you are trying to achieve, rather than whether you can see a mine from your drill rig.

Some exploration is more like 'resourcing' and involves the search for the most efficient way to prove up an area of mineralisation that is reasonably well known to exist. Such work is common in well-studied brownfields areas, however the 'elephant-hunting'[1] sub-set of greenfields exploration critically falls into this category too. Here explorers follow up a discovery in a new area in search of similar types of deposits likely to also exist in proximity. As the saying goes – you look for elephants where elephants are found.

In both the above cases, this combines relevant scientific-economic and engineering factors to establish the most efficient route to discovery. The key to discovery effectiveness resides in risk/reward understanding and the prioritisation of the most promising hypotheses to deliver resource growth. This is the Dana Scully approach to exploration. Ultimately however, because the best discoveries are usually made early on, it most often delivers diminishing returns over the long run as the quality of new discoveries declines (unless the search space can be materially expanded).

Going to elephant country to hunt elephants is all well and good if there are still some elephants to shoot, but finding the next 'big game' is a wholly different matter. This presents the second type of exploration – the first-mover[1] or Fox Mulder type – trying to find something completely new, and in the explorers' parlance, open up entirely new search space[2]. Such exploration has the potential for very high returns, as the best deposits are usually amongst the first discoveries in a given search space. However, the potential for high return is counterbalanced by the ubiquitous presence of numerous false 'leads' (Mulder's conspiracies).

To make a genuinely new discovery (by definition) you need to look where no one else has looked before – or at the least look from a radically new perspective. Fox Mulder and most explorers would recognise the geographical version of this – trekking into deepest jungle, furthest desert, up the highest mountain and so on. New search space can be generated in supposedly mature mineral districts too however with new ideas, concepts and technologies. Hence 'Mulder exploration' is far from redundant in the near-mine brownfields environment.

Fox Mulder exploration involves operating in the unknown world and generating ideas or hypotheses about what could be (rather than what is proven to be). This type of work is arguably less scientific, demonstrably more creative and certainly less easy to quantify and measure than the exploration world of Dana Scully. Exploration investors gravitate towards Scully's rational approach and are prone to lose patience with Mulder's hunches.

As Fox Mulder put it at the beginning of 'The X-Files Movie: Fight the Future'(1998), whilst conducting some typically Clint-type[3] exploration in looking for the bomb on the building across the road from where the bomb-threat was called in:

> "*Whatever happened to playing the hunch, Scully? The element of surprise. Random acts of unpredictability. If we fail to anticipate the unforeseen or expect the unexpected in a universe of infinite possibilities, we may find ourselves*

at the mercy of anyone or anything that cannot be programmed, categorised or easily referenced."[4]

So did Mulder find the bomb, or was this just another conspiracy-theory leading him and Scully astray? Is your exploration team onto something or is it just another false-lead?

To be continued...

---

1 Hronsky, J.M.A. & Groves, D.I. 2008. Science of Targeting: Definition, Strategies, Targeting and Performance Measurement, *Australian Journal of Earth Sciences*, 55, (1), p3-12.

2 Hronsky, J.M.A. 2009. *The Exploration Search Space Concept: Key to a Successful Exploration Strategy*. Centre for Exploration Targeting (CET) Quarterly Newsletter, June, p14-15.

3 See short chapter 73, "Which exploration personality are you?" in Part Seven: "On Exploration Management".

4 Fox Mulder, 'The X-Files Movie: Fight the Future', 1998, 12min to 15min.

61. THE X-FILES ON NEW EXPLORATION SEARCH SPACE

1 Feb 2016 Strictly Boardroom and Jon Hronsky continue their investigation into The X-Files and mineral exploration, looking at how Mulder and Scully would go about opening up new search space.

In the previous short chapter we left Fox Mulder atop a skyscraper looking for a bomb, across the road from the building to which the bomb threat was directed, and posing the question:

"Whatever happened to playing the hunch, Scully? ..."[1]

Of course, Mulder was right and the bomb was in the building he was looking in – and critically – not the one mentioned in the bomb threat. In a metaphor within a metaphor the discovery of the bomb eventually leads to an even bigger discovery of an alien nature. Discovery begets discovery. Success breeds success.

Earlier we used Mulder and Scully as an analogy for the two main types of exploration process. Scully had a scientific, hypothesis-testing approach, essentially optimising the exploration search algorithm, whilst Mulder was more creative, generating new hypotheses and aiming to open up entirely new search space[2,3,4].

The Scully-like optimisation work of exploration is well understood in principle, if not always in practice, by explorers, their managers and mining executives. In contrast however, the Mulder-type work of continually seeking to open up new exploration search space is less well understood and perceived as more difficult to manage. This in part is because, by definition, it involves doing what everyone else is not doing.

So how might Fox Mulder see potential in the world of exploration where others 'fear to tread'?

- **Geographically inaccessible regions:** very high, cold, hot, remote, dense jungle, etc. If it can suddenly be newly accessed this can be a fertile area for exploration. Mulder will be amongst the first on the ground. Infrastructure improvements can be critical in this new search space process. For example, the James Bay hydro-power scheme in Quebec resulted in roads that opened up remote parts of the state and eventually led to the discovery of the Eleanore gold deposit. A century earlier, the construction of the Trans-Canadian railroad led to the discovery of the giant Sudbury nickel deposit[5]. Helicopters have also proved a valuable aid to explorers in this regard[4], as has 'technical support' from advances in satellite navigation and geo-imaging, even if Mulder's alien intelligence leads haven't yet paid off.

- **Politically inaccessible regions:** due to war, unfavourable regimes, etc. Conceptually similar to the above, though with different causes. A change of government can allow foreign investors into a country (alongside Mulder) leading to new mineral discoveries. Chile in the Pinochet-era is a good example[4]. Myanmar could potentially be a contemporary example[6]. An important caveat comes in that the insiders who were conducting in-country exploration whilst the region was in isolation must only have been able to undertake unsophisticated exploration focused on the obvious outcropping opportunities, otherwise the new arrivals will find that the most prospective locations are already identified. This is arguably one of the reasons why exploration in post-Soviet states since the '90s has not been as successful as many predicted.

- **'Under cover' regions:** piercing the exploration veil of cover rocks – the final physical way of opening up new search space. Most mineral discoveries have been made when either mineralisation or distal parts of the deposit have surface expression. We are only now acquiring the technology and conceptual abilities to explore under thick regolith, where there are no 'Scully-like' clues to the deposit at surface. Exploration under cover in the interior regions of Australia, Canada and in Scandinavia's north all represents new search space. A focus upon this type of exploration is the aim of the UNCOVER scientific research programme in Australia[7].

- **New exploration technology:** a variety of geochemical and geophysical technologies helping unveil new mineral deposits that were previously undetectable. These improvements can be as simple as greater resolution gold assaying that allows for soil anomaly sampling across wide areas of the Australian gold fields[8]; or lower cost drilling making it cost-effective to explore for giant porphyry deposits[4]. The constantly improving 'X-ray' vision from higher resolution and deeper penetrating geophysical techniques will aid both Scully and Mulder explorers too of course.

- **New exploration concepts:** new ideas, as well as new technologies unveiling deposits. The idea is to predict using scientific theory what may be present in a new region – traditional greenfields exploration. The discovery of Olympic Dam in South Australia is the archetypal example. However, the development of the porphyry copper model also aided the discovery of Escondida and other major South American copper deposits in the latter part of the 20th century[4]. No doubt the series 10 instalments of The X-Files in 2016 will include many ideas considered 'out there' but for which exploration analogies abound.

- **Reframed exploration concepts:** new ideas helping us change what we think about supposedly well-known areas. One of the best examples of this exploration reframing is the discovery of nickel in the Eastern Goldfields of Western Australia in 1966. The Kambalda nickel camp was found right in the middle of an old gold mining region and the nickel boom followed.

- **New extraction technology:** advances in mining, processing and other 'above ground' extraction technologies making previously uneconomic deposit types viable, and therefore worth exploring for. Examples in this case include the development of solvent extraction electrowinning (SXEW) to process oxide copper deposits leading to a boom in such mines in the latter 20th century[4], or the development of Carbon-in-Pulp (CIP) processing which was instrumental in resurrecting the Western Australian Goldfields in the '90s[9]. Historically, porphyry deposits themselves were not economic and required a variety of bulk mining and processing technological improvements in the early 20th century, in addition to the development of the Panama Canal (which led to the commercialisation of bulk-earth moving equipment), before such deposits became a worthwhile exploration target[5].

- **New commodities:** the modern industrial complex uses a far wider range of commodities than 100 years ago, and even just 50 years ago. As such, explorers are now looking for metals that previous explorers would not have thought to look for[5]. This can lead to the re-generation of very old mining districts, where exploration would not have been conducted for elements that were either unknown or valueless at the time. For example, exploration for lithium and rare earths is underway in the Erzgebirge region of Germany and the Czech Republic – the tin mining region that was the focus of Agricola's 16th century mining text, *De Re Metallica*[9]. Indeed, in the recent rare earths boom (2011 to 2012), many deposits were 'discovered' simply by re-assaying drill core of likely deposits, but this time checking for the presence of rare earths. Zinc and nickel are other more historical examples of metals ignored in early-European base metal mines, until the required technological improvements were developed to process these metals. Many of the first nickel and zinc mines in Europe were therefore the waste dumps of old base and precious metals mines.

Of course, the opening up of new search usually involves a combination of the developments. For example, the resurrection of the Western Australian goldfields in the 1990s required at very least the development of CIP processing to allow the mining of low-grade oxide deposits, and high resolution gold assaying facilitating soil sampling for gold, and therefore allowing for their discovery. Similarly, the re-generation of the Chilean copper industry in the late 20th century was based on newly permitted foreign investment in exploration, cheaper drilling technologies, infrastructure improvements in the remote Atacama region, the development of the porphyry geological model and in some cases the development of SXEW processing technology.

Hopefully this list provides some inspiration for would-be Fox Mulder type explorers looking for new exploration ideas and for the hard pressed Dana Scully types seeking some kind of quality control and conceptual understanding of what on earth is going on. However, as a warning, the most innovative explorers' efforts will not fit on this list. Just like Fox Mulder they will be doing something we have not yet thought of to list here, and by definition we will have to wait until posterity for classification and addition to the list.

The truth (and your next mineral discovery) is out there.

---

1 Fox Mulder, 'The X-Files Movie: Fight the Future', 1998, 12min to 15min.

2 Hronsky, J.M.A. & Groves, D.I. 2008. *Science of Targeting: Definition, Strategies, Targeting and Performance Measurement*. Australian Journal of Earth Sciences, 55, (1), p3-12.

3 Hronsky, J.M.A. 2009. *The Exploration Search Space Concept: Key to a Successful Exploration Strategy*. Centre for Exploration Targeting (CET) Quarterly Newsletter, June, p14-15.

4 Sykes, J.P. & Trench, A. 2014. *Finding the Copper Mine of the 21st Century: Conceptual Exploration Targeting for Hypothetical Copper Reserves.* Society of Economic Geologists (SEG) Special Publication 18: Building Exploration Capability for the 21st Century, Chapter 11, p273-300.

5 Sykes, J.P., Wright, J.P. & Trench, A. 2016. *Discovery, Supply and Demand: From Metals of Antiquity to Critical Metals.* Applied Earth Science, 125, (1), p3-20.

6 Gardiner, N.J., Sykes, J.P., Trench, A. & Robb, L.J. 2015. *Tin Mining in Myanmar: Production and Potential.* Resources Policy, 46, p219-233.

7 UNCOVER: www.uncoverminerals.org.au

8 Hronsky, J.M.A., Suchomel, B.J. & Welborn, J. F. 2013, Senior Exploration Management course, 18-21 June, Centre for Exploration Targeting and Western Mining Services.

9 Agricola, G. 1950. *De re metallica.* Translated by Hoover, H.C. & Hoover, L.H. Dover Publications, New York. Originally published in Latin in 1556.

62. CORPORATE EXCELLENCE IN EXPLORATION

29 Sep 2014 Strictly Boardroom attempts to understand how companies get really great at exploration.

In this short chapter, Strictly Boardroom attempts a textbook answer as to the corporate elements that give a company a realistic chance of achieving exploration excellence. The success factors are similar for small, mid-tier and for large companies. Achieving and sustaining all of them is clearly a major challenge in practice however.

1. Exploration as a clear company aspiration

Companies that aim to be good explorers set a clear focus on exploration as a preferred means by which the company will create value. So ask yourself whether exploration is part of your company's clear aspiration? Put simply, does exploration success form part of the company's vision and mission? If the answer is yes then this will energise all involved to that end and inspire day-to-day activity – everyone just 'gets it'. If the answer at your organisation is more cryptic in that the company "aims to deliver shareholder value by doing A, B, & C plus X, Y and Z" – none of which are expressly exploration – then the task is all the harder for such goal ambiguity. Most companies fall into the latter group.

2. Exploration at the boardroom table

The best mineral explorers will be attracted to those companies where exploration clearly matters and where explorers are valued. The same goes for any key function in an organisation. So if a mining company aspires to become the 'Toyota of Mining' then such a vision will help it to attract the best engineers. If in contrast a company is dedicated to great mergers and acquisitions then it should say so – and it will attract excellent commercial and financial people as a result. How does one signal that exploration matters in terms of organisational structure? Easy. The board should have a director of exploration. Additionally, there should be at least one influential non-executive director with an exploration background in the boardroom. It is not hard to measure either of these things. Many larger companies fail the test. The challenge here is having a board and management that actually believes that exploration adds value. While most acknowledge that a new discovery is the cheapest path to growth, few mining companies follow through in adopting exploration as a core strategy.

3. Swinging for the fences: Greenfields exploration

The best mineral deposits create disproportionally greater value than do lesser orebodies. The 80:20 rule applies – and may actually be closer to 90:10. Brownfields discoveries are usually (but not always) incremental in their value addition. Greenfields exploration on the other hand can change the game – even for large companies when significant high quality mineral discoveries are made. Newcrest Mining once had the distinction of mining only gold orebodies that it had discovered – a rare case study indeed. The short-run incentive of incremental resource growth will drive a focus towards brownfield work. Sometimes this is appropriate but often not. Don't forget greenfields if you strive to be a great explorer. Most of the industry has done so, unfortunately, in recent years.

4. Continuous drilling and funding

It takes drillholes to discover and delineate mineral deposits – so keep on drilling. That means staying funded – or in larger companies continually winning a suitable exploration budget to advance the exploration portfolio. Good communication skills as to the potential exploration upside in value terms are critical. Such communication needs to involve serious analysis of the potential value creation and of the return on investment from exploration. So concepts such as expected monetary value (EMV) do matter. If your company has never mentioned EMV in the boardroom it is certainly not a best practice explorer. Staying funded can sometimes pull you to short-term thinking whereas true swinging for the fences (as described above) involves a serious timeline.

5. Exploration is both commercial and technical

The science of exploration is critical, but companies targeting exploration excellence also need strong commercial exploration skills. Forming exploration joint ventures is a critical skill-set for an explorer. Win-win deals take considerable skill to craft. Once the right target area is selected, the commercial aspects of exploration become as critical as the scientific side. Does your company value the exploration commercial skill-set and resource it appropriately?

That's it, simple really. How did your company score? Did it ace the test?

63. LARGE COMPANY VOLUNTEER REQUIRED: EXPLORATION CHAMPION

06 Jul 2015 Strictly Boardroom joins with Campbell McCuaig to develop a three-point plan to help solve the global exploration crisis but it still needs a corporate volunteer in order to give it a fair go.

Great news, the mainstream dialogue in the mining sector is now finally turning to the global exploration crisis. Witness the release by Boston Consulting Group[1] of a study into exploration success factors in organisations as one high-profile recent example.

The exploration crisis is typically summarised both in terms of input and output factors – namely a poor recent discovery track record for world-class assets (the key output), driving a consequent lack of funding and corporate/investor interest in greenfields exploration (the key inputs).

Related factors that may have prompted the rise in the level of industry commentary include the poor mergers and acquisition (M&A) track record of the major miners in recent years with cumulative asset write-offs approaching $100 billion.

Debate between M&A and exploration as alternative pathways to drive value is however not the focus for this discussion. Clearly when well-executed both pathways can deliver value.

The focus here is to instead suggest an implementation plan should the industry take up the challenge of exploration-led value growth. At a high-level, the following three-point plan is one solution. It goes something like this.

1. Wire the organisation to make exploration a priority

Successive studies since McKinsey in 1975[2] have pointed to the importance of exploration leadership in a company. Leadership needs to come from the top – from board level. So an exploration director appointment is needed as the first step.

To clarify, this appointment is an executive appointment and not just a token independent director who once sat near a drill-rig (although few large miners even have that). So how many large companies have an executive director of exploration at present? We know that answer – and think you can guess at it.

2. Obtain a strong long-term mandate

Greenfields exploration is a long-term endeavour. Successive studies have shown that too. So seek a mandate from shareholders to undertake such an endeavour, and cost it out. Put a resolution to the annual general meeting seeking shareholder approval for exploration investment.

A decade-long exploration investment will cost a very small fraction of the company write-offs from M&A (write-offs that accumulated in far less than a decade). If shareholders approve the resolution then you get on with it.

3. Redefine exploration best practices

The Boston Consulting Group study referred to above paints a picture of exploration best practices recounted by industry veterans responsible for some of the world's great discoveries of recent decades.

We agree with those best practices, which, beyond leadership, have been summarised as: exploration strategy; exploration management; innovation; and talent development and people management.

Note, however, that these factors are principally sourced from the last generation of explorers and that the road ahead will require a new level of exploration prowess. This will redefine what best practice means to an organisation, including the way that exploration spans the boundaries of economics, mining, metallurgy and even social science.

The next generation of mineral discoveries will look different to the obvious pipeline of lower grade, larger scale, energy intensive and socially challenged projects that we see ahead now.

So there you have it. A three-point plan that is easy to articulate but difficult to implement. The plan is so difficult that nobody has even tried it. Our contention is that the future is bright – at least for any large company willing to seek to become the next generation exploration champion in the sector.

Do we have any volunteers?

---

1 Koch, A., Schilling, D. & Upton, D. 2015. *Tackling the Crisis in Mineral Exploration*. The Boston Consulting Group. June.

2 McKinsey and Company. 1975. *Successful Management of Minerals Exploration in Australia: Report to Survey Participants*. June.

64. MYSTERY IN THE EXPLORATION BOARDROOM

03 Feb 2014 Strictly Boardroom looks at wiring a boardroom for exploration success – and finds that systematic research into the matter is far from definitive, actually non-existent.

A favourite television show of Strictly Boardroom is the Stephen Fry-hosted 'QI', where QI stands for "quite interesting". QI is a comedy panel show that has achieved great popularity – it is now into its eleventh year. The game is somewhat quirky but at the same time very insightful. Panels of contestants each week aim to make "quite interesting" observations on a vast variety of subjects – and score points for doing so. One specific aspect of the game in recent seasons is that each panellist is pre-armed with a special card that can be played only once during the show – a joker of sorts. This special card reads simply "nobody knows". The card can be played by the panellist in response to a question where they believe there is no proven scientific answer to a particular conundrum.

Fans of the show will recall that some of the facts revealed on QI are very interesting indeed. In the majority of circumstances, of course, the facts of the matter are also extremely obscure too.

Did you know, for example, that good decision-making skill is enhanced when a person desperately needs to visit the toilet? That is, the call of nature somehow focuses the mind in more ways than one. Rational thought is made all the easier by that other pressing commitment: 'quite interesting' indeed. As to whether any company board has made use of this fact to improve its boardroom decision-making is not yet a matter of public record!

Now to the quite interesting (actually make that very interesting) subject of 'wiring' a mineral exploration boardroom for success. How is that done exactly?

First consider the following questions:

- "Is it better to have a geologist as an exploration company managing director or someone with a commerce or legal background?"

- "Should the chair be a lawyer, or an accountant – or a geologist again – or does it make no difference whatsoever?"
- "What is the optimum size for an exploration board that typically accompanies business success – three, four, five, perhaps more?"
- "What is the right mix of executives to non-executives?"
- "What is the optimum experience profile for a mining board – a mix of experienced heads and young guns, or a specific weighting towards either the former or even perhaps the latter?"

If you responded that "nobody knows" to all the above questions then you would be absolutely right.

That is, while everyone has an individual opinion on what makes for an effective mineral exploration or mining sector boardroom – with enlightening anecdotes as supportive evidence – when it comes to systematic research, the work just hasn't been done as yet.

As Stephen Fry would say, the answer is simply that nobody knows!

Hopefully this curious situation will one day be remedied.

KEY INSIGHTS: ON EXPLORATION STRATEGY

- True exploration is about finding 'better' mineral resources, not 'more' mineral resources. These better quality resources will form the next generation of mines.

- Exploration has a high level of technical failure (in that discoveries are infrequently made), however when effectively stage-gated and managed it is of low risk to a mining corporation as a whole.

- The numerous false leads that are generated in exploration before the one successful lead is revealed are the defining characteristic of the business of exploration.

- Exploration fits into two broad types. One is focused on developing efficient exploration practices, and one is engaged in generating new discoveries – the former is a more scientific task, the latter more creative.

- Opening up new 'search space', which can be physical or conceptual, increases the likelihood of making major new mineral discoveries.

- Exploration is a long-term endeavour (akin to research and development in other organisations) so it requires high-level corporate support in both large and small companies, combined with stable funding over the long term. Those companies who drill the most holes (test the most hypotheses) make the most discoveries.

- Excellence in exploration requires good scientific understanding, most obviously in geoscience, but also good corporate skills, particularly in constructing optimal joint-venture agreements.

- The importance of exploration to a mining company stems not just from the discovery of new mineral resources, but as a starting point in the development of social licence and as a hot-house of technology and innovation.
- There is, however, still much to learn about the business of exploration. For example, little research has been conducted into the best structure of an exploration company board – what is the best blend of expertise and experience?

PART 7
On Exploration Management

P art Seven "On Exploration Management" looks into the critical factors of running a minerals exploration company. This part covers thoughts on the key tasks of managing an exploration portfolio, sequencing exploration techniques, building a team of explorers and incentivising the team, which in turn relies on appropriate measures of exploration performance.

We start with "Goldilocks on exploration portfolio management" which alongside many areas of life and business management suggests balance is the key – the right amount of opportunity for the right amount of cost, with a little bit of "X-factor" thrown in. Managing an overseas exploration portfolio is an even greater challenge, but with around half of Australian exploration companies operating projects outside of their home country, it is a task exploration boards have to be comfortable with. "The wheat from the chaff of overseas exploration" suggests that building an overseas exploration portfolio requires a greater commitment of time, funds and engagement than for a domestic exploration portfolio. For the many junior exploration companies which rely purely on equity funding, it is critically important the exploration company board members know "What explorers should ask brokers" about their exploration portfolio to ensure they receive the required investment advocacy.

Successful mineral explorers drill more holes and thus have a greater chance of beating the odds. To do this they must spend their limited funds efficiently, using appropriate tools to focus quickly on the best areas to drill. Such a razor-sharp focus is not yet industry-standard, however, as the short chapter "Battleships – the all-new exploration game" demonstrates. Poor exploration choices can be very expensive. "Exploration drill targeting – the sequel" argues that few in the industry apply best practice techniques to optimise the probability of finding mineralisation with their drilling. As the "Sequencing of exploration techniques matters" chapter highlights, at least part of the challenge lies in deploying the right tools at the right time.

Exploration is however more than just the science and economics of drilling holes. As "My Prospect (Kitchen) Rules" highlights it is just as important that explorers have capabilities in community engagement, environmental permitting and project management. "Trivial Pursuit – Special mineral explorers' edition" builds on this aspect, suggesting a range of core capabilities for explorers including: knowledge of country-by-country minerals endowment and policy; corporate governance procedures; discovery and mine case histories; good scientific processes; and team and people management skills. Unsurprisingly, a broad range of skills requires a diverse cast of exploration team members, introduced in "Which exploration personality are you?"

Delivering effective exploration via diverse teams requires some way of measuring performance. "Measuring success – in sport and exploration" highlights that because every exploration project and every exploration company is different the measures of success are likely to differ too. Managing directors of an exploration company should therefore have their performance measures aligned with the goal of delivering exploration excellence – an issue covered in "Make a discovery stupid: On measuring exploration company MD performance" and "On exploration remuneration – the hard line".

65. GOLDILOCKS ON EXPLORATION PORTFOLIO MANAGEMENT

08 Jun 2015 Strictly Boardroom looks at the challenge of enhancing an exploration portfolio and suggests three factors are critical to successful decision-making.

Taking steps towards optimising an exploration portfolio of properties is very easy on paper but far more difficult in practice. The real challenge is to acquire those rare value-adding projects that conceal juicy new discoveries, while at the same time rejecting and disposing of the majority of projects that are (at best) also-rans in terms of value addition, and at worst destroy considerable value in a futile search for non-existent prizes.

Exploration and mining company boards across the length and breadth of the Australian Securities Exchange face this very challenge right now. Project valuations are down across the board, for everything from early-stage exploration concepts through to well advanced projects. So there is no shortage whatsoever of potential deal-flow opportunities.

Those companies that sit on their hands now may regret doing so in future when the current window of opportunity inevitably closes.

So what would you have to believe in order to make a move in the market and adjust your exploration portfolio?

Here, once again, the answers on paper are simple – although a comprehensive evaluation needs to go beyond simply spotting the proverbial 'diamonds in the rough' out there.

Three ticks on the acquisition scorecard are required.

1. Is the new ground 'just right', neither too difficult to explore nor already explored?

Clearly an answer to that toughest of all exploration management questions is needed. That is, will the potential new project addition host a potential prize that truly adds value through discovery? Getting to an answer is far from simple. Considerations here should include whether the appropriate prize even exists within the project awaiting discovery. Assessment of mineral endowment can assist there of course. Next, a critical question is not simply whether hidden 'gems' indeed exist (which an endowment study can reveal), but whether they can be found with sufficient cost-efficiency? That is, will a plethora of false positives for example burn up so much exploration capital as to make the whole exploration effort value destructive? The technical challenge of successful exploration has never been easy. Whether at the top or bottom of the mineral cycle, that challenge remains critical.

2. Is the deal 'just right', meaning both doable and affordable?

Despite the difficult market times for junior companies, some potential win-win deals inevitably still fall into the 'too hard basket'. That is, some boards will not contemplate sell down of an interest in their key properties. These boards stand firm with Churchill-like resolve to repel all commercial approaches, friendly or otherwise. Whether such resolve is correct or else misplaced nevertheless rules out this entire cohort of opportunities. Deals clearly need to be doable to advance the value of an exploration portfolio – so selected counterparties need to be ready to deal. Deals need also to be affordable of course. So to the list of boards that won't deal at any cost, add a further list of boards that will not deal at a reasonable price despite the market downturn in valuations. The commercial challenge in exploration was never easy. Despite the tough times, the commercial challenge remains a further hurdle to overcome.

3. Is the X-factor 'just right', such that the market both 'gets it' as an acquisition and future corporate leverage exists too?

The all-too-often forgotten element of optimising an exploration portfolio is what might be termed an X-factor to any acquisition. That is, the process of optimisation does not stop simply at making the right technical and commercial decisions that add to portfolio value. The third factor, the X-factor, is more difficult to define but is very real. It has particular importance for those companies reliant upon continued market support in order to advance their exploration efforts. The X-factor includes whether the market 'gets it' in terms of seeing value in the acquisition. Separately, the X-factor can include whether there is a likely future deal flow to on-sell the property for example, a consideration which sits beyond a simple definition of whether the ground is 'just right' (decision 1) and also whether the price is 'just right' (decision 2). Analogies to real estate have relevance here. Does the property have potential sale value in the future as a 'special buy' for example, where it may become critical to another party's growth aspiration in the region? Good exploration deal-makers see such X-factor value in portfolio acquisitions that other companies do not.

So there you have it. If the answers to all these three questions are positive, then your exploration portfolio will be all the better for making the potential new acquisition. The aim is to position the overall portfolio as being 'just right' for your company.

Determining what is 'just right' is not easy of course; it never has been. That said, Goldilocks would have made an excellent exploration director.

66. THE WHEAT FROM THE CHAFF OF OVERSEAS EXPLORATION

14 Oct 2013 Strictly Boardroom looks at what drives success in managing overseas exploration – and struggles to find clear guidance.

Your scribe was asked in a boardroom recently what makes the difference between wiring a company for future success rather than failure in overseas exploration.

No doubt there are those among the readers who can bring far more experience to this issue than yours truly, so you are invited to add comment to the sketch below.

From personal experience the list of 'dos' and 'do nots', is at least in part, a normative argument. That means, while there is as yet no overwhelming proof of what does indeed work (although individual case studies are always helpful), one can logically make a case as to what *should* work.

So here are some apparent 'dos' of managing for future overseas exploration success:

- Make the overseas exploration effort one of the principal focus areas for the company.
- Make a material commitment to the overseas initiative: two years and an initial A$2 million commitment is a rough guideline.
- Concentrate upon building in-country relationships – working as relentlessly hard on these as on the technical aspects of exploration.
- Build a high-quality, in-country technical and administrative team comprising locals supplemented by imported expertise.
- Aim to acquire the best exploration properties possible, including a focus on those that might at first appear 'too expensive'.
- Create win-win commercial arrangements with overseas partners, including staged payments to in-country tenement holders where joint ventures are formed.
- Manage to clear exploration milestones – getting holes in the ground and giving exploration projects a realistic chance to shine.
- Direct exploration activities largely in-country – including maintaining extended rosters in the field.

Now to the corresponding 'do nots':

- Believe that overseas success will come from just 20% of the overall exploration portfolio activities.
- Expect material success inside six months and well within a $500,000 budget.
- Regard in-country relationships simply as a chore that accompany the technical side of overseas exploration.

- Rely solely upon imported exploration prowess.
- Insist on JV earn-ins wholly based on exploration expenditure.
- Build an exploration strategy around acquiring vacant ground that those closest to the action (the locals) have failed to see the full potential of.
- Rely solely on low-cost surface exploration while waiting for a big brother JV partner to miraculously appear with a drilling budget.
- Direct exploration from afar – with overseas field visits via global stopovers en route.

Simple on paper, isn't it? But also certainly worth regular self-audits as to whether the simplicity on paper still aligns with practical reality.

Like many things in the management arena, it is easy to think you are doing the right thing when in practice you no longer are doing so.

So what do you think?

67. WHAT EXPLORERS SHOULD ASK BROKERS

12 May 2014 Strictly Boardroom looks at why people invest in exploration and suggests the answer is seldom crystal clear – in fact, not even close.

A corporate colleague who recently returned from an investor roadshow was pleased to report a good hearing and feedback from all brokers. The key message was that broking firms were interested in the company on behalf of their clients and that the company was travelling very well indeed. The brokers all thanked management for the briefings and were pleased the company was not seeking to raise further capital in the near future. That's a good result, right? In this market it is.

Taking a broader perspective, however, further granularity would help the company all the more to determine just which future actions in coming months would likely have more shareholder impact than others.

The old saying in marketing springs to mind here: marketing professionals are often quick to admit that around half their marketing budget is wasted annually but the problem is that they are never quite sure just which half is wasted!

A similar rationale can apply to broker dialogue with exploration companies. Sometimes the key messages are lost in the superlatives that the company is doing a good job in very difficult times. Exploration companies would do well to seek answers to some simple questions whilst on the road. A five-minute, real-time survey would provide structured data as input to company strategy.

Below are some suggested questions to ask brokers on your next visit, along with just how much stock in the company their clients hold, that is. If the answers to these questions hold no surprises for the company then that's fine, but if the answers do contain surprises perhaps that is an even better outcome?

Here are three simple questions to ask:

1. Company X is a diversified explorer: what is your main interest in the company's assets, commodity-wise? Tick one only:
   - Commodity A is our main interest.
   - Commodity B is our main interest.
   - That Company X has more than one commodity in its exploration portfolio is why we like it.
   - We would prefer if Company X made a choice between commodities A and B rather than continue exploration for both.

2. What are the key attraction factors of Company X? Please rank the following from 1 to 3:
   - 100% or majority control of its principal exploration projects?
   - Company X has a tight geographic focus?

- The fact that Company X uses the majority of its funds on exploration not administration.
3. What would you like the management and board of Company X to be doing that they are not doing already? Pick one only:
   - Cutting costs further?
   - More drilling?
   - Talking to you about capital raisings?
   - Other – please indicate a preference (for example, share consolidation, management/directors buying more stock, a deal into an advanced exploration asset or other commodity)?

Experienced heads in the exploration space will know that company strategy is not quite this simple but knowing the answers to the simple questions nevertheless helps.

68. BATTLESHIPS – THE ALL-NEW EXPLORATION GAME

29 Apr 2013 Despite decades of experience in exploration Strictly Boardroom comes clean and admits to not having the tools to optimise reconnaissance drill targeting to maximise cost-benefit – and neither does anyone else, it seems.

It is time we changed our industry. We are still living in the 1950s when it comes to drill targeting efficiency in mineral exploration. Give a bunch of geologists a map, replete with some anomalous areas that could host economic mineralisation and you'll get as many answers to how to plan the drilling effort to reveal and then test targets as there are geologists in the room.

That's not a good situation.

Actually, it is worse than that. It is downright scary. How can we expect investors to trust us with their risk capital when drill targeting is based on thumb-suck experience from past successes, as opposed to rigorous three-dimensional spatial statistics and geometry (in addition to the benefit of hindsight that comes from experience)? We need new tools to help us. Right now we aren't quite on the ball, so-to-speak.

Here is a recent example for you. Your scribe taught a class of international geoscientists in 2012 and gave each of four groups in the class (with a typical group comprising four to six geoscientists) a 'stylised' cartoon geological map. The map area was 50km by 100km by recollection – so there was plenty of room to 'hide' even very large mineral deposits.

The exercise was akin to an exploration version of the children's game of Battleships, where you first hide your fleet from your opponent and then declare whether the various attempts to sink the naval fleet based on torpedoes fired at specified grid coordinates were successful or not. The exploration version is not dissimilar, except this time you are hiding mineral deposits rather than ships and submarines.

First to the good news. The entire map area was indicated as prospective for orogenic gold occurrences, diamonds, nickel sulphides and volcanic-massive-sulphide (VMS) copper-zinc deposits, with various historical occurrences indicated to help the targeting along.

Not all mineral deposits are equal, of course. One might consider a diamond mine to be the equivalent of a submarine in Battleships, as it is a small target that is hard to find. An orogenic gold system, on the other hand, may leave a far larger spatial footprint – akin to a destroyer or aircraft-carrier in the Battleships gaming analogy.

Now for the bad news. While approximately half the map was indicated as lying in residual terrain – including all the historical mineral occurrences – the other half of the map was indicated as entirely covered by younger sediments, with a thickness of some 50m to100m. For this area of the map, the prospective rocks lay beneath the younger cover rocks.

To the results then. Despite an accompanying dataset provided with the map that indicated the median initial public offering (IPO) capital raising for a listed junior explorer was only A$5 million, the various groups still proposed many times that spend in their respective exploration campaigns. Costing the campaigns was very high-level, but with different drill costs based on depth and type of drilling.

The proposed work plans included permutations for drill-spacing for reconnaissance work in the covered areas. Also, various geophysical surveys were proposed for those readers who hail from a geophysical background (as were stream sediment sampling, soil geochemistry and rock-chip sampling for the geochemists who are reading). One group even breached the A$100 million mark in proposed exploration spend for the map area!

If anyone wants a copy of the Exploration Battleships geology cartoon, then feel free to contact Strictly Boardroom and the geological sketch is all yours.

On a more serious note, however, the Centre for Exploration Targeting (CET) at The University of Western Australia is in the process of developing the new tools required. The CET has developed a far more sophisticated Exploration Simulator (as opposed to Strictly Boardroom's Exploration Battleships game) using real exploration data and serious computing power to achieve the same objective of up-skilling our collective approach to exploration targeting. Now that really is worth seeing.

---

* http://www.cet.edu.au/research-projects/geophysics-and-image-analysis/projects/the-cet-exploration-simulator-assistive-technologies-for-exploration-decision-making

69. EXPLORATION DRILL TARGETING – THE SEQUEL

06 May 2013 The previous chapter on "Exploration Battleships" prompted great feedback from readers when originally published in our weekly column. So Strictly Boardroom took the thinking a little bit further with mathematical input from colleague Jose Saavedra-Rosas. Do you know your real chances of exploration success?

As noted, Exploration Battleships provided interesting feedback to your scribe. In response to the 'fun for all ages' exploration targeting game, a number of colleagues expressed their frustration at the lack of available tools across our industry to more effectively target exploration drill programs in a rigorous manner.

Spurred into action, Strictly Boardroom worked closely with a mathematical engineering colleague, Jose Saavedra-Rosas, to throw some numbers at the problem[1].

However, rather than looking at regional exploration targeting, we focus here on the nitty gritty of drill spacing at a tightly defined prospect. "Tightly defined" is always a relative term, of course.

Whereas last time the search area was some 50km by 100km, this time we're down to just 600m by 600m. Surely we can't miss? Before you think that the job is done though, some numbers illustrate the difficulty of hitting small targets even within such a modest search area.

Here's the analogy. Faced with a regolith-covered terrain in the Eastern Goldfields and a reasonable drill budget in an area of good gold host-rocks and structure, what drill pattern would you recommend for initial drill testing of the targeted area to pick up a regolith gold signature?

Let's be hard on ourselves and suggest that the target is a mere 50m by 50m horizontal plate hidden at the base of the regolith[2] and sitting atop a narrow bonanza-grade gold vein. Would you favour laser-like reverse circulation drilling of structurally defined targets? What about grid-based aircore first perhaps? If the latter is your preference, then what grid spacing do you recommend?

The maths behind such a conundrum is not difficult to solve. In fact it was solved long ago for ellipsoid targets by the Russians way back during the Space Race – but the exploration industry has yet to widely adopt that methodology.

Part of determining an answer is to look at the statistical likelihood of hitting the said geometric target. Here are some quick results.

If you chose a broad 400m by 80m drill-pattern then your chances of getting a hit would be under 8% (based upon iterative sampling of computer-generated drill-grid patterns of those dimensions covering the entire search area).

Those who opted for 320m by 160m would be looking at a statistical result below 5%.

Those selecting 320m by 80m would hit roughly one time in 10, so 10% – whereas an 80m by 80m grid raises the statistical likelihood to around 40%.

Those explorers with a preference to use fence-lines and existing tracks for easy access pay a statistical penalty for doing so – with random drill-spacings performing below regular grids on average hit-miss rate for an equivalent number of drill tests.

None of the above bode too well for confidence in hitting the target. Of course those willing to commit to a 50m by 50m grid-spacing will always hit their target by definition. That selection yields 100% success but at the cost of more drill metres.

Critically, the grid spacing does not need to widen much in order to lower one's probability of success materially, however. At just a 55m by 55m grid, the probability of a successful drill hit has already declined to just 83%.

Would you change your drill pattern armed with the above statistical information?

At the least you are now better informed and have an extra decision-making tool at your disposal.

Of course this example is over-simplistic, but such tools can be made far more sophisticated to estimate outcomes for other geological analogies. It depends whether your target more closely resembles a rectangle (in areas of known strike/structure), a cylinder, an inclined, plunging pipe, or perhaps an ellipse – you name it.

So why have we not advanced towards the use of such tools over the last 50 years?

Your feedback would be welcomed to answer that conundrum.

In order to lift the cost-efficiency of exploration drilling – and more critically improve the discovery rate when testing new target areas – we first need to accept that the industry has a problem.

So do we?

---

1 This example is illustrative only. The principles of drill optimisation can be applied with effect to far larger areas than in the example described.

2 Regolith is a general term used by geologists to refer to the near-surface weathered rocks where oxidation and chemical changes to the rocks can render surface samples unreliable as a true indicator of the rock-type and mineralisation at-depth. The depth of regolith is variable but can be many tens of metres in thickness until fresh underlying rocks are reached by drilling.

70. SEQUENCING OF EXPLORATION TECHNIQUES MATTERS

16 Jun 2014 Strictly Boardroom casts his mind back to the nickel mines in Kambalda and suggests there are key lessons for effective exploration in the Fraser Range region, despite the vastly different nickel mineralisation styles.

It is a quick virtual odyssey for Strictly Boardroom in this short chapter. First, recent activities in South Korea have relevance and then it is onward via the classic Kambalda nickel fields, south of Kalgoorlie in Western Australia to finally arrive at the emerging Fraser Range nickel province, east of Norseman, also in Western Australia.

In South Korea, your scribe rolled out the Exploration Battleships* mineral discovery game again with geoscientists drawn from many different developing countries. In Exploration Battleships, exploration teams first receive a cartoon geological map and are then asked to design exploration programs to search for volcanic massive sulphide (VMS), nickel sulphide, gold and diamond deposits.

Your scribe was especially devious this year in hiding difficult targets on the map, in some cases outside the reach of surface geochemical techniques. Would-be discoveries were buried 200 metres below surface and then (in part at least) further hidden by some near-target conductive shale horizons intended to introduce the concept of 'false positives' into ground geophysical data.

The results of the exercise were as expected. Most of the groups did well to locate even one of four economic deposits that were carefully hidden on the map despite what was in essence a limitless exploration budget.

In the real world of course, exploration budgets are far from limitless. As such, the efficient sequencing of drilling and other techniques becomes all the more important. Getting the optimal sequence saves your company a great deal of money and can fast-track the exploration process by years, not merely months.

Stretch the memory cells back to nickel sulphide exploration at Kambalda. The WMC Resources' explorers there conceived a number of contrasting exploration sequences for geoscience and drilling techniques based on the various geological situations encountered.

Without going into great detail these included: whether a key geological contact was already proven to be prospective for nickel (an intact basal contact in the Kambalda sulphide model); whether there were conductive shales in the ore environment, which complicate surface EM (electromagnetics), but which can be far better resolved in drillhole EM; and whether the geology was one of either residual soils or else covered by younger rocks.

Depending on the combination of the above parameters you might either: proceed straight to a diamond drilling program (rather than shallow pattern drilling); design a reverse circulation (RC) drill program essentially as a drillhole EM platform supported by hard rock geochemistry; or alternatively kick things off with surface geophysics combined with mapping-style air core drilling.

The details do not matter here, what does matter is that the most effective and efficient answer in each case was vastly different depending on the local geological situation.

This brings Strictly Boardroom neatly around to the Fraser Range and to finding the next Nova-Bollinger nickel discovery. Debates are emerging as to the best way to explore the province. There has been no shortage of alternatives proposed.

Some companies are set on repeating the exact same sequence undertaken by Sirius Resources to locate Nova-Bollinger, while other companies argue for a cookie-cutter, stage-gating of different techniques that may keep their shareholders on tenterhooks for several years to come.

The 'right' answer, as alluded to earlier, will be very different – depending upon the local geology of each company's project tenure.

The debate is for the most part a red herring. There is no single best way to explore the Fraser Range. The sequencing of techniques depends entirely on the local geology.

Some ways to sequence exploration are however a lot faster, have greater effectiveness and deliver at far lower cost than others.

Identifying and then choosing the most efficient exploration pathways is one key challenge to unlocking the next discovery in the Fraser Range, sooner rather than later.

Each local exploration puzzle has a different answer, but there are many lessons for the Fraser Range from Kambalda and even perhaps from the cartoon-style exploration challenge that is Exploration Battleships.

---

* See short chapter 68, "Battleships – The all-new exploration game" earlier in Part Seven.

71. MY PROSPECT (KITCHEN) RULES

11 Feb 2013 Strictly Boardroom reviews the prospects for a radical new TV show next year – one featuring the joys and the challenges of the Australian mining sector.

Australians are in love with cooking. But a recent poll suggested that Australians are not quite so in love with mining. Indeed, the poll found that a majority of the public do not even trust our industry to look after the nation's best economic interests. The medium of TV could hold the answer to mining's public relations problem. Forget Sunday night boutique channel mining documentaries, mining needs to get onto the primetime network channels.

So for next year, here is an idea for a TV show to bring mineral exploration and mining into every household; a show provisionally entitled *My Prospect Rules*[1].

The primetime show might go something like this. Teams of mineral explorers represent the various states, with the exception of the Australian Capital Territory (ACT), that is – which proves no great loss as Canberra seems to know very little about mining.

Teams then take it in turn to showcase various mineral prospects from their state in front of the other teams and, of course, in front of an experienced judging panel, too.

The first episode features a team from Western Australia (WA), with a menu that kicks off with an exciting gold prospect out the back of the historic mining centre of Kookynie. We see the members of the team desperately rushing to have a first round of aircore drill results ready in time for the judges.

Unfortunately, a significant part of the exploration budget has been consumed expediting a heritage survey. An argument in the team over what appear to be exorbitant legal fees adds to the tension. The outcome leaves precious few funds left to actually drill any holes. Things don't get all that much better when the assays get stuck in the laboratory. What great TV. Will the results be ready in time? An ad break interrupts the nervous tension. On return, we hear that Team WA has now paid for the samples to be expedited at the lab – at further unbudgeted cost.

Finally, the assay results arrive: initial 4m composites are returned with a number of coherent 0.5 grams per tonne (gpt) to 1gpt gold results. The judges suggest that the assays are tantalisingly tasty – and can't wait for the next course: reverse-circulation (RC) drill testing.

Now for the main course. Team WA decides to move away from the traditional fare of gold and attempts to dish up a neat little uranium project up near Leinster. The judges nod knowingly to each other, however. "No Greens for me please", advises one judge. But how on earth could a new uranium project possibly be permitted in time for the show to go to air on time?

The main course indeed runs over time. The other teams sit patiently around the table, with the New South Wales team in particular very empathetic about the delays in getting a project approved – even for coal, let alone for uranium. The results are as expected. Another delay in the approvals process means that the uranium main course is not quite ready in time (you can't keep Canberra off the show entirely). Team WA could be evicted unless it lifts its game here.

To the dessert then – after another short ad-break, that is. Team WA has decided to serve up a feast of Direct Shipping Ore (DSO) lump and fines; a traditional state speciality. Portions will no doubt be ample. The guest judges from China express their preference for lump over fines, adding as an afterthought for Team WA to "go easy on the phos[2]."

The dessert is delicious and good value for money at around $150/tonne. "A touch less silica next time," says one judge as the closing credits roll.

That's it from 'My Prospect Rules' this week. Next week's show features Queensland, with the team promising far more than just a sprinkling of coking coal.

---

[1] *My Kitchen Rules* is a popular television cooking series – which commenced in 2010. To date, no minerals-sector equivalent series such as 'My Prospect Rules' has been commissioned.

[2] Phosphorus is an impurity in iron ore that can adversely impact the steel-making process.

72. TRIVIAL PURSUIT – SPECIAL MINERAL EXPLORERS' EDITION

19 May 2014 Strictly Boardroom takes a new slant on an old board game: Trivial Pursuit – Mineral Exploration edition.

Exploration companies very much need multi-talented people, as the challenge of making mineral discoveries, let alone raising equity capital to continue drilling, is not getting any easier.

To pass away the hours waiting for the next round of funding to come through, explorers must keep their minds honed towards meeting the many commercial and scientific challenges that accompany the business of mineral exploration.

Trivial Pursuit – Mineral Explorer's edition, if commissioned, could be just the thing to keep everyone on top form.

The object of the game is to move around the boardroom table while correctly answering the many and varied challenges of the mineral exploration business across a number of key categories.

Companies each move their playing pieces along a series of exploration tracks (assuming track clearance permits are in place) towards the ultimate goal, a new discovery. Each company's progress along the exploration tracks is clearly demarcated using brightly coloured flagging tape – with the aim to find that rare exploration track that leads the explorer to a new mine.

When a player's counter passes a piece of coloured flagging tape, the company must correctly answer technical and commercial questions according to the respective colour of the tape. Each coloured flagging tape corresponds to one of six exploration-slanted categories being geography, entertainment, history, literature, science and leisure.

If the company correctly overcomes the challenge, the exploration program continues.

The categories in the Trivial Pursuit – Mineral Explorers' edition are:

- **Geography (blue flagging tape)** – the explorers' knowledge on the metals and mineral endowment and mineral policy in different states and countries of the world is tested here. A special prospector-level edition also includes questions down to the detail of individual prospects.

- **Entertainment (pink flagging tape)** – company annual reports, stock exchange announcements and investor slide-packs and briefings are the principal source of the questions in this category. Explorers must avoid releasing any technical information that is not Joint Ore Reserves Committee (JORC) compliant, must identify technical errors and omissions in company slide-packs prior to their release and demonstrate a clear ability to construct stock exchange releases where the key corporate and technical messages are sufficiently clear and simple.

- **History (yellow flagging tape)** – the explorers' knowledge of the discovery case histories of key mines and projects in and around the exploration district is under scrutiny here.

Historical datasets are also the subject of careful analysis. Are there mineral discoveries hiding in plain sight among historical data?

- **Literature (brown flagging tape)** – previously reported technical literature on an area is a key input to the exploration process too. Academic literature also comes into play. Good explorers are expected to be fully cognisant of all the reported literature for a prospective area.
- **Science (green flagging tape)** – good science is a given in exploration but will you be able to answer all the questions that exploration poses? Is 2,000 parts per million of nickel significant in fresh rock within reconnaissance exploration drilling for the devil's metal, for example? Some explorers would say yes and others no – it depends. Good explorers need to know why.
- **Leisure (orange flagging tape)** – questions here relate to the likes of work–life balance and other choices as they impact on exploration activity. What is a good roster for explorers in the field for example? Six-on, one-off perhaps? But is that measured in days or in weeks?

The new edition of the game includes a boardroom table, playing pieces, question cards, a box, small plastic chip trays (for playing pieces) and many rolls of the dice.

Of course, the only real way to roll the exploration dice in practice is to keep on drilling!

73. WHICH EXPLORATION PERSONALITY ARE YOU?

13 Jul 2015 Strictly Boardroom and Doug Brewster team up to consider the psychology of mineral exploration – introducing some interesting personality profiles that usually exist in a successful exploration team.

Forget all you have learned about Belbin[1] team roles and Myers-Briggs[2] personality types, a good exploration team is often populated by many colourful characters who could be well overdue for a stint on the psychiatrist's couch. Here are pen profiles[3] of a few of the explorers that Strictly Boardroom has met over the last 25 years. It certainly takes (or used to) all sorts to make an effective exploration team.

Neville – "The Data Junkie" – If there was ever a degree in naval-gazing then Neville would have finished it two years early with Honours. Neville focuses upon whether there is a levelling error or floating point problem in the geological database – and spends weeks trying to resolve this without telling anyone there are several multi-element combinations in the recently received data that could be a significant future discovery.

Clint – "The Enigmatic Loner" – Take Clint on a geological field trip and if most people in the party go in one direction then Clint takes his cue to head away from the pack on a totally different compass bearing. Clint is intent on being the first to a new rocky outcrop. Clint's approach to all exploration theory and data is the same – ignore anything that looks significant to the rest of the team and focus, for reasons apparent only to him, upon a small anomaly or area that everyone else considers uninteresting. Consequently, Clint has an enviable but inexplicable discovery record.

Haydn – "The Not-Quite-A-Geophysicist" – Despite being innumerate, Haydn has developed what he considers a 'knack' for divining things in geophysical data that others cannot. When it comes to signal versus noise, Haydn is all about the noise, blissfully perceiving profound significance in fifth vertical derivatives. Stretch a dataset beyond any credible reliability and Haydn will be there quickly to observe the 'critical' patterns. Haydn always wants to collaborate with Clint.

Noel – "The Noel Knows" – A proud member of the dull man's club. Noel is a library of information on things that he knows – and especially things he does not know. For example, Noel knows about 'known unknowns' and 'unknown unknowns' but seems to have particular trouble with his 'unknown knowns'.

Anna – "The Rocket Scientist" – Anna is orders of magnitude ahead of everyone else in manipulation of data. Everyone in the team, except Noel, knows that Anna is the 'go to' person in helping others 'fix' their file formats, data-analysis, quality control and image processing.

Don – "The Rock Doctor" – Don is a specialist in magmatic systems. He has multiple PhDs in sedimentary processes, metamorphic systems, geochronology, mineralogy, palaeontology, even anphiblicriliosis – you name it, Don is the world (or only) expert. With a brain twice the size of Uluru, Don is always the smartest person in the room. Don does not suffer fools gladly and has the people skills of a shearer's cook with a hangover. Clint rarely understands anything Don says.

AB – "The Bureaucrat" – Administration of exploration is the focus for AB, especially since elevation to the role of exploration studies co-ordinator. Want a new hand-lens? AB will decide if you qualify to apply for one – via complex forms required in triplicate. AB is oblivious to the fact that successful exploration and bureaucratic process are not necessarily synonymous. AB aspires to be an exploration manager, knows the company vision and mission by heart and admires accountants.

Agatha – "The Sleuth" – Agatha has many attributes of the characters of famed novelist Ms Christie. With Marple-like skill, Agatha has an attention to detail for data, for reading people (critical to exploration debate) and resolving team conflict. The mystery and art of exploration strategy is Agatha's strength – although few fully recognise her prowess and team influence. AB is secretly impressed by Agatha's neatly completed hand-lens application forms.

Wal – "The Dependable Veteran" – If the best geologist is the one who has seen the most rocks then Wal is the venerable master in the team. Wal has been in the field since the first nickel boom. He is always quick to volunteer for remote overseas postings, the task of mapping the highest hill-tops and fly-camping in malaria infested swamps for extended periods. Everyone, especially the exploration manager, loves Wal.

Petra – "The Exploration Manager" – Petra now has a permanent twitch and has worked for many big mining companies as the result of being routinely retrenched after making a big discovery. Once a teetotal fitness fanatic, Petra took up chain smoking to cope with an ever-increasing exploration compliance reporting and corporate administration workload (despite delegating mines department paperwork wherever possible to AB). Petra went to school and duelled for dux with Don but has long ago forgotten what a rock looks like.

So there you have it. Which exploration personality are you? What critical team members are missing? The perplexed graduate? The driven future CEO?

Somehow, when brought together, our team of misfits actually find the mines that are the future of our minerals industry.

The challenge to sustain and grow our industry is to convince company boards and fund managers to back this eclectic lot as being fundamental to major wealth creation. Not an easy task, especially when the directors meet them! When astutely managed to focus resolutely on ore discovery, the above cocktail of people-chemistry can work miracles for the share price and dividends. Extraordinary outcomes require extraordinary people.

What do you think?

---

1 Belbin team roles – A self-test devised by Dr Meredith Belbin to measure an individual's preference for specific types of roles within a team. www.belbin.com

2 Myers-Briggs – A self-report questionnaire designed to indicate psychological preferences between people in the way they make decisions and engage with each other.

3 Any resemblance to actual persons, living or dead, is purely coincidental but quite possible.

74. MEASURING SUCCESS – IN SPORT AND EXPLORATION

10 Feb 2014 Strictly Boardroom looks at how we track success and finds that some measures are far better than others.

A summer of fantastic sport, notably in cricket and tennis, now gives way to the winter sports – including the rugby codes and the AFL.

Australia certainly did well in the cricket: it would be hard to make a case that the England team were up to their straps – or reputation for that matter. Whatever cricketing metric is used, England bordered on the abysmal – couldn't bat, bowl or field better than your average pub team second XI.

In mining and exploration, the blowtorch is being applied to measures of success too – most notably of late when it comes to mining cost declarations and their true meaning.

Key performance indicators (KPIs), whether in sport or industry, all have common pitfalls – with some far better than others. The insight is less around the elusive search for that 'silver bullet' KPI that doesn't really exist – and more about knowing when to use which combination of the plethora of KPIs available.

In tennis, for example, one can measure any number of metrics:

- First serve percentage
- Unforced error count
- Propensity to double fault
- Conversion rate on break points – perhaps even sponsorship and endorsement potential!

In soccer there is an equally large number of possible KPIs which apply at different times during a season or even during a single game:

- Number of corners won
- Time in opponent's half
- Possession time
- Yellow cards
- Pass completion rate

- Total goals scored, goals conceded and goal difference – perhaps even propensity towards 'sexy' entertaining football.

In cricket, aside the above-mentioned generic prowess at batting, bowling and fielding, one can look at specific areas within each discipline of the game:

- Batting average
- Runs per hundred balls
- Over-rate
- Number of dropped catches
- Run outs.

The same holds true for rugby – taking league as an example – perhaps:

- Total metres gained
- Completed set of six tackles.

Finally in Australian Rules Football (AFL) there is kicking accuracy – both in the field of play and when targeting the goal-posts. A high number of goals to behinds is a good thing.

Back to mining and exploration. One can measure costs – with the market focused on that area, profit and loss and share price performance, which are as close as it gets in mining to the sporting equivalent of 'scoreboard pressure', and any number of internal metrics.

In exploration, the process can be measured by time in the field (and not in West Perth), amount of budget spent 'in the ground' on drilling and assaying (and not on administration). Then there are impact measures, such as number of high priority geochemical anomalies, number of high-grade drill intersections and resource/reserve growth.

Where companies – and investors – need to be wary of course is that no single metric or combination of metrics is perfect. Share price is certainly not perfect – and can even be misleading, which financial economists would term 'market inefficiency'.

When it boils down to it, sporting teams have it easy. The final score is the ultimate measure – leading ultimately to ladder position. For explorers and miners it is not that simple. The market, as umpire, can be demonstrably wrong – for long periods of time too – with no cricket-style decision review system either.

The answer? One clear insight is that "process precedes impact", so aim to get the process-linked KPIs right first.

Explorers should worry less initially about their share price, an impact measure, and focus more instead on elements of exploration process – meaning to "bowl at the stumps" (read drill) and also about "scoring runs quickly" (read testing new prospects).

Eventually that way you win the game. Success will come, as it did for the Australian cricket team this year.

75. "MAKE A DISCOVERY STUPID": ON MEASURING EXPLORATION COMPANY MD PERFORMANCE

22 June 2015 Strictly Boardroom looks at the challenge of setting effective key performance indicators for exploration company managing directors.

A colleague recently asked whether Strictly Boardroom had a standard template available for evaluating managing director (MD) performance at an exploration company. For those close to the governance of listed companies, standard templates are all the rage these days in the disclosure of performance and competency. That said, Strictly Boardroom advised that a customised – not a standard – key performance indicator (KPI) set would represent the best way forward. One size does not quite fit all in the exploration scene.

Here are five managing director KPIs that can be customised to most exploration company situations.

1. **More drill hits:** More formally put, this may read as "substantially advance one or more company exploration projects via ore grade intersections of mineable width in a geologically compelling environment thus leading towards an initial mineral resource".

2. **Stronger company support:** Improve the share register through introduction of additional investors where appropriate and strengthening relationships with existing holders; the introduction of project joint venture partners as appropriate; and completing successful capital raisings in excess of the company's proposed annual exploration expenditure at a board-approved issue price.
3. **Stronger share price:** The company's share price will be tracked over a 12-month period relative to that of a basket of 12 peer companies. The KPI will be deemed to have been achieved in the event that the company finishes in the top quartile of the performance of these stocks as measured by share price movement in the calendar year.
4. **External endorsement:** Successfully apply for government incentive grants for exploration where matching funds amount to at least $100,000[1].
5. **Keep everyone safe and engaged:** Some would argue that all things related to both safety and people should be at the top of any KPI list and not the bottom. In response, Strictly Boardroom simply advises those with such a concern should just re-order the list. That is, no specific hierarchy of KPIs is implied here. The 'safety and people' KPI can have a variety of wordings – principally along the lines of: a) that "the MD will proactively manage safety systems and culture such as to record better than industry-average safety performance" and b) that "the MD will seek to foster a culture of continuous professional development and provide tangible evidence thereof".

So there you have it. Measuring performance of exploration leaders is not rocket science. So what is missing from the five-point KPI plan above?

---

[1] Several state governments have competitive grants that can cover at least part of the cost of exploration drilling programs.

76. ON EXPLORATION REMUNERATION – THE HARD LINE

13 Jan 2014 Strictly Boardroom looks at remuneration for listed mineral explorers and unfortunately finds gross inequity.

Times are very tough in the mineral exploration world. Never again did your scribe think we would return to the days of the exploration geologist-turned-taxi driver across Australia. Unfortunately, however, we appear once again to be at that key low point in the exploration market cycle.

So 'GeoTaxis'* are back on the streets – with mineral explorers having been at the wheel over the festive season. One such 'explorer-turned-driver' voiced his frustration to your scribe last weekend. A bush-bashing four-wheel drive is by far his preferred mode of transport and not the two-wheel drive licensed vehicle with a yellow light atop that he is currently driving during unsociable hours.

His key complaint was not that the exploration and share market cycle for mineral resources had turned down such that geoscience jobs were once again very thin on the ground. These issues he saw as just temporary and that the market would indeed pick up again – it always does.

His more acidic observations were reserved for the well-heeled, 'non-explorers' of the exploration scene at present who run listed 'lifestyle explorers'.

Who are these people exactly?

The said taxi driver noted that there was a large number of listed mineral explorers led by executives from a non-exploration backgrounds who are still paying themselves good coin to do very little at all at present it seems. Very little, other than, he suggests, employing casual contract geologists at knock-down rates to meet minimum exploration expenditure commitments on their mineral projects.

Suffice to say that non-technical managing directors (MDs) who pay themselves A$300,000 and more to run listed mineral exploration companies are not particularly popular in the fast-growing world of the licensed GeoTaxi.

One example pointed out to Strictly Boardroom by the said GeoTaxi driver last week was of an explorer with no actual exploration projects actually managed by the company at all – just joint venture (JV) exploration interests managed by other companies.

"The MD knows less about exploration than my 10-year-old yet is paid $300,000-plus a year. I earn less than $50,000" the GeoTaxi driver said.

"The non-executives – in combination – take home another $250,000 between them too."

"None of them are even geologists – they are all accountants and lawyers. They are just pen-pushers."

Your scribe had to agree that just watching a JV partner explore your tenements on your behalf is not the sort of thing for which one would rationally expect to get paid more than $300,000 a year.

The message here is very clear to us all.

Board and executive remuneration across the mineral exploration sector is under very close scrutiny indeed – both from those who are 'in the know' (including the said GeoTaxi driver), and rightly from the general investment community also.

Directors of listed explorers who choose to pay themselves excessively should cease and desist right now from doing so.

To misquote the purported Chinese proverb, "we live in inequitable times".

Strictly Boardroom expects there are many remuneration reviews in progress among explorers in January 2014. The market view is to take a big hair-cut if an exploration MD earns more than $250,000 per annum. Non-executives should clearly make a real contribution to exploration if they sit on exploration boards.

Investors will vote accordingly come annual general meeting time – it's not rocket science really.

---

* A GeoTaxi is an informal label for a taxi cab (or Uber) driven by an out-of-work geologist.

KEY INSIGHTS: ON EXPLORATION MANAGEMENT

- A well-built exploration portfolio consists of exploration upside, acquired at an appropriate cost, with some 'x-factor' remaining. The opportunity in exploration lies in the uncertainty.

- Overseas exploration portfolios are necessarily more difficult to manage, even if they may provide better opportunities. It is vital that if pursued, an overseas exploration portfolio is a main focus of the company's efforts with material time, money and people devoted to it, alongside substantial 'in-country' time building relationships on the ground.

- Brokers are critical for maintaining support for exploration from equity investors. Ideally an exploration company's portfolio should match the brokers' and investors' interest in the company.

- Effective exploration requires a good understanding of how best to sequence exploration tools for optimum efficiency and discovery effectiveness. The appropriate exploration sequencing will differ for each region and potentially even each prospect.

- Minerals exploration requires knowledge of global minerals prospectivity and an up-to-date understanding of relevant discovery case histories and geoscience and exploration technologies.

- Explorers need collective team capabilities that encompass project management, people management, community engagement, environmental and minerals policy, law and permitting, and corporate governance.

- Team members and importantly the managing directors' key performance indicators need to align with the key activities of an exploration company – conducting optimal exploration, generating funding and support, and keeping everyone safe and happy.

PART 8
Of Mineral Economics and Finance

Part Eight tackles the intertwined topics "Of Mineral Economics and Finance". It starts by looking at "The commodity cycle sundial", noting that whilst all commodities do not rise and fall at the same time, they do follow a repeatable pattern from one business cycle to the next. Industries at different stages of the 'sundial' present different strategic and operational opportunities and challenges to managers.

Understanding mineral markets however is more than commodity prices and demand from China or emergent new demand-side technologies that require mineral commodities as key constituents. "Beyond China – why some commodities are profitable (and others not)" describes the key structural factors in minerals market supply and demand that facilitate mining industry profitability. Factors such as price inelasticity, recycling, substitution and oligopoly market structure can have a major bearing on a market's inherent profitability. "Getting into bismuth" and "Reasons to love uranium" provide case studies on how these economic factors can interact in different mineral markets. The minerals sector goes through 'fashion seasons' too, with one commodity passing into fashion for often quite literally a summer, before investors lose interest and move on to another commodity. Understanding this fact of the business is addressed in the case study of "The ultimate hot metal – radium".

Mineral economics and the financial markets inevitably overlap. In "Mining investment myth busters" we look at a couple of common assumptions made by equity analysts that may not ring true when factual support is sought. For example, the jury is still out as to whether directors holding a significant interest in their company leads to better performance. Similarly, the simple 'grade is king' mantra, at least in the context of Australian gold mining, may not drive the cost function down. The actual data look more complex. "Gearing up for mining's future leaders" looks at another common misunderstanding at the nexus of finance and economics – that low-cost companies should be highly leveraged and vice versa. Investor influence on commodity prices, both in driving them up beyond economic fundamentals in the boom, and then subsequently below fundamentals in the bust has become a major issue in the mining industry over the last decade. The mining industry can collectively respond with a focus on factors they can control – and improve – rather than those market factors beyond their control, as reviewed in "The market is abysmal – so what must change?"

77. THE COMMODITY CYCLE SUNDIAL

21 Oct 2013 Strictly Boardroom teams up with Paul Robinson to take a look at commodity price cycles and finds an easy analogue with the times of the day.

There are many challenges to passing high-level, one-size-fits-all judgments on the state of the mining sector. There are a number of commentators who either declare the mining boom to be already over or just about to enter a new growth phase. Neither group of proponents is entirely right or wrong in its assertions. All face the same dilemma that commodity prices and mining margins do not all move up and down synchronously.

Certainly we have witnessed a China-led commodity-wide boom since the turn of the century but when it comes to the price of metals and minerals, they can be simultaneously night and day.

Don't believe me? Just ask those companies in the uranium sector versus those in say copper or iron ore right now.*

So for some metals and minerals the sun may well be shining at a given point in time, whereas for others the better analogy refers to the dark of the night – or at least to twilight.

To help highlight and explain these contrasts, CRU Group has developed a commodity heat chart which determines whether future prices for specific commodities will either heat up (rise) or cool down (fall).

The heat chart has its limitations, however – with forecast percentage changes in prices not specifically linked to (or indicative of) the relative margins available at given points in time across the commodity spectrum.

The commodity sundial overcomes some of these limitations. It describes the microeconomic forces at work as the mining business cycle plays out separately for each commodity. That is, the four stages of the day are a useful analogy here – dawn, noon, evening and twilight.

In a commodity price context, the day evolves as follows:

Dawn – commodity is among those viewed as the 'next big thing'.
- Price at around long-run marginal cost (equilibrium level)
- Solid producer margins attract interest
- Strong and easily understood demand story – for example, Chinese growth, technology-led demand
- Supply concerns on tightening market
- Market opportunity for early movers.

Noon – commodity is considered "hot".
- Price above the cost curve
- Record producer margins (price-driven), particularly in the first and second quartile

- Producers focus on volume growth over cost control
- Consumers respond via substitution and economisation
- Reliability of supply an industry issue
- New production technologies, low grades, tailings rework all considered 'viable'
- A market optimism that proclaims market conditions as 'the new normal'.

Evening – commodity is still in favour but doubters emerge.

- Prices gradually eroding
- Strong margins (volume-driven)
- Demand growth solid but not spectacular
- Supply growth rates meet and exceed demand expectations
- As short-term signals weaken optimists have to rely on 'medium-term fundamentals' to maintain optimism.

Twilight – commodity is out of favour.

- Prices well down 'into' the cost curve, third and fourth quartile assets fight for survival with state-owned 'protected' assets
- Margins squeezed across the industry
- Producers sacrifice volume for cost reductions
- Demand-side, even if healthy, fails to influence price
- Supply growth and future expectations far higher than demand growth
- Supply (and stocks) overhang
- A market pessimism that proclaims market conditions as 'the new normal'.

So where are the different commodities right now? You guessed it – it depends. Iron ore and copper are enjoying a long balmy evening*. Conversely, uranium and nickel are very much in the twilight zone, zinc and metallurgical coal both wait for their new dawn, whereas tin is perhaps approaching noon already.

Simple really, isn't it? So is the mining boom over then?

It depends, of course, upon the specific commodity for which the question is being asked.

* Since the time of writing of this short chapter, both iron ore and copper markets have progressed from their respective periods of evening sun and into the twilight zone.

78. BEYOND CHINA – WHY SOME COMMODITIES ARE PROFITABLE (AND OTHERS NOT)

01 Jun 2015 Strictly Boardroom shares some thoughts on what the ideal mineral market might look like, from a producer perspective.

Strictly Boardroom recently had the great pleasure of working with a cosmopolitan group of delegates visiting the International Mining for Development Centre (IM4DC) at The University of Western Australia.

In a session which focused on understanding mineral markets, discussion turned to what made for a perfect commodity through the lens of the private sector. The perfect commodity from a public sector perspective may well be different, but with the resources sector struggling to make good profits these days, the session's focus was on the capture of economic rent and on maximising profits.

Over the last decade, industry practitioners and even mineral economists have perhaps forgotten that the answer to the question of "why your industry is so profitable" is not always "demand from China".

Many sub-factors exist within the broader themes of supply and demand that can allow companies to extract more economic rent (aka profit). Strong demand does not necessarily itself equate to high profits for miners.

Veterans of the industry will remember the low prices across all metal commodities in the late 1990s, yet at the time the world was consuming more of these metals than ever before. Consumption has increased again significantly since this time (mostly due to China), but with various other market characteristics in place there has been a better flow through of commodities demand all the way to profits for miners.

Industry strategists and mineral economists would therefore do well to understand exactly what characteristics make their industry profitable. Future strategies should build on these characteristics, thus increasing profits, and at very least, should not seek to destroy these characteristics, thereby reducing profits. In this light, our discussions with the IM4DC participants are worth sharing on this wider forum.

To avoid blushes from miners in specific commodity industries, we'll look at a fictitious new metal named "pricyum", that is the sort of ideal commodity market described by the IM4DC participants. Profitable commodity markets, such as that for pricyum benefit from the following favourable market characteristics.

Inelastic demand: When the price of pricyum goes up, then the demand-side does not diminish. Think of pricyum as a critical metallic input to end-use applications such as heart pacemakers and you get the general idea here. It doesn't matter whether the price rises, buyers still have a strong willingness to pay.

Derived demand: Most metals are not consumed by society in of themselves. Instead, they contribute as a raw material to some kind of end-use product which is then consumed. The proportion of raw material costs in this final end-use is an important determinant of demand elasticity. Thus, although tantalum prices have been known to experience spikes, because they only make up a few cents of the average cost of producing an iPhone, Apple does not pay much attention to tantalum prices – Apple's demand is therefore very insensitive to supply scarcity in our ideal commodity pricyum.

Demand growth: 'Peak Pricyum' is an oxymoron on the demand side. New applications with rapid market growth projections underpin an accelerating demand-side growth outlook.

Diverse end-use segments: As introduced above, new uses for the ultra-light metal emerge with regularity. Pricyum uses abound in traditional heavy industry and in manufacturing whilst new applications exist across multiple emerging and high technology sectors.

Diverse end-use geographies: For similar reasons as above, pricyum is consumed across the world and is not too reliant on one country or economic block. In general, the industrial infrastructure-orientated economies of Asia use a different 'recipe' of commodities than the consumer-product orientated European and North American economies. Even the type of steel alloy can matter with vanadium steels still used more commonly in the West than in China. Pricyum as an ideal commodity market is important to economies across the world.

High barriers to entry: It takes a massive capital outlay to build a pricyum mine and processing plant. Successful extraction then requires highly trained specialists who have mastered complex mineral processing stages, many of the latter being patent-protected and subject to stringent regulatory controls. As a consequence, new supply-side entrants cannot easily tip the supply-demand balance for pricyum.

No substitutes: Most metals have substitutes that limit the price upside. For example, when copper prices rise relative to aluminium, market share is lost by the red metal to the lighter, cheaper metal. Pricyum suffers no such substitution alternatives even when prices rise.

No thrifting: Rare earth markets are an example of what can happen when prices rise sharply. Consumers find innovative ways to use less and less product. With pricyum however few such opportunities exist. Demand is not unduly impacted by thrifty consumers.

Steep cost curve: Pricyum producers are smart enough to keep those high-cost producers of the metal in the market – ensuring that economic rents for those at the low-end of the cost curve are protected by the continuing requirement for high-cost players to provide metal to market too. Think iron ore as it used to be, not as it is now.

No recycling: The secondary metal markets are more important for some metals than for others. Lead is among the most recycled of metals but steel, aluminium, copper, nickel and tin all have significant scrap production. More akin to zircon, rutile and ilmenite however, pricyum is not recycled in quantity as it is not easily recovered from end-use applications.

Main product mines: There is a saying in mineral economics that "nothing beats a by-product (on costs)". Pricyum is produced as a main product, however, such that neither by-product nor co-product production impacts upon market balance. Mines can therefore respond to price weakness directly should it occur, without having to overcome ongoing, price-insensitive production from either by-product or co-product producers.

Oligopolistic supply: Niobium is one of Strictly Boardroom's favourite metals from a supply-side perspective. Around 85% of supply comes from a single mine, Araxa, in Brazil. Fringe producers operating at higher cost fill out supply and provide an alternative to consumers. Now that's an oligopoly which has remained stable for many years but which, like most favourable market structures, remains under constant threat. Pricyum enjoys a similar market structure. Think iron ore but if there was just a 'Big One' producer rather than three or four. Petroleum and diamonds are more often cited when it comes to concentration on the supply-side – but niobium (and pricyum) take out the prize.

Power of buyers: It is all very well having an oligopolistic supply-side but some commodities face a concentrated set of buyers (oligopsony) that evens out the power of the mines in negotiating attractive offtake. Tantalum is the most obvious example of a concentrated demand-side where the number of buyers globally could fit into a single phone box.

Power of suppliers: Miners can face single supplier challenges on occasions allowing those suppliers to capture a share of the economic rents for a project. Provision of lime to gold mines in Western Australia is one such example on a small scale, albeit lime makes up only a small fraction of total costs. Unionised labour prone to industrial action is a more common threat to economic rent. Pricyum faces neither challenge at its operations – with competitive supply available for all key input factors of production.

So there you have it; the ideal mineral commodity market for miners. Did we say that pricyum was particularly difficult to discover too? We should have done. But what else did we miss that characterises the perfect commodity in which to make consistent above-normal profits?

It goes without saying that from a consumer perspective 'pricyum' is a non-ideal market. Consumers would be interested in the market for 'cheapium' though, with pretty much the opposite characteristics to those listed above.

Finally, as with everything in business, the competitive advantages arising from the market characteristics above are only ever temporary. High prices and abnormal profits will eventually be brought back to equilibrium by the market (what goes up, must come down). Though whether this equilibrium is found within one month, one year, one decade or the length of your career is clearly important.

79. GETTING INTO BISMUTH

7 Dec 2015 As an illustrative case study, Strictly Boardroom looks at bismuth and suggests that as an industry, we would collectively benefit from a deeper understanding of the economics of bismuth and other key minor metals markets.

Downturn or not, Strictly Boardroom suspects that greater interest in the economics of the minor metals is going to become an increasingly common theme across the global mining industry. Whilst the industry has a clear preference for 'clean' single-commodity primary metal deposits, due to their economic and metallurgical simplicity, increasingly the minerals sector faces the development of complex polymetallic deposits across the future project pipeline. Multiple revenue streams from such deposits represent future market opportunities. However, increased technical and boutique market risks present associated threats.

As society becomes ever more conscious of environmental impacts, letting heavy metals and other contaminants pass through the processing plant and out into tailings or waste will come at ever greater cost: the industry will aim to respond by turning such cost into opportunity.

Finally, the modern world uses an ever wider range of minor metals, as exemplified by the typical mobile phone, which now contains something in the order of two dozen different metals.

There are actually quite a lot of potential by-product metals that could be future sources of revenue. For example, bismuth, cobalt, germanium, indium, molybdenum, rhenium, scandium, selenium, tellurium and rare earth elements are all currently recovered, or have the potential to be recovered, from common base metal ores.

This therefore raises the question of "is it worth it?" If it were so easy to make money out of these by-products surely all miners would already be doing this? Indeed, the track records of proponents of the 'next big thing' amongst the smaller minerals markets have inevitably found market entry harder than anticipated.

Success at the smaller end of the mineral market spectrum clearly takes more than just pointing to demand from China and some exciting high-technology uses. Amongst the myriad of microeconomic factors at play, the end-use structure of demand, supply and pricing in the industry must, like Goldilocks' porridge, be 'just right' – or at least tolerable.

Using the example of bismuth, we consider the state of play for one of the potential by-products listed above – from the perspective of a potential bismuth by-product miner.

Demand-side good news:

1. **Healthy:** In bismuth's case, the health on the demand side for the metal has a literal meaning. Bismuth is a major constituent of the household medicine PeptoBismol, amongst a wide range of pharmaceutical applications, which make up around 40% of global demand. Beyond the obvious attraction of exposure to the health sector, with rapidly ageing populations in Europe, North America, China and Japan, more importantly, consumption in the healthcare sector speaks to potential inelastic demand – people don't start buying less antacid due to rising bismuth prices!

2. **Clean:** Unlike bismuth's close heavy metal associate lead, bismuth is non-toxic, making it a clear substitute for lead

(and other heavy metals such as cadmium) in many applications. These include water piping, electronic solders, steel alloys, display screens and a variety of paints, ceramics and pigments. This not only makes bismuth a 'green metal' of the future, but one with a broad range of uses, making demand for the metal more stable.

3. **Exciting:** Research suggests that bismuth is a candidate for deployment in lithium-ion batteries as an efficient anode. The future of said batteries is the driving force behind the market's enthusiasm for lithium. In addition, bismuth could also potentially be used in superconductors, permanent magnets, nuclear power stations, Maglev trains and 3D printing 'ink'. Again this indicates the potential for broad and fast-growing uses.

4. **China:** Yes, don't worry, bismuth is exposed to China too, with the country consuming about 40% of the world's bismuth.

Supply-side good news:

1. **Scrap:** About half the world's annual supply of 16,000 tonnes of bismuth is derived from recycled production.

2. **By-product:** The bismuth supply that is derived from mining is entirely sourced as a by-product of other ores (though primary mines have operated in the past). Lead smelters have traditionally recovered bismuth from lead concentrates, whilst in China it can also be extracted from tin and tungsten ores. More recently, the removal of bismuth from copper concentrates (where it is traditionally a penalty element) is also opening up a new frontier of supply.

3. **Chinese controlled:** Like many minor metals, China mines and refines about 90% of the world's annual supply of bismuth. Partly for this reason, both the British Geological Survey and Geoscience Australia classify bismuth as a 'critical metal', and thus parties in these governments may be interested in developing domestic sources of bismuth supply.

4. **Domestic potential:** Whilst China may control the bismuth market at present, amongst the supply-side candidates sits Australia. Bismuth occurs with gold in Tasmania, with copper-gold at Tennant Creek in the Northern Territory and in the Telfer copper-gold field of Western Australia too.

5. **Not insignificant:** Even with bismuth prices falling in 2015 alongside most other metals, the value of bismuth remains material. The heavy metal currently trades for around US$10,000 per tonne (/t) – akin to the price of nickel. This makes the global refined market worth about US$160 million. Like nickel, bismuth has traded at far higher prices in the recent past – peaking over US$40,000/t in 2006.

So bismuth has potential for would-be by-product miners. It is an in-demand metal with stable, inelastic and growing demand and a supply structure that supports market entry.

Specifically on the supply side, the bottom half of the cost curve is made up of by-product miners insensitive to bismuth price movements. The top half of the cost curve is filled with scrap producers who react rapidly to any bismuth price movements, trimming or increasing supply as required. Thus, in theory, once a new by-product miner enters the market, scrap production should adjust down to accommodate the new, low-cost, by-product mine supply.

Conversely, the large market share of bismuth scrap production provides a substantial buffer of marginal supply that will absorb falling demand. In theory, over 50% of demand must disappear before production adjustments by miners are required (and as long as the price is above zero, they don't necessarily need to make the cuts).

Finally, bismuth's status as a 'critical metal' means any potential non-Chinese by-product bismuth miners may find a helping hand from a concerned Western government or industrial firm in securing offtake deals – a welcoming market indeed.

The inevitable bad news:

- **Volatility:** Bismuth is vulnerable to severe price volatility, with at least four spikes and crashes since 2006. This discourages demand growth and makes it difficult for potential new suppliers to set up off-take deals.

- **Manipulation:** Like many metals, 2015 prices are down sharply. However, this time a stock overhang courtesy of the collapse of the Fanya Metal Exchange in China is making the situation particularly uncertain. With a year's supply rumoured to be held on the Fanya exchange, near-term price upside is limited.
- **Opacity:** Last but not least, the bismuth market remains a relative unknown (this short chapter aside). This is more a negative than a positive for potential market entry – that is, both bismuth trade and the details of the value chain through to end-user consumption are largely opaque.

On balance, however, bismuth is the sort of by-product market that looks set to play a far greater role than it does at present in the mining industry. So consider going into bismuth.*

---

* Note that the global bismuth market is currently too small to be of interest to sizeable mining companies.

80. REASONS TO LOVE URANIUM

25 Nov 2013 Strictly Boardroom teams up with Ian Hiscock to do a quick fact-check on aspects of the uranium market which could use a little help with both prices and public relations.

With both the spot and long-term prices struggling to make any headway in 2013, uranium needs all the positive publicity it can get. That's not a hard ask when one looks to the actual facts of the matter – a fact-check on uranium reveals plenty of causes for optimism in future. That said, the price turnaround is not imminent, but the outlook is positive.

Here are some key uranium facts to consider.

1. **The uranium demand outlook is strong** – with a compound annual growth rate for global uranium demand of around 4%

is forecast out to 2035. That a nuclear facility is essentially 'CO2 free' and provides reliable, secure, fixed-price baseload energy for 60 years adds to the demand-side appeal.

2. **The demand requirement is front-end loaded** – so read growth rates for the next decade that will exceed 5% per annum.
3. **Asia is the driver of new uranium demand** – with more than 70% of forecast long-term demand growth (to 2035).
4. **China – you guessed it – is the principal constituent of Asian demand,** at more than 65% of Asian growth and approaching half global demand growth to 2035. The China story remains in its infancy for uranium, unlike most other commodities.
5. **China is set to become the world's largest uranium consumer,** overtaking the US, by the end of the decade – and to kick on further from there. India enters the top three consumers by 2035. China's low cost of capital makes nuclear a most attractive option.
6. **Chinese and Indian demand growth for uranium are both forecast to grow at double-digit rates** in percentage terms out to 2035. India edges out China on a compounded annual growth rate (CAGR) basis, but it is starting from a far lower base.
7. **In 2012, mine supply fulfilled more than 70% of uranium demand** – with the rest from secondary sources, including the high-profile 'megatonnes to megawatts' (M2M) program that closed out in 2013 – taking with it a large slug of secondary supply. In the next decade, uranium mine supply will need to more than double to satisfy demand.
8. **Stockpiles and inventories are a key part of the uranium equation** – and actually represent another source of demand in the current context of the industry. Expect inventory build per annum to be material – equivalent to more than 8,000 tonnes uranium per annum.
9. **Lead times to new uranium mine supply are lengthy,** as the mine permitting process is particularly acute compared to other commodities. It takes a decade to advance from

discovery to first production – often far longer. Project timescales reported by developers are inevitably a 'best case' scenario.

10. Incumbent producers may not love the prevailing market conditions but the **permitting challenges faced by aspiring new producers nevertheless represent a material barrier to entry to the sector.** Brownfield expansions can be actioned far quicker than greenfields developments to capture new supply contracts.

11. **Currently operating mines are set to decrease production from 2017** as mines deplete. Significant new mine supply is needed to fulfil demand growth.

12. Kazakhstan leads all-comers in mine supply, accounting for 38% of the market. However, despite being the big supply-side 'mover' of recent years, **Kazakhstan has relatively few new projects on the horizon** compared to Australia and Canada and is less likely to expand significantly.

13. **The majority of new uranium developments that are considered 'probable' are in Australia and Africa** – so Australia has a big role to play going forward. Canada hosts the largest quantum of 'possible' new uranium projects.

14. **Nearly 70% of new mine supply to 2025 will come from established jurisdictions** in Australia, Canada and Namibia.

15. **Kazakhstan will remain a supply-side force,** however, there is potential downside, with Kazakh in situ recovery uranium projects typically not delineating long-term reserve inventories ahead of annual production.

16. **Australia's future position in the uranium market is highly dependent on decisions regarding Olympic Dam's future expansion.** Australia's loss could be Canada's gain (once again) if additional South Australian development does not occur. That said, the shelving (for now) of the Olympic Dam copper (and uranium) expansion is a positive for the supply-demand balance.

17. Overall, the future supply-side contains committed projects and possible projects – with little in between. A 'gap' in the project pipeline exists. That said, a 'dark horse' for new mine supply is Niger – where the Chinese state giants in China National Nuclear Corporation (CNNC) and China General Nuclear Power Corporation (CGNPC) are active.
18. **Supply to the uranium market is quite concentrated** (pun intended). In 2012, there were only 23 significant companies in the world that were actively operating uranium mines. Passive equity participants in uranium mines include governments, utilities (consumers) and trading companies.
19. **Barriers to entry to the uranium supply-side are high.** Cameco (Canada) and KazAtomProm (Kazakhstan) lead the producer statistics, with both companies having claim to top spot depending upon whether 'managed' or 'equity interest' tonnes are used as a basis for ranking now and in the future. AREVA is also a key player with the top four supply-side companies accounting for around 60% of supply.

So beyond the current uranium price – which to state the obvious remains weak – things are far from all doom and gloom in the uranium world.

81. THE ULTIMATE HOT METAL – RADIUM

02 Sep 2013 Strictly Boardroom looks again at the concept of fashionable metals with a glance back at the public excitement that first accompanied radium's discovery.

The concept of 'fashion' in the metals and minerals space is far from new. From time to time in the mining investment cycle, certain metals seem to catch the imagination of investors leading to a commodity-specific speculative boom.

The exuberance of the Australian – or, as is it known, the 'Poseidon' nickel boom[1] – is of course the historical standout example of modern times. But the likes of tantalum, vanadium, uranium, the rare earths, nickel (again) and of late graphite have all had their respective days in the sun in recent years.

Contenders for the 'next big thing' proliferate across the lesser known corners of the periodic table – with antimony, scandium, tungsten, cobalt, lithium, molybdenum, rhenium and rhodium among those commodities that all have their strong supporters.

With the modern sophistication of stock exchanges, there are numerous opportunities for speculative investors to get on board and become dedicated followers in the minerals fashion stakes when a commodity steps into the limelight.

New explorers for the latest hot commodity spring up quickly, commodity-specific exchange-traded funds appear and polymetallic explorers 'rediscover' the potential for the 'commodity du jour' on their existing mineral leases.

Seldom, however, does the excitement extend beyond the stock exchange itself, the associated investor chat rooms and even those hot tips for which cab drivers are now infamous. That is, the investor-focused excitement for the far reaches of the periodic table does not typically reach the broader non-investing public.

The story of the discovery of radium is one outstanding example of fashion among metals that did lead to widespread community speculation and recognition – as described in *Periodic Tales – The Curious Lives of the Elements*.[2]

Radium, an explosively reactive as well as radioactive metal, burst into the limelight following Marie Curie's discovery and was seized upon by the public as an element with miracle properties, only to later dramatically fall from public view.

Radium as a destroyer of tumours was too good to leave just at that. It was quickly exploited as a 'therapy' for many and varied human ailments of the blood, bones and nerves.

But it went even further than that.

The next time the market gets excited about a specific mineral commodity or metal, you are invited to compare the hype of modern times to the following list of products that emerged following radium's rise to prominence.

Radium fever spawned some interesting consumer products – including but not limited to the following:

- Radium butter
- Radium beer
- Radium chocolate
- Radium cigars
- Radium toothpaste
- Radium condoms
- Radium suppositories
- Radium contraceptive jelly
- Radium fertiliser
- Radium chicken feed
- Radium hair tonic.

This scribe's view is that the above assemblage of exotic consumer, radium-bearing products trumps even the hype of the nickel boom for speculative interest – a feat that is unlikely to be repeated in future.

Of course, there is actually nothing to stop the future rise of molybdenum-alloy condoms any time soon but somehow I think they will not really catch on.

What do you think?

---

1 Named after Poseidon NL which made a significant mineral discovery near Laverton, Western Australia in September 1969, leading to a speculative stock frenzy, first across other nickel stocks, then mining stocks in general. The bubble collapsed in February 1970. The mine did however go into operation but struggled with the company forced to delist in 1976. The mine was subsequently taken over by WMC Resources and operated until the 1990s.

2 Aldersey-Williams, H. 2012. *Periodic Tales: The Curious Lives of the Elements.* Viking, New York.

82. MINING INVESTMENT MYTH BUSTERS

10 Nov 2014 Strictly Boardroom looks at what should be in mining investment – but isn't. Be careful not to fall into the myth traps of mining investment.

At a recent mining investment conference a presenter confidently advised the assembled 400-strong audience to prioritise those companies where management and directors had a material stake in their company – suggesting that these companies would outperform peers in which management held lesser stakes.

No evidence was presented and no questions were asked on the issue. The only problem with such counsel is that it doesn't stack up in the data. During the last year, your scribe had a student work exceptionally hard to uncover such a relationship from empirical data across the junior resources sector.

The outperformance of companies in which directors hold a significant stake versus those where they do not is very hard to find indeed. No end of statistical efforts could unearth it in any way, shape or form. This is not to say that such a relationship does not exist of course, but it does suggest that commentators who proffer such counsel need to be careful. One day someone will ask for the data!

In some ways, the whole tenet of level of ownership is something of an insult to hardworking management and directors who do not happen to own several percent of the stock of the company. Do management teams who hold only a few shares in a company not try as hard? In Strictly Boardroom's experience there is occasional anecdotal evidence of that from company to company – but seemingly not to the point where it shows up in the total shareholder returns data.

So until I can find it – or anyone can show me a study that illustrates it – your scribe will not issue such counsel to investors. Take that not perhaps as the myth being busted but certainly that the jury is still out.

That high-grade drives high-margin is another obvious investment mantra we all hear very often. Regular Strictly Boardroom readers would realise that the latest available data from the Australian gold industry show this is not the case either.

There is no relationship in the current crop of Australian gold mines – some 50 in all – between grades and cost. How do you explain that one? Actually it is pretty easy.

While grade determines whether you have a mine or not (this scribe has yet to see a gold mine with no grade), it doesn't tell you whether it is a good mine. Only costs do that.

The grade advantage conferred by high-grade lodes is actually engineered away in the mine design. Higher-grade stopes take some getting to – which normalises their cost advantage. Of course, high-grades within a mine should make for lower costs when accessed, but variations in grade between mines count for little in determining competitiveness and deposit quality. Indeed, Australia's lowest-cost gold mine at Cadia* is among the very lowest in grade domestically.

Once again take this not perhaps as the high-grade myth being busted, but certainly that high grade is only an advantage in certain situations – or not in all. Once again, the jury is still out.

Let's leave it there for now. If you cannot rely on whether management appear committed through share ownership – or that high-grade mines will outperform lower grade ones – what can you actually rely upon in making mining investments? That's perhaps is a story for another day.

---

* Cadia also benefits from copper revenues that lower but also complicate the reporting of true gold production costs.

83. GEARING UP FOR MINING'S FUTURE LEADERS

21 Dec 2015 Strictly Boardroom looks at the recommended relationship between cost curve position and gearing levels and finds that prevailing industry practice is far from optimal.

Strictly Boardroom looks to the future again – to 2016 and beyond – in order to contemplate what the next generation of senior executives and boards at our major miners might do differently from the currently prevailing management practices.

Specific answers to potential changes at the corporate, portfolio and asset level would of course be purely conjectural. From a strategic level viewpoint there are indeed areas where our industry could learn from the current market challenges and change itself in future for the better.

Let's consider then two areas critical to the future health of our industry. The first area is the none-too-trivial matter of transparent and factual mining costs and their relativity versus competitor companies. The second area is the equally critical matter of best practice balance sheet management from the bottom to the top of the cost curve.

So let's recap as to how the current industry is positioned on both costs and balance sheet right now. The answer is none too flash unfortunately, unless you believe that corporate spin should hold sway over the actual facts of the matter and the underlying guiding principles of corporate finance and economics.

By way of example, last week your scribe heard the leader of a significant mining company claim that his company was far better positioned than its competitors to ride out the current market doldrums. You can likely guess as to the reasons given for this assertion but here they are anyway.

Firstly, the company's long-life mining assets were trumpeted as residing in the lowest cost quartile of the respective industry supply curves. No surprises there; almost every company makes that claim after all (but should not do).

Secondly – and you can probably guess this one too – the company claimed to have a 'very strong balance sheet', meaning that it had a consequent lower gearing ratio than its major competitors.

Anyone who sees no paradox between these two linked statements should think them through carefully once again from first principles.

As noted above, astute observers of mining companies would be well aware that a large number of companies have a nasty habit of taking a rose-tinted view of their production costs relative to others. Indeed, the rule of thumb that applies is that around 75% of any commodity industry producers will claim to reside within the lowest cost quartile of the entire industry. Clearly that maths doesn't work.

Let's assume however that in this rare case the company is correct in its low-cost claim. Let's also cede that the company has a factual basis for its claim to hold long-life assets too. So for the avoidance of doubt then let's agree that this particular company's mining assets do indeed lie in the respective lowest cost quartiles for the various commodities in which they operate.

So if this is true what is paradoxical then with the claim made in the very next sentence that a low gearing ratio gives the company an advantage over its peers? Any suggestions? The answer is that truly lowest-cost, longest-life assets and low-gearing should not actually go hand-in-hand as a corporate strategy; contrary as that statement might seem versus the popular market wisdom of 2015.

That is, if the company did truly have confidence that its assets resided in the lowest cost position on the industry cost curves then it should be the most geared company on those same cost curves and not the least geared. Why? To maximise the return on equity to the company's shareholders of course that's why.

The 'all debt is bad' mantra of the current market is not entirely without merit. Indeed, there are several large miners in all sorts of trouble due to inappropriately high debt loads in a period of weak commodity prices.

So again let's take a step back to understand the present situation.

Fact one is that those miners that should actually use effective gearing, meaning the truly lowest cost miners, have for the most part chosen not to gear-up assets to maximise returns on equity to their shareholders.

Fact two, albeit somewhat ironic, is that the very miners that should not be overly geared given their higher cost-curve positions are in fact the companies that are the most aggressively-geared and carrying too much debt.

Put simply, the current financial management of mining assets by mining companies is almost the perfect antithesis of that situation which the principles of microeconomics and corporate finance would consider optimal.

It may take a while to sort this situation out – at least all of

2016. Hopefully, by the time the next generation of mining leaders arrive, the mining industry will better resemble a group of companies with a rational financing structure – and that ideally only the truly lowest cost companies will claim that status.

84. THE MARKET IS ABYSMAL – SO WHAT MUST CHANGE?

22 Apr 2013 Very few investors who follow junior companies are doing well at present. Even those who have had some recent wins admit that times have been far better in the past. So Strictly Boardroom asks what must change?

Of late, your scribe has been on the wrong end of a nasty ear infection and has also spent a lot of time listening to company administrators – with the former affliction apparently unrelated to the interactions to the latter. So much for the mining boom 2013-style.

Leaving aside the challenges of the Eustachian tube – and of company administration travails too for that matter – things seem to have got more than a little gloomy in the mining world in recent days and weeks.

So who is to blame for all this? A natural inclination when things aren't going quite to plan is to blame someone else. The government is usually near the top of any hit list and then comes just about everyone else from A through to Z – hopefully accompanied by a look in the mirror too.

A recent comparison of copper prices is illustrative. In a presentation on behalf of CRU Group recently, your scribe had a good excuse to compare copper prices in 2011, 2012 and 2013.

Back in March-April 2011, with the copper price up around $US9,500 per tonne (/t) (remember those good old days?) CRU's econometric analysis of the constituents to the copper price returned a result of just $5,500/t of the copper price at the time originating from market fundamentals. For fundamentals, read supply/demand, inventories, China import/export balance, currency effects and energy movements. Conversely, the remaining $4,000/t originated from investment effects (the various influences of index funds, hedge funds and short-term traders).

Fast forward to March-April 2012 and the situation had changed. Now the copper price came in at around $8,500/t – but with fundamentals actually up to around $6,500/t and investment effects down sharply to $2,000/t.

By March-April 2013 and a $7,000 to 7,500/t copper price, the fundamentals were holding ground at $6,000/t but investment effects had collapsed further to just $1,000 to 1,500/t.

So who sets the prevailing copper price?

Clearly fundamentals play a major role but investment effects are the principal driver of the prices at the margin.

So who then is to blame?

The answer it seems in this example is all those who trade in the copper market as investors. Blame alone does not reside with professional investors in commodities for the broader market challenges of course.

Here then is the long list of who should be doing what – but isn't.

Governments should promote and support (not impede) a national industry that has competitive advantage – such as the resources sector – as opposed to propping up losing industries with no comparative or competitive advantage.

Universities need to get closer to industry in order to produce more industry-savvy graduates – quickly. Industry should play an active role in this outcome too of course.

Mining companies need to be clear and transparent on their costs and on project timelines. Incorrect costs and unrealistic timelines are still an industry-wide challenge.

Explorers need to target funds towards good projects with high impact pay-offs to company value – not towards over-drilling of prospects where the pay-offs are most likely sub-economic.

Let's first start with fixing ourselves.

KEY INSIGHTS:
OF MINERAL ECONOMICS AND FINANCE

- All mineral commodities are different in terms of their microeconomics: Thus, whilst the overall attractiveness of the commodities sector can rise and fall over time, the price impact on individual commodity markets can be markedly different.

- Predictable patterns emerge as a commodity makes its way through the commodity cycle. The impacts of the twin forces of supply and demand are predictable at high level as are market perspectives and expectations as the cycle evolves.

- There is more to analysing a commodity market than the potential for high prices via strong demand. Understanding the scale and structure of supply and breadth of end-use demand segments are both key to the inherent profitability potential of a minerals market.

- Demand is not a single concept. Demand-side factors to a mineral market are manyfold. For example, price (in)elasticity of demand, the nature of derived demand, and absolute and relative demand growth, as derived from the range of end-use sectors and geographies, substitution and thrifting, and buyer power are all important factors in their own right.

- Supply too is a complex subject. High barriers to entry, the shape of the cost curve, the amount of recycling, by and co-product supply and supplier consolidation can all be important market determinants.

- Boutique minerals markets can be both exciting and excruciating at the same time. Volatility, potential market manipulation and opacity can all make a minor minerals market more difficult to operate in than a mainstream metal market.

- Some metals markets are too small to be of material interest to major mining companies.

- Commodity markets are susceptible to investor 'fashions'. The minor metals are a good example – with uranium, lithium, rare earths and graphite having all been fashionable at one point in the last decade. Market entry into these markets can be very difficult, even when the economic fundamentals are attractive.

- The mining industry is not optimally structured in terms of its collective use of financial leverage (i.e. by gearing up low cost assets) and conservatively financing higher cost assets.

PART 9
Of Mineral Policy and Mining Regulation

The final part of this book tackles the 'last but not least' topic "Of Mineral Policy and Mining Regulation". Regulation and industry economics go hand-in-hand. Those close to the industry will know all too well that the role of government in industry differs from place to place, and it can also change rapidly with time. Achieving best practice solutions for the equitable sharing of economic rents between all of society and the industry itself is clearly a difficult goal to deliver upon. We have a long way to go as yet, with improvements required from industry, from governments and from each and every one of us as contributors to society to achieve better outcomes for all.

The mining industry has a key role in building developing world economies, as outlined in "Three rules to build a resource economy". Geology, policy and economics interact here, in that because the best assets in the industry are responsible for such a large share of economic value, countries should focus on their discovery and development. Part of the challenge of developing a minerals economy therefore is balancing policy so that is attractive enough for new investment, but economic rents are divided equitably between public and private sectors. Alas in minerals policy the focus too often falls on dividing up rents, rather than trying to grow the domestic mining sector as a way of providing larger economic rents – as reviewed in "The forgotten economic potential of new mineral discovery".

Attracting new minerals investment is reviewed in "Quiz time: Where in the world is your state?" Different jurisdictions obviously have very different minerals policy, geological attractiveness and other in-country factors unrelated to policy (infrastructure, civil strife, etc.) which together makes up a country's overall attractiveness to minerals investors. "Global competition for the exploration dollar" looks at the basic steps governments can implement in attracting exploration investment. The collation and free distribution of 4D (3D over time) geological prospectivity information is a precursor "Towards the most competitive exploration on Earth". There is of course much work still to be done in improving the investment climate, particularly in stakeholder engagement as discussed in "A report card to Australia's mining ministers on exploration: Could do better".

The next short chapters look at the challenges of dividing up minerals industry profits. "The emperor's new royalties" looks at the total effective tax rate across the life of a mine, dependent on jurisdiction. In a similar manner to developing policy to attract minerals investment, devising a sensible mineral royalty scheme once again relies on the nexus of geology, economics and policy. Perhaps the most important rule therefore, as explored in "Countdown to a new Western Australian gold royalty: 4, 3, 2, 1…" is that both royalty and wider mining taxation policy should recognise the different geological and therefore economic quality of deposits in setting payability thresholds. This principle also forms part of the thinking underlying "The three golden rules of mining royalties", alongside keeping royalty regulation simple and that reviews should be pre-planned and not reactionary.

The book concludes on one of the major contemporary issues in the mining industry – social licence to operate. Two short chapters provide different perspectives on this issue. "The perception of mining – a social licence reality check" provides an outsider's view of the industry. Despite lots of improvements in safety and environmental management within the industry, this is not necessarily recognised by broader stakeholders. Finally, "Social licence – a NIMBY perspective" suggests that even the most ardent supporters of the mining sector can on occasion be prompted to question its social licence to operate.

85. THREE RULES TO BUILD A RESOURCES ECONOMY

20 Apr 2015 Strictly Boardroom looks at the rather large topic of building emerging economies through mineral resource development.

Strictly Boardroom chooses to tackle the daunting subject of nation-building – more specifically the economic growth that can come from mining wealth and new mineral discovery.

Forget the decades-long 'resource curse' and Dutch Disease rear-view mirror debate that has stunted forward-thinking in development-focused mineral economics. If managed properly, mineral resources are a blessing to an emerging economy. The clear challenge of course is that the word "if" looms very large in that statement "IF managed properly". Therein lies the challenge.

Readers unfamiliar with this subject are referred to the recent seminal works of Sir Paul Collier[1,2] whose influence on government thinking in the poorest economies of the world looks set to do far more to alleviate poverty in Africa than his more famous knighthood peer, Sir Bob Geldof.

Where Collier still needs a bit of help however is to understand and communicate knowledge of geological economics to decision-makers in developing nations, whether in parts of Africa or elsewhere across countries that host the 'Bottom Billion'[2].

The following perspectives may assist Sir Paul – and will also aid Strictly Boardroom and their academic colleagues in the delivery of an upcoming course on mineral economics and policy to be presented later this month. The imminent mineral policy and economics course will welcome representatives of a number of emerging nations via the International Mining for Development Centre (IM4DC) to The University of Western Australia.

A short-form version of Strictly Boardroom's 'three rules' of development economics in resource economies goes something like this, when aspects of geological economics are added into the equation.

1. **It is the 20 that rules, not the 80:** Mineral deposits have materially different economic impacts by their very nature. Fewer than 20% of the world's mineral assets generate over 80% of the economic value across the minerals sector. Discovering a mineral deposit capable of reaching this 'top 20' club is a potential game-changer for a developing economy. Development geoscience, meaning that the provision of easy-to-access, high-quality, public domain, regional exploration datasets in advance of private sector exploration, is a major catalyst to success.

2. **Think 'great to good' more so than 'good to great':** That is, great mineral assets create potential for economic value; good mineral policy unleashes it. The economic value of a mineral deposit to a country is a function of global industry-level and asset-level attributes – on to which localised mineral policy is then superimposed. The size of the economic pie from a mineral deposit is principally determined by the quality of the asset itself on a global comparative basis, then next by the forces at work in the particular commodity market. Mineral policy acts to unleash that latent value and to divide the spoils between stakeholders. It is not an end of itself, merely a catalyst to release value.

3. **Mineral policy is 'EC' not easy:** That is, successful mineral policy is both Equitable and Competitive (EC). Governments usually achieve neither E nor C in designing policy on the fly. The key to successful mineral policy is simply to achieve just these two outcomes. Firstly an equitable split of economic

rent across the many stakeholders in the public sector – meaning from local, regional and then up to national-level – leaving sufficient surplus for the private sector to invest. Secondly, implementation of the national mineral policy must be competitive with key overseas jurisdictions for the commodity of interest – else capital will flow elsewhere. Achieve both these outcomes and project development will not be unnecessarily delayed – everyone wins.

Building a successful resource economy is simple in theory but seldom achieved in practice unfortunately. There are pathways to improve the success rate. One way starts with education and communication. Sir Paul has made a pretty impressive start.

---

1 Collier, P. 2008. *The Bottom Billion: Why the Poorest Countries are Failing and What Can Be Done About It.* Oxford University Press, Oxford.

2 Collier, P. 2011. *The Plundered Planet: Why We Must – And How We Can – Manage Nature For Global Prosperity.* Oxford University Press, Oxford.

86. THE FORGOTTEN ECONOMIC POTENTIAL OF NEW MINERAL DISCOVERY

04 May 2015 Strictly Boardroom looks at further ways to develop the minerals sector across emerging economies.

Strictly Boardroom has been neck-deep in delivering a mineral policy and economics course at The University of Western Australia. The course forms part of the activities of the International Mining for Development Centre (IM4DC).

Certainly getting to know representatives from Cameroon, Fiji, Indonesia, Ghana, Malawi, Mongolia, Nigeria, Papua New Guinea, Philippines, Uruguay, Zambia and Zimbabwe is proving a great experience and an education.

The focus of the 2015 IM4DC course is the same as for previous years. It is to raise the capacity of these countries to develop a healthy mineral resources sector upon which to base breakout economic growth. That lofty goal remains a challenging one, with baby steps still very much the order of the day.

To get there, governments of these nations must share in the economic surplus that successful mines can create. Paradoxically, in doing so, they must not stifle the growth of the minerals sector at the outset by demanding too much of that economic surplus. Minerals left in the ground represent a latent but unrealised opportunity.

One exercise, with the group, aimed to provide insight into this paradox. It was pretty simple, and went like this. The group was asked to suggest answers to the following question:

> 'What are 10 ways to raise extra revenue in a country from the minerals sector?'

The answers were predictable. For the record, the exercise took all of 12 minutes to get to an initial list of (more than) ten items along the following lines: raising royalty rates; imposing import tariffs on mining equipment; lifting corporate taxation rates; undertaking more thorough government audits; limiting the proportion of expatriate workers at mines to encourage use of local employees; requiring community projects to be funded as part of mine activities; making miners pay for maintaining the roads which they use; raising charges for any pollution and water usage; enacting greater penalties for breach of operating conditions; raising withholding taxes; and increasing government administration charges and levies.

Another 12 minutes would undoubtedly have doubled the length of this list. The insight here is straightforward. The entire list of items shows a mindset that relates to taxing *existing mines* by one means or another. The forgotten prize of course lies in the development and benefits that flow from *new mines* – to 'grow the economic pie' in colloquial terms.

So Strictly Boardroom's answer to the conundrum was to suggest that there are only ever two principal ways (not 10 or more) to raise government revenues in the minerals sector:

- To raise revenue from the existing stock of mines; and
- To discover and develop new mines from which to raise revenues.

The former strategy splits the economic pie between the private and public sectors, usually at a hefty cost to both sides in terms of reaching agreement. By contrast, adding to the number of operating mines grows the economic pie benefiting both the private and public sectors.

So the takeaway from the session was simple. There are only two ways to lift economic gains from mining for developing nations. Governments in the developing world must not forget about one of them!

87. QUIZ TIME: WHERE IN THE WORLD IS YOUR STATE?

10 Mar 2014 Strictly Boardroom draws an alternative world map of Australia's states – aided by the latest Fraser Institute country rankings.

Canadian think-tank The Fraser Institute[1] produces a survey of mining company executives each year to determine which jurisdictions around the world are most attractive to the mining sector. The survey is watched closely by industry insiders to see where respective jurisdictions rank each year.

However, the fact that the survey assesses each Australian state separately but most other countries as a whole allows us an unusual opportunity to place each Australian state in a global context.

On that basis, Strictly Boardroom has chosen to redraw the state map of Australia by comparing each state to a similarly ranked sovereign nation in one of Africa, Asia, Europe or Latin America[2].

For the key Fraser Institute survey indices reflecting policy environment, geological potential and the overall attractiveness (combining policy and geology), Strictly Boardroom has selected a near-neighbour sovereign nation in the rankings for each state.

Some 'artistic licence' applies in selecting near-neighbours from the survey to allow choices of the more well-known countries for best illustration.

So which Australian state has a mineral policy that most closely resembles the ranking of Turkey? Not sure?

Then how about which Australian state ranks, on geology alone, as most similar in attractiveness to the Democratic Republic of Congo? Still struggling?

OK then, in terms of overall investment attractiveness, one Australian state ranks most closely to France! Any ideas which one?

To help you along a bit further, here are the results of the comparisons for each of three of the most critical Fraser Institute survey indices. All you need to do is match which of the Australian states and territories fits which of the country answers in the right order.

First, to the "policy perception index": this considers each jurisdiction purely on the merits of its regulatory environment and business climate – ignoring that actual geological potential.

Which of these countries matches an Australian state or territory with a mining sector (i.e. with the Australian Capital Territory excluded)?

- Botswana
- Chile
- Ireland
- Namibia
- New Zealand
- Norway
- Turkey.

Second, to the "best practice mineral potential index": this asks how jurisdictions would rate, if all applied "best practice" policy. That is, which are most attractive on geological potential alone?

In this case, the economic geology of which Australian states corresponds with which of the following countries?

- Chile
- Democratic Republic of the Congo
- Ireland
- New Zealand
- Peru
- Poland
- Zambia.

Finally, the combined overall "investment attractiveness", which considers both the policy environment and the geological potential.

Which of the Australian states are therefore most similar to the following nations in the world of mining investment attractiveness?

- Botswana
- Chile
- Finland
- France
- Ireland
- Peru
- Zambia.

So to the answers: for mining policy environment, with the answers ranked in the order they come in the survey, first being the best:

- Ireland (Western Australia)
- Norway (South Australia)
- New Zealand (Northern Territory)
- Botswana (Queensland)
- Chile (Tasmania)
- Namibia (Victoria)
- Turkey (New South Wales).

Now onto the geological attractiveness, again in order of best to worst:

- Chile (Western Australia)
- Peru (Queensland)
- DR Congo (Northern Territory)
- Zambia (South Australia)
- Ireland (New South Wales)
- Poland (Tasmania)
- New Zealand (Victoria).

Finally, the overall investment attractiveness considering both policy and geology, again in ranking order:

- Finland (Western Australia)
- Chile (Northern Territory)

- Ireland (South Australia)
- Botswana (Queensland)
- Peru (Tasmania)
- Zambia (New South Wales)
- France (Victoria).

A surprisingly mixed bag of results.

Western Australia is now seen to be as attractive as Finland, perennial leader of these (and other similar) surveys. Congratulations to 'Team WA'.

Plaudits also go to the Northern Territory, now apparently as attractive as Chile.

Let us hope that this result encourages more minerals investment in the Northern Territory, although it has a long road ahead to match the Chilean mining sector for scale as well as mere attractiveness.

---

1 Green, K.P., Wilson, A. & Cervantes, M. 2013. *Annual Survey of Mining Companies*. Fraser Institute, March 13, [online], http://www.fraserinstitute.org/research-news/display.aspx?id=20902 [updated annually].

2 Sykes, J.P. & Trench, A. 2014. Australia versus The World: The Perceived Attractiveness of Australia's Mining Industry in a Global Context. *CET Quarterly Newsletter*, June, p6-9.

88. GLOBAL COMPETITION FOR THE EXPLORATION DOLLAR

22 Apr 2014 Strictly Boardroom looks at the race between jurisdictions to entice mineral sector investment through pre-competitive geoscience investment.

State governments are very much in the global investment attraction game, with drilling co-investment the most popular incentive tool being pulled out of the investment toolkit in various guises.

Such initiatives show how geoscience in Australia has evolved over many decades – such that the ready availability of basic geoscience information is now taken as a given by the private sector seeking to explore in Australia. To attract a greater share of the exploration investment pie, the competing jurisdictions are looking for that extra incentive that first brings in the incremental dollar of exploration activity but then hopefully leads to new discovery.

On tour in South Korea last week and working with delegates drawn from the geological surveys across a number of emerging international destinations, Strictly Boardroom stitched together the following high-level framework to attract exploration dollars to a country. The framework is akin to building a house. You start with the foundations and go on from there.

Here is a simplistic view of how emerging resource economies around the world can position themselves for private sector exploration success, initially via the provision of public sector geoscience information. This was the counsel given by Strictly Boardroom to delegates from countries as far afield as Cameroon, Chile, China, DR Congo, Laos, Malaysia, Mozambique, Myanmar, Peru, South Africa, Thailand, Turkey and Vietnam:

1. **Lay the foundation stones** – Understand and publicise the history of mining and exploration in a country, including the economic impact of mining upon country-building development and infrastructure. The aim here is twofold. Firstly, lay out the grounds for future prospectivity analysis by minerals companies seeking to explore in the country. Perhaps more importantly, however, this information helps build awareness of mining and educate the broader public in a country (including Australia as an aside) as to how critical is the role of mining to the economy – past and present. This 'pre-wires' a country towards future successful mine development.

2. **Build the architecture** – Data and mapping. Obtain country-wide new primary field datasets, encompassing geology, geophysics and geochemistry. There are both right and wrong ways to do this technically but plenty of technical assistance is available to avoid pitfalls. For the private sector to be able to value properties for future investment, base-case regional datasets are a must. With such data, the public and private

sector can determine the correct value of mineral property rights to conduct exploration. Without such data, exploration will not eventuate. Or perhaps worse-still the value of key mineral property rights is in greater danger of misappropriation.

3. **Open the doors** – Provide access to online information: It is no good having geoscience data and mapping (and a working mineral licence system) if people cannot either see or use the information easily. This is a key failing in many emerging jurisdictions. Getting data online is like opening up a shop front.

4. **Invite guests in** – Showcase your prospectivity and mineral policy benchmarked against others and the concessions available for early entrants. In emerging jurisdictions this may mean lower lease commitments for early birds. In advanced mining jurisdictions it may mean the likes of state co-funded drilling grants.

5. **Put on a show** – Beyond concessions, commence state-funded 4D (3D over time) geoscience work to unlock the more challenging geological mineralised provinces (loop this information back into point 3).

Simple really, yet seldom executed without many complex challenges along the way. There is no perfect one-size-fits-all answer of course – but some answers out there in the global exploration landscape are certainly better than others. It is to those jurisdictions with the better solutions that the incremental exploration dollars will flow. Watch that space.

89. TOWARDS THE MOST COMPETITIVE EXPLORATION ON EARTH

17 Aug 2015 Strictly Boardroom looks towards what might constitute the most competitive exploration jurisdiction on the planet and finds planet Earth still lacks a clear winner.

Every serving politician on the planet wants a thriving domestic economy – and to either a greater or lesser degree also sees the mining sector as a potential contributor towards that goal.

Competition therefore exists among jurisdictions globally to attract the exploration dollar as a pathway to future resources-fuelled prosperity via long-life mines and mineral processing facilities. Everything from exploration incentives to future tax breaks on production can get into the policy mix as de facto cash benefits in aiming to attract investment.

Rather than just offer more money to entice exploration and mining investment however, jurisdictions are also getting smarter in seeking out the future 'new mines' opportunity.

Pre-competitive geoscience data are the flag-bearer here. Australian states, via their respective geological surveys, are among the global leaders in now adopting a mineral systems approach to designing new data acquisition on a scale that assists explorers in their regional area selection.

So if a strong pre-competitive geoscience program is already being smart, then what might constitute being even smarter?

In addition to acquiring new pre-competitive technical data, jurisdictions now also have opportunity to quantify exploration outcomes in economic terms, and therefore lift the veil on true exploration return on investment at a scale of relevance to explorers. Unfortunately, thus far this opportunity remains untapped; there is as yet no global leading jurisdiction in this regard.

Even those few economic analyses of mineral exploration that do exist fail to engage directly with the resources sector at a scale of relevance to the private sector explorer.

High-level studies into the multiplier effects from exploration form the prime examples. They also constitute a form of 'policy trap' as the strong temptation for governments is to view such high-level economic studies as the end-game in themselves.

While rating well in terms of political sound bites, such economic impact analyses stop well short of true exploration impact. The greater opportunity lies in granular 'live' linkage of pre-competitive exploration datasets to ongoing exploration investment on an intra-jurisdiction, geological province scale.

Such provincial-level exploration economic studies still sit beyond the current horizon of jurisdiction-led mineral exploration intelligence provision. The potential benefits parallel those from pre-competitive geoscience surveys.

Indeed, unveiling the true exploration economics of geological regions prospective for mineral discovery could inform government decision-makers in 'real-time' as to the actual effectiveness of pre-competitive exploration programs.

Even more critically, such studies would better inform industry by providing key data on empirical exploration outcomes (including probability data, false positive frequencies, prospect and target distributions and types).

The basis for better communication of exploration economics and impact to broader stakeholders also lies within reach if such analyses were to hand.

Ironically, empirical probabilities of exploration outcomes in different regions of a jurisdiction do actually exist, but only unfortunately in the category of 'known unknowns'. That is, such probability data lie dormant in historical exploration results from prospective areas.

The clear opportunity is to 'data-mine' exploration records through the lens of exploration economics. The detail is important here – just as for any exploration-related activity. Analytical 'boundaries' to such data-mining should be geologically defined rather than simply on the scale of whole jurisdictions.

Exploration probabilities are a key, if not the principal 'missing link' from which industry can better determine effective exploration choices.

So will any jurisdiction take up the challenge to go to the next level and become the most competitive exploration jurisdiction on the planet? The first step is to realise that the current pre-competitive data push is missing a vital element – it is called the assessment of empirical exploration economics.

90. A REPORT CARD TO AUSTRALIA'S MINING MINISTERS ON EXPLORATION: COULD DO BETTER

09 Jun 2014 Strictly Boardroom tells it like it really is for exploration compliance in Australia.

The worst thing that could have happened to Australia in the latest Fraser Institute* global rankings was to do well.

For those unaware, all our various states actually did do very well indeed. We think we are good!

Strictly Boardroom can't quite understand that outcome. The rest of the planet must be doing really badly if exploration in Australia is viewed as such a favourable environment for mineral explorers to operate in.

With thanks to an anonymous source, Strictly Boardroom thought the anecdote below on the difficulties of actually doing exploration in Australia from a company perspective is illustrative. The example is sanitised but the message is still clear.

Strictly Boardroom's anonymous source advises that he remembers attending the annual general meeting of a large diversified international mining company a couple of years back and was lucky enough to be able to have a cup of tea with the CEO and ask a few questions as a small-time shareholder.

The key thing discussed was that our source noted nearly 90% of profit for the year in question came from Australia yet there was no mention of Australia in the review of the company's exploration program.

He asked why, especially in light of the very strong statement about the company's preference for stable, first-world jurisdictions.

He thought the answer was well informed, direct and disturbing. The CEO said the trouble with Australia was as follows:

> *"The prospectivity is fine but when geologists get a good idea or identify a good target in Australia, by the time we have processed the native title, heritage, environmental, stakeholder liaison, the property-holder access compensation agreements, ground water and any other compliance approvals it has taken a couple of years.*

"Those same geologists have by then forgotten why they wanted to go there in the first place.

"So we like other jurisdictions where we can just do a deal with the landholder and get on with our work in a timely way.

"In a nutshell, sure, we make all our money in Australia (based on resources discovered many decades ago) but land access risk is too high for us now – Australia is yesterday. Other parts of the world are tomorrow."

Strictly Boardroom agrees. All the high quality and easily obtained data provided by the various state surveys are irrelevant if actually undertaking exploration is so convoluted, complex, time-consuming and costly.

According to our source, it's like going to the races and saying I would like $100 to win on horse 4 in race 6 and the bookmaker looking you and up and down and saying: "Sorry, your clothes are not pressed and your shoes are not shined, please go to the laundry and fashion service-provider down the road and get cleaned up first, its only $50, then I can think about taking your bet."

The number one hurdle to Australia's competition for the world exploration dollar is land access and operational compliance – and the erosion of the spending power that exploration dollar has to be spent on it.

Sobering stuff. We can of course look for the positives here and actually choose to do something about this.

Strictly Boardroom would advise jurisdictions to measure and to benchmark the absolute parameters of conducting exploration, not just relative perception measures. The aim then is to improve the metrics over time.

What should we measure exactly? Start with time-based measurements such as land access time and time to tenement approval. Indeed, some early work is already being championed here by several Australian states as it is a focus of attention.

Next the more difficult cost-based measurements, such as access cost (inclusive of heritage, environmental, legal, et cetera) need to be far more transparent.

We'll get there – but it is clear there is still a long road ahead.

---

* Green, K.P., Wilson, A. & Cervantes, M. 2013. Annual Survey of Mining Companies. Fraser Institute, March 13, [online], http://www.fraserinstitute.org/research-news/display.aspx?id=20902 [updated annually].

91. THE EMPEROR'S NEW ROYALTIES

12 Jan 2015 Strictly Boardroom and Chris Gemell turn to the subject of mineral royalties and to the relativity of government-take – with considerations both home and abroad.

The recently announced Western Australian iron ore royalty relief package has been well-received across the sector. As Strictly Boardroom understands the proposal, assistance will be in the form of a 50% rebate on eligible iron ore royalties for up to 12 months, subject to the iron ore price remaining below an average of A$90 per tonne.

Deferred and rebated royalties will then be repayable to the government over two years. Lower commodity prices have meant that WA state royalty revenue is fast disappearing – reminiscent of the Emperor's new suit of clothes in Hans Christian Andersen's famous tale.

The royalty relief at this time is therefore what Sir Humphrey Appleby of 'Yes Minister' fame might term a "bold decision" if also a welcome one.

Structuring mineral royalties effectively is a very difficult challenge indeed. While any move to provide relief to those producers most impacted by the low iron ore price is commendable, the recent move also serves to illustrate that the prevailing Western Australian royalties system still has a few warts attached to it.

For those unfamiliar with the term, "warts" in this context, when used in economics it is somewhat akin to the technical term "fubarite" so often used in geology (refer to Chapter 24 for a reminder of fubar).

Strictly Boardroom takes an interest in the mineral regulations, fiscal policy and royalty structures across mining jurisdictions both at home and abroad. Not surprisingly, many jurisdictions face legacy issues in their respective mining codes that make life disproportionally harder for some miners than for others.

The overarching aim to re-engineer royalty structures to flex pay-offs to both the local state and to producers with differing cost bases is not unique to Western Australia.

Indeed, studying mineral royalties is a bit like painting the Sydney harbour bridge. No sooner do you think you are nearing completion than you need to start over again. In the case of mineral royalties this is because the rules are subject to change so often. At any point in time a rule of thumb is that around half the jurisdictions within a particular study will be considering changing their mineral policy – whether at the granular royalty level or elsewhere in the broader taxation of minerals revenues.

Before things change further then, the current dialogue provides a timely opportunity to list some preliminary outcomes of a recent look at selected overseas jurisdictions and their mineral policies in gold. Royalties are only one part of the equation of course. Miners also pay 'normal' taxes like any other business.

Here's a simple question for you. If you constructed a similar mine, say a mid-size gold mine with capital and operating costs around the median for the industry, in each of the following 10 countries, which would have the lowest overall government-take? The 10 countries comprise five from Africa and five from South America. In alphabetical order, they are: Brazil, Burkina Faso, Chile, Colombia, Ghana, Guyana, Mali, Peru, South Africa and Tanzania.

Don't know the answer? Neither did Strictly Boardroom. With the help of some modelling however, average effective tax rates calculated for the fictitious gold project (including royalties, income taxation, mineral policy and related government taxes) suggest relative 'winners' and 'losers' across the jurisdictions, depending on whether you take a government perspective or a private sector one*.

The estimates for the life of mine tax and royalty-take vary significantly from country to country, from lows below 40% overall government-take to over 60% government share of the mine-generated total value.

From most attractive to least attractive to the private sector, the rankings of the 10 countries for a median-cost gold mine asset development were as follows:

1. South Africa
2. Chile
3. Brazil
4. Peru
5. Burkina Faso
6. Colombia
7. Tanzania
8. Mali
9. Guyana
10. Ghana

Of course, notwithstanding the relative levels of government-take in the various mineral sector jurisdictions, there is always that small matter of finding a viable gold deposit in the first instance! That task is even harder than understanding the prevailing mineral policy.

So how does Western Australia stack up against the overseas competitors in terms of government-take in the gold sector? The answer to that question requires knowledge of the future royalty levels affecting WA gold assets. Let's hope someone runs the numbers ahead of making any changes close to home.

---

* Trench, A., Gemell, C., Venables, T., Curtis, M. & Sykes, J.P. 2015. *Evaluating the Attractiveness of Fiscal Regimes for New Gold Developments: African and South American Peer Country Comparisons.* International Mining for Development Centre (IM4DC), Action Research Report, May, [online], http://im4dc.org/wp-content/uploads/2015/07/Fiscal-Regimes-for-New-Gold-Developments-Completed-Report.pdf

92. THE THREE GOLDEN RULES OF MINING ROYALTIES

09 Dec 2013 Strictly Boardroom looks at what makes a good royalty system for the government and mining sector alike. There are just three golden rules to follow, which most systems do not.

Mineral royalties remain a contentious issue across the global landscape of the resources sector. Royalties are something that everyone has an opinion on, like politics. And just like politics, some opinions are founded in economics, while others are founded in self-interest.

Strictly Boardroom takes the view that just three things are required to develop a working royalty system that is fair to both state and mining companies. The three golden rules of mineral royalties are founded in the basic principles of commodity microeconomics, in revenues and costs – but also, critically, in the nuances of global geology.

Here are the three rules. They are very simple. Why then do the vast majority of jurisdictions fail to score three out of three in implementing them? That is where the self-interest factor comes into play, which is distorting mineral policy globally, to the detriment of miners and broader society. That we can get something so simple so horribly wrong is a sad reflection on where the mining world sits within present society. Your scribe hopes for that situation to be resolved, but the likelihood of that actually happening is perhaps more a dream than reality.

1. 'One-size-fits-all' royalty rates do not fit all minerals

Geology has no borders. Some countries have good deposits, such as high-grade, near-surface minerals; others do not. What is obvious is that some jurisdictions have world-class assets in some minerals, but a paucity of quality deposits in other minerals. Yet most jurisdictions set mineral royalties using a one-size-fits-all principle across the periodic table. That's dumb. Having no regard to where a country's assets sit on a global cost curve leaves some commodities able to carry higher royalties and others unduly penalised. Fail!

2. Keep it simple – so a 10-year-old can understand it

Even PhD economists struggle to articulate the nuances of an economic rent-based approach to mineral royalties. Such systems are elegant in theory – and economically the most efficient, too. But in practice, they are open to many forms of abuse (among other issues, they can rely on complex accounting edicts and agreed cost of capital). Perhaps more critically, even if the PhD economists 'get' economic rent-based royalties, the broader public does not. Simple revenue-based royalties as a percentage are far less prone to abuse – and can be explained to a 10-year-old. Many jurisdictions fail here, too.

3. Plan ahead for transparent royalty review

Things change over time in the minerals world. The minerals sector is highly volatile in price terms. New discoveries are made that change the shape of cost curves. These new discoveries may be world-class Tier 1 assets or more often, marginal Tier 3 assets. A transparent system is therefore needed such that mineral royalties can be periodically reset to accommodate movements in price and cost curve. The Chinese economic miracle has been based upon successive five-year plans. Something similar is needed for mineral royalties – for example, being subject to periodic five-year review, critically with certainty at all times in between. Most governments are prone to review royalties every time the price moves rather than at set five-year intervals. This destabilisation of the sector must stop. Five years is not a long time in mining, especially when it can take a decade or more to get a new project up and running. You guessed it: most of the world fails on royalties policy, too.

It is all so simple really, yet such a long way from current practices. Even if governments would just keep their hands off the controls, it would be better than today's reality. How about a five-year moratorium on royalty rates globally? Is that virtually impossible? Most probably. What do you think?

93. COUNTDOWN TO A NEW WESTERN AUSTRALIAN GOLD ROYALTY: 4, 3, 2, 1...

07 Oct 2013 Strictly Boardroom jumps into the Western Australia royalty debate with some thoughts on simultaneously raising – and lowering – gold royalty rates.

The Western Australian (WA) government is on the lookout to raise revenue, signalling higher receipts from the mining royalties as one potential avenue to that end.

So what is a fair gold royalty? That is the million dollar question, or over A$200 million question in Western Australia's case.

State gold royalties in WA are set at 2.5%. But is this fair? Actually, it's not particularly. An across-the-board gold royalty of 2.5% penalises those producers at the top end of the cost curve over those at the bottom.

For a marginal mine with revenues of $100 million and of the order of just $10 million per annum operating cash flows (in the absence of any royalty), the royalty becomes a 25% impost of itself – leaving aside other aspects of government- take, corporations tax being the largest.

Conversely, a 2.5% royalty impost on a $100 million revenue mine that would otherwise enjoy a $50 million cash margin is just more manageable, at an effective 5% levy on margin.

Most government attempts the world over to vary royalty systems result in one of two outcomes. There is either markedly increased inequality, or significantly increased legislative complexity that requires intestinal fortitude in order to decipher.

Neither outcome is all that flash.

Hypothetically speaking, a royalty hike to 5% would clearly raise inequality among miners. The numbers in the above simplified example would rise to an effective 50% impost on the margins of our fictitious high-cost gold producer and a 10% impost to the margins of the low-cost producer respectively.

Now let's take an economic rent-based approach to royalty revision. Many such attempts often sit very well in economic textbooks but far less well in reality. The Mineral Resource Rent Tax (MRRT) was one such example. The added complexity is the principal major hindrance.

Producers struggle to 'get it'. The public can't follow it, and both government and the private sector waste an inordinate amount of time administering it. Perhaps the only winners are the multitude of compliance and financial advisers who take the business opportunity that comes with the implementing of any new complex system.

Here is a simpler way forward.

Your scribe would seriously consider setting royalties on a sliding scale from 4% (for any companies in the lowest quartile of global gold production costs), through 3% (second-quartile producers), 2% (third quartile) and then just 1% (for the highest-cost, fourth-quartile marginal gold producers).

So if WA's gold mines are of high quality, being better than the global average in terms of their cost-efficiency, then the overall government-take rises under such a system (versus an across the board 2.5% model in this instance). Conversely, if WA's mines are of lower than average global quality, reflecting an average higher production cost than the global average, then the government-take would fall and also act to stimulate the industry.

Simple really – yet perhaps still with sufficient complexity to leave some consulting fees on the table for royalty advisers. An added side benefit would no doubt be a reduction in mines massaging their cash costs to appear as low as possible.

Economists will not like it because this is far too crude. Miners will not like it either, moving the goal posts is never welcomed. Governments in those jurisdictions with high-cost gold mines may not like it because their share of the pie falls.

So your scribe doubts this suggestion will be all that popular. Pity that, because it would be a fairer system than the one that operates in WA now.

What do you think?

94. THE PERCEPTION OF MINING – A SOCIAL LICENCE REALITY CHECK

24 Nov 2014 Strictly Boardroom looks at the mining sector from an outsider's perspective and concludes that external perceptions are very different to internal views on mining.

Your scribe accepted an invitation to stand in at late notice as a replacement keynote speaker at an international management forum not so long ago. The participants were career academics from Australia, New Zealand and Asia researching all aspects of business activity, from human resources practices through to organisational behaviour, business strategy, accounting, finance and e-commerce. You get the general idea. Put simply, this was very much NOT a mining sector audience – but it was certainly a highly intelligent audience.

The presentation task was straightforward. It was to speak to an overview of the global economy as it impacts upon aspects of minerals demand, to discuss the supply-side response to this demand in Australia and elsewhere and then to consider the respective market outlooks for precious metals, base metals and bulk commodities. All this is pretty standard stuff.

What differed markedly from presenting similar content to a mining sector audience was the question and answer session however. Rather than focus upon the outlook for iron ore, for the price of gold or for the Chinese economy, the questions quickly zeroed in upon aspects of mine safety and environment.

Don't get me wrong here. This was categorically NOT a group of anti-mining activists, but there was a clear undertone from the questioning that the external perception of mining among this group held that a "production first, safety and environment later" management ethic existed in our sector.

Attempting to change that perception was the most valuable takeaway from the day. Having worked at different mine sites on two separate occasions when underground fatalities occurred is something that I will never ever forget. Feeling the impact on everyone in a mining town is very real – and fades very slowly. When one of your soccer team does not turn up to Monday night training because they are in a coffin it is too close to home.

Many in the mining sector will unfortunately have had similar experiences in the past. After that has happened, safety-first as the way of doing things takes on a whole new higher meaning. NEVER, in a 25-year career, have I seen an operations manager prioritise anything other than a safety first culture at a site.

The same logic applies to the environment, although with lesser immediate consequences. All miners are environmentalists – but we are pragmatic environmentalists and not environment romantics. Somehow that is not the view of mining externally however. Externally we are viewed by some as ambivalent to mining's impacts on the environment.

This experience from the management forum highlighted that while we may talk amongst ourselves about such things, we do so far less often to the broader community with the consequence that the mining industry is misunderstood. The perception of mining suffers as a result.

The forum was an unexpected opportunity to share internal mining perspectives on safety and environment externally with an intelligent audience. This is not to say by any means that the industry is anywhere near perfect. We can improve of course in both safety and environmental performance and must do so.

The lesson was clear though. The travails of weakening iron ore prices and of slower Chinese economic growth rates suddenly didn't matter that much anymore.

95. SOCIAL LICENCE – A NIMBY PERSPECTIVE

30 Mar 2015 Strictly Boardroom thinks NIMBY (not in my back yard) and sees the Western Australian government as needing to lift its game.

Strictly Boardroom is a long-term resident of the DRG – that's the Democratic Republic of Gnangara to those not familiar with the acronym – located around 22km north of the Perth CBD as the drone flies.

Renowned for its extensive groundwater and shallow sand resources, the DRG has served the CBD and its surrounds well – contributing to the city's water supply security in an overall dry climate alongside the provision of high quality sand for construction and infrastructure needs.

In recent years however the DRG residents have grown restless, and now converse as to the potential for secession from Western

Australia due to the inappropriate exploitation of its valuable resources in the total absence of community consultation. Indeed, should secession transpire in future, Strictly Boardroom may even consider standing for election as the inaugural mineral resources and foreign minister for the DRG.

For those unfamiliar, the DRG has two co-existing communities. One is a local Aboriginal mission, just known as 'the community' in the local area. The second is one of semi-rural residents who commute across the DRG border to work elsewhere throughout Western Australia and beyond.

Why the community restlessness? The DRG has been subjected to recent sand mining – without due notice – by an oppressive and faceless Western Australian government regime. That is, the latest sand mine just appeared from nowhere, although now it is nearing its end after around three years of local community disruption.

Next generation land use on the mine site is arriving in the form of a light industrial estate that is now selling fast (at least that is what the advertising hoardings say). The previous far more aesthetic land use for the area, which included a rolling grass hill that was 'sustainably mined' as a turf farm is unfortunately no more.

Speculation is that the plans for sand mining were published by the state government and that the community indeed was duly notified and consulted.

No source has yet been verified for this notification however, and no compensation for the loss of amenity has been proffered. The current rumours are that a past issue of the Northern Suburbs Train Spotters' Journal did once purportedly contain a crossword where the answer "Gnangara" fitted a five-across clue along the lines of "site for an imminent disruptive sand mine".

Light-heartedness aside, the story of the DRG shows clearly that we need to lift our game as a mining industry. Strictly Boardroom has always been and remains staunchly pro-mining but the events in the DRG have severely tested that resolve.

For Western Australia to continue to rank highly in such eminent surveys as that published by Canada's Fraser Institute*, we need to do far better than this in terms of maintaining a social licence to operate as a sector. Sorry, let me re-phrase that statement: the Western Australian government needs to do far better than this.

Letters to the relevant ministers from DRG residents were met with the usual polite *"clear off there's nothing you can do about it"* response – *"due notification was given in the cryptic clue to five-across of the crossword"* or words to that effect.

The issue must have resonated somewhere however – as the Western Australian opposition leader Mark McGowan even turned up during the last state election campaign. Well done to Mark on that one. Of course there was precious little he or anyone else could do about the issue: The die was already cast.

If the DRG (read Western Australia) is going to continue to lead the DRC (read Democratic Republic of Congo) in mining circles as a jurisdiction where there is strong community support for mining then things need to vastly improve.

Strictly Boardroom remains a staunch supporter of mining, but how can we as an industry expect to build community support when governments behave in this manner?

The bar clearly needs to be raised. Actually in this instance there was no bar to speak of at all – so beating past performance should be an easy win. In the next Fraser Institute survey Strictly Boardroom won't be voting for Western Australia as the best mining jurisdiction on the planet. What do you think?

---

* Green, K.P., Wilson, A. & Cervantes, M. 2013. *Annual Survey of Mining Companies*. Fraser Institute, March 13, [online], http://www.fraserinstitute.org/research-news/display.aspx?id=20902 [updated annually].

KEY INSIGHTS:
OF MINERAL POLICY AND MINING REGULATION

- Effective minerals policy and mining regulation is based on an understanding of the nexus between geological, economic and policy factors.

- Because a small proportion of mineral deposits carry most of the economic value in the mining industry, policy should focus on finding and developing these resources.

- Governments can choose to generate revenues from the mining sector in two broad ways: either by focusing on taxing existing assets or by fostering the discovery and investment that leads to the development of new assets. In general, contemporary minerals policy (unfortunately) focuses far more on the former than the latter.

- Ultimately effective minerals policy requires a balance between investment attractiveness and equitable distribution of minerals revenues back to the populace.

- Countries and regions have vastly different levels of investment attractiveness to the minerals sector based on geological, policy, and other in-country (political stability, infrastructure, etc.) factors.

- Pre-competitive geoscience data provision is regarded as best practice in attracting exploration investment, though even this is now evolving, as co-drilling and other incentive schemes become more common. Even industry-leading regions can improve their investment attractiveness.

- Mineral industry taxation should recognise that different deposits are of different geological and therefore economic quality. Some mining assets can support higher tax rates (and indeed should) – whilst other assets cannot.

- Ideally mineral royalty and taxation policy should be simple, be predictable, and subject to periodic pre-planned review.
- Social licence to operate has become one of the most important concepts to be embraced by the industry.
- Both outsider and insider perspectives on the mining industry's collective social licence to operate suggest there is room for improvement.

BIBLIOGRAPHY

Books

Agricola, G. 1950. *De re metallica*. Translated by Hoover, H.C. & Hoover, L.H., Dover Publications, New York.

Aldersey-Williams, H. 2012. *Periodic Tales: The Curious Lives of the Elements*, Viking, New York.

Baghai, M., Coley, S. and White, D. 2000. *The Alchemy of Growth: Practical Insights for Building the Enduring Enterprise*. Basic Books, New York.

Boyett, J. & Boyett, J. 2000. *The Guru Guide: The Best Ideas of the Top Management Thinkers*. Wiley, Hoboken, NJ.

Carnegie, D. 1936. *How to Win Friends and Influence People*. Simon and Schuster, New York.

Collier, P. 2008. *The Bottom Billion: Why the Poorest Countries are Failing and What Can Be Done About It*. Oxford University Press, Oxford.

Collier, P. 2011. *The Plundered Planet: Why We Must – And How We Can – Manage Nature For Global Prosperity*. Oxford University Press, Oxford.

Eberts, J. & Ilott, T. 1990. *My Indecision is Final: The Rise and Fall of Goldcrest Films*. Faber & Faber, London.

Handy, C. 1995. *The Empty Raincoat: Making Sense of the Future*. Random House Business Books, New York.

Horne, D. 2008. *The Lucky Country*. Penguin Australia, Docklands, Vic.

Kahneman, D. 2013. *Thinking: Fast and Slow*. Farrar, Straus and Giroux, New York.

Kay, J. 2007. *Foundations of Corporate Success: How Business Strategies Add Value*. Oxford Paperbacks, Oxford.

Mauborgne, R. & Kim, W.C. 2015. *Blue Ocean Strategy: How to Create Uncontested Market Space and Make the Competition Irrelevant, Expanded Edition*. Harvard Business School Press, Watertown, MA.

Nalebuff, B.J. and Brandenburger, A.M. 2003. *Co-opetition*. Profile Books, London.

Peters, T. and Austin, N. 1989. *A Passion for Excellence: The Leadership Difference*. Grand Central Publishing, New York.

Porter, M.E. 2003. *Competitive Strategy*. Free Press, New York.

Porter, M.E. 2004. *Competitive Advantage: Creating and Sustaining Superior Performance*. Free Press, New York.

Ramirez, R. & Wilkinson, A. 2016. *Strategic Reframing: The Oxford Scenario Planning Approach*. Oxford University Press, Oxford.

Rumelt, R.P. 2011. *Good Strategy / Bad Strategy: The Difference and Why It Matters*. Crown Business, New York.

Silver, N. 2015. *The Signal and the Noise: Why So Many Predictions Fail – But Some Don't*. Penguin Books, London.

Sunter, C. & Ilbury, C. 2011. *The Mind of the Fox: Scenario Planning in Action*. Human & Rousseau, Cape Town.

Tetlock, P. 2006. *Expert Political Judgment: How Good Is It? How Can We Know?* Princeton University Press, Princeton, NJ.

Tetlock, P. & Gardner, D. 2006. *Superforecasting: The Art and Science of Prediction*. Crown, London.

Thomson, P. and Graham, J. 2005. *A Women's Place is in the Boardroom*. Palgrave MacMillan, London.

Trench, A. 2013. *Strictly (Mining) Boardroom: Management Insights from Inside the Resources Sector*. Major Street Publishing, Highett, Vic.

Waterman Jr., R.H. 1993. *Adhocracy*. W.W. Norton & Co., London.

Papers

Arvidson, G. 2015. The Case for Exploration as Strategy: An ASX Top 80 Mining and Metals Case Study, Centre for Exploration Targeting Discovery Day, Fremantle, WA, 24 February.

De Assuncoa, J.C. 2013. Economic Insights from a Cost Analysis of Gold Production in Australia from 2008 to 2012. Capstone Individual Research Project, MSc in Mineral and Energy Economics Programme, Curtin University.

Gardiner, N.J., Sykes, J.P., Trench, A. & Robb, L.J. 2015. Tin Mining in Myanmar: Production and Potential, Resources Policy, 46, p219-233.

Gerken, A., Hoffman, N., Kremer, A., Stegemann, U. and Vigo, G. 2010. Getting risk ownership right. McKinsey Working Papers on Risk, #23.

Green, K.P., Wilson, A. & Cervantes, M. 2013. Annual Survey of Mining Companies, Fraser Institute, March 13, [online], http://www.fraserinstitute.org/research-news/display.aspx?id=20902 [updated annually].

Hronsky, J.M.A. & Groves, D.I. 2008. Science of Targeting: Definition, Strategies, Targeting and Performance Measurement, Australian Journal of Earth Sciences, 55, (1), p3-12.

Hronsky, J.M.A. 2009. The Exploration Search Space Concept: Key to a Successful Exploration Strategy, Centre for Exploration Targeting (CET) Quarterly Newsletter, June, p14-15.

Kanakis, M. 2014. Grade Expectations: Exploring the Cost-Grade Hypothesis in Australian Gold Production, CET Quarterly Newsletter, September, p14-17.

Koch, A., Schilling, D. & Upton, D. 2015. Tackling the Crisis in Mineral Exploration, The Boston Consulting Group. June. [online], https://www.bcgperspectives.com/content/articles/metals-mining-tackling-crisis-mineral-exploration [updated annually].

Lauritsen, V. 2014. Gender diversity in the Australian minerals sector: Key insights from a labour force statistical review, Capstone Individual Research Project, MSc in Mineral and Energy Economics Programme, Curtin University.

McKinsey and Company. 1975. Successful Management of Minerals Exploration in Australia: Report to Survey Participants. June.

Reeves, M., Moose, S. and Venema, T. 2014. BCG Classics Revisited: The Growth Share Matrix. Boston Consulting Group Perspectives, 4 June [online], https://www.bcgperspectives.com/content/articles/corporate_strategy_portfolio_management_strategic_planning_growth_share_matrix_bcg_classics_revisited

Sykes, J.P. & Trench, A. 2014. Australia versus The World: The Perceived Attractiveness of Australia's Mining Industry in a Global Context, CET Quarterly Newsletter, June, p6-9.

Sykes, J.P. & Trench, A. 2014. Finding the Copper Mine of the 21st Century: Conceptual Exploration Targeting for Hypothetical Copper

Reserves, Society of Economic Geologists (SEG) Special Publication 18: Building Exploration Capability for the 21st Century, Chapter 11, p273-300.

Sykes, J.P. & Trench, A. 2016. Using Scenarios to Investigate the Long-Term Future of Copper Mining and Guide Exploration Targeting Strategies, AusIMM International Mine Management Conference, Brisbane, 22-24 August, in press.

Sykes, J.P., Wright, J.P. & Trench, A. 2016. Discovery, Supply and Demand: From Metals of Antiquity to Critical Metals, Applied Earth Science, 125, (1), p3-20.

Trench, A., Gemell, C., Venables, T., Curtis, M. & Sykes, J.P. 2015. Evaluating the Attractiveness of Fiscal Regimes for New Gold Developments: African and South American Peer Country Comparisons, International Mining for Development Centre (IM4DC), Action Research Report, May, [online], http://im4dc.org/wp-content/uploads/2015/07/Fiscal-Regimes-for-New-Gold-Developments-Completed-Report.pdf

Trench, A., Packey, D. & Sykes, J.P. 2014. Non-Technical Risks and Their Impact on the Mining Industry. Australasian Institute of Mining & Metallurgy (AusIMM) – Mineral Resource & Ore Reserve Estimation, Monograph 30, Chapter 7, p605-617.

Trench, A., Sykes, J.P & Robinson, P., Edge of tomorrow: A tour of 2016-2020 mineral commodity markets, AusIMM New Zealand Branch Annual Conference 2015, Dunedin, p481-494.

Trench, A. & Sykes, J.P. 2014. Perspectives on Mineral Commodity Market Cycles and Their Relevance to Underground Mining. AusIMM 12th Underground Operators Conference Proceedings, Adelaide, 24-26 March, p19-31.

Whittington, R. 2012. Big Strategy / Small Strategy, Strategic Organization, 10, (3), p263-268.

INDEX

2014 Mining World Cup 143
2015 Paris Climate Summit 93
2016 Chinese Financial Crisis (CFC) 88
2016 Marrakesh Climate Summit 101
3D printing 168, 237

Abydos iron ore 172
'adhocracy' 158-160
affiliations 132
Agricola 5
All-In-Sustaining Costs (AISC) 116, 147
Andersen, Hans Christian 269
Anderson, Gillian 177
Andy Well gold mine 66, 147
Anglo American 94
AngloGold Ashanti 139-140
annual general meeting (AGM) 12, 119
Apple 137, 168, 232
Appleby, Sir Humphrey 269
Arvidson, Graham 58
asset level strategy 45
assets 62, 65, 164, 202
assets, non-core 46
Atkins, Alex 31
Atlas Iron 173
auditing 14
Australia's mining ministers 267-269
Australian Football League (AFL) 218-220
Australian Securities Exchange (ASX) 16, 56, 58, 60, 64-65, 97, 110, 197

Bamforth, Shannan 173
Ban Houayxai gold mine 66
Barrick Gold 85
Battleships 203-205, 208
Bayesian 75
Belbin 214
benchmarking 43
Bennett, Mark 173
Beresford, Steve 31
Bernard Shaw, George 31
BetExploration.com 103-105
BHP Billiton 85, 139-142, 170
bias 78
Black Butte copper project 66
Blue Ocean Strategy 105
boardroom, conundrums 20-22, 38
boardroom, effectiveness 7, 31-33
Bonaparte, Napolean 31
Boston Consulting Group 42, 187-189
Bowie, David 127
Brewster, Doug 31, 214
British Geological Survey 237
brokers 201-203
Buffett, Warren 3
bureaucracy 158-160

business conditions 41
business model innovation 67, 106
by-products 237-238

Cadia Hill gold mine 147, 246
Cameco 242
capabilities 153, 164, 225
capital 47-48, 148
carbon emissions 93
Carnegie, Dale 27, 32
Carrapateena copper project 66
Centre for Exploration Targeting 53, 139, 205
China 90, 98, 100, 229, 231-235, 237-239, 249, 273
China General Nuclear Power Corporation (CGNPC) 242
China National Nuclear Corporation (CNNC) 242
China, uranium 239-240
Christie, Agatha 173, 174
Churchill, Winston 32, 198
Cloncurry copper project 67
Cluedo strategy 43, 70
coal 59
cobalt 236, 243
Coldeco 90
Collier, Sir Paul 255
Collins, Michael 31
Commodity Crusade scenario 91-95
commodity
– market 142, 251-252
– new 183
– prices 50, 77, 86, 93, 96, 122, 151
– profitable 231-235

– sundial 228-231
communication 35, 125-126, 187
competing business objectives 41
competition 137, 169, 264-266
competitive advantage 40-41, 43, 154
compound annual growth rate (CAGR) 240
conduct 23
copper 59, 82, 86, 90, 230
copper mines 94
corporate governance 7, 15, 16, 21, 32
corporate leverage 198
cost curves 43
cost focus 119-121
cost, mining escalation 121
costs, business 117-118, 219
costs, corporate 117-118
costs, economic 117-118
costs, site 117-118
Counting House scenario 95-99
Craske, Tim 173
CRU Group 150, 229, 249
Curie, Marie 243

De Re Metallica 183
decision-making 31, 38, 106
Deflector gold deposit 66
de-globalisation 90
DeGrussa copper mine 66, 174
Dell, Michael 68
Democratic Republic of Gnangara (DRG) 277-279
desalination plants 97

diamonds 208
Direct Shipping Ore (DSO) 212
diversity 15, 17, 18, 83, 84
Doepel, John 31
Doray Minerals 66
drill targeting efficiency 203
Duchovny, David 177

Eastern Goldfields 206
Eberts, Jake 31
economies, emerging 257
electromagnetics (EM) 209
Emmerson Resources 173
Empty Raincoat, The: Making Sense of the Future 120
energy sector 12
engineering, procurement, construction management (EPCM) 86
environmental issues 89, 97
Ernest Henry copper mine 172
equitable and competitive (EC) 256
equity analysts 79-81
Evolution Mining 67
Exco Resources 67
expected monetary value (EMV) 187
exploration 12, 38, 56-57, 60-63, 69, 80, 97, 170-172, 192-193
– big 175-177
– boardroom 190-191
– competitive 264-266
– corporate excellence 185-187
– crisis 187-189
– dollar 262-264
– drill targeting 205-208

– governance 13-18
– management 195-226
– measuring MD performance 220-221
– new concepts 183
– new technology 182
– overseas 199-201
– personalities 214-217
– portfolio management 197-199, 225
– reframed concepts 183
– remuneration 222-223
– search space 180-185, 192
– sequencing techniques 208-210
– technology 182, 225

fact-based assessment 13
Fanya Metal Exchange 239
financing 59, 109
Flanagan, David 173
Flying Fox nickel mine 172
Ford 140
forecasting 75, 77, 106
forecasting resolutions 77-79
Fraser Institute, The 259, 267, 278-279
Fraser Range 208, 210
Fry, Stephen 190
FUBAR 75
funding 13, 60, 186

game theory 42, 70
Geldof, Sir Bob 255
Gemell, Chris 269
gender balance 8, 24, 84-85
Geographic Information Systems (GIS) 93

Geoscience Australia 237
GeoTaxi 222-223
Gillard, Julia 40-41
Glasenberg, Ivan 65
Glencore 94
gold 59, 80, 138, 208
gold mine 51, 53-54
gold, Australian industry 146-147
Goldberg, Arthur 32
Goldfields 9
Google 137
Gosowong gold mine 172, 174
governance 13, 14, 15-17, 220
government 250
government policy 253-259
government, Western Australia 274-275, 279
grade 156-158
graphite 59
greenfields 149, 167, 175, 182, 186, 188, 241
growth 38, 41

Handy, Charles 120
Harmony gold mine 172
Harvard Business Review 105
Heather, Steve 31
Hiscock, Ian 239
How to Win Friends and Influence People 27
Hronsky, Jon 177, 180

Ilott, Terry 31
Iluka Resources 96, 173
inaccessible regions, geographically 181
inaccessible regions, politically 181

Independence Group 66, 96
individual expertise 7, 32
infrastructure 148
initial public offering (IPO) 204
inside running 47-48
Integra Mining 67
International Mining for Development Centre (IM4DC) 231, 232, 256-257
intra-board communication 25
iron ore 59, 138, 168, 230, 233
issue analysis 42

Jacinth-Ambrosia mineral sands mine 172, 174
Jackson, Colin 31

Kahneman, Daniel 76
Kanakis, Matthew 146, 156
Kazakhstan 143-145, 241-242
KazAtomProm 242
Kennedy, John F. 129
key performance indicator (KPI) 129-131, 218, 220-221, 226
Keystone Cops syndrome 112-113
Kim, W.C 105
Kindle 3
known knowns 32
known unknowns 75, 266
Krasnoff, Rich 53

Langhorne Clements, Samuel 109
lateral thinking 154-156
Lauritsen, Vikki 161
Layman, Sally-Anne 53
liquid natural gas (LNG) 96

lithium 59, 237, 243, 252
London Alternative Investment Market (AIM) 97

Macquarie Bank 53
management mentoring 7
management, downturn 132-134, 136
Managing Director (MD) 9, 220-221
manganese 59
market challenges 246
market conditions 38
market disruption 85
Master of Business Administration (MBA) 7, 22, 65
Mauborgne, Renee 105
McCuaig, Campbell 187
McGowan, Mark 279
McKinsey & Company 47-48, 188
measuring success 218-220
megatonnes to megawatts (M2M) 240
mentor support 13
mergers & acquisitions (M&A) 38, 57, 63, 70, 86-87, 96, 98, 149, 171
mid-tier miner 66, 85
mine management 109-112
mineral commodity analysis 42
mineral deposits 186-187, 204
mineral exploration 103-105, 109, 177-180, 212-214, 222
mineral markets, boutique 251
mineral markets, global 59, 90

mineral policy 253-280
mineral resource companies 56-60
mineral resource development 255-257
Mineral Resource Rent Tax (MRRT) 274
mineral resources 192
mineral royalties 269-275
mineral sands 59
mineral, economics 37, 227-253
mineral, finance 227-253
Minerals Boardroom 7-37
minerals sector 12, 138, 140, 142
mines, foreign-owned 89
mining companies, large 148-150, 167, 187
mining company boards 12
mining, costs 116
mining industry, Australia 128
mining industry, future 90, 246-249
mining industry, growth 64
mining investment companies 69
mining juniors 150-152
mining regulation 253-280
mining, external perceptions 275-277
mining, investment 244-246
mining, real-time 94
Miss Marple 174
Mitsubishi 140
Modi, Narendra 93
Monty copper deposit 66

morale 123-124, 136
Mount Monger gold operations 66
Mulder, Fox 178-185
My Prospect (Kitchen) Rules 210-212
Myers-Briggs 214

natural ownership 38, 47-48
net present value (NPV) 80
networking 13
Newcrest Mining 173, 186
Newmont Mining 139-140, 173
nickel 59, 138, 144-145, 184, 208, 230
niobium 234
non-core assets 38, 46-48
non-executive directors (NEDs) 9, 16, 186, 223
Northern Star Resources 67, 96
Northern Suburbs Train Spotters' Journal 278
not in my back yard (NIMBY) 277-279
Nova-Bollinger nickel deposit 66, 208

oligopolistic supply 234
Olympic Dam copper mine 145-146
Osborne, Rocky 173
Oxford Scenario Planning Approach 88, 91, 95
OZ Minerals 66, 86, 96

PanAust 66
pay it forward 132-133

Peasants' Revolt scenario 100
Periodic Tales – The Curious Lives of the Elements 243
Phu Kam copper mine 66
Pilbara iron ore district 168
platinum 59
Poirot, Hercule 174
policy perception index 260-262
Polymetals 67
portfolio analysis 42
Porter's Five Forces 42
Precedent, Analogy, Numbers, Empathy, Logic (PANEL) 26
precious metal 63
pricyum 232-234
problem-solving 42
project development 57
Prominent Hill copper mine 66

QI 190
quartz 157

radium 242-244
rare earths 59
Real Housewives of Mining 161-163
regions, 'under cover' 182
relationships 23
research and development (R&D) 89, 92, 97, 167
resources economy 255-257
Rio Tinto 85, 141-142, 170
risk 45, 47-48, 133, 149, 170
Robin Hood 37-41
Robinson, Paul 228
Rocky's Reward nickel mine 172, 174

Roxy Music 127
Royal Dutch Shell 159-160
royalties, gold rates 273-275
Rumsfield, Donald 32, 75

Saavedra-Rosas, Jose 205, 206
Sandfire Resources 66, 86, 96, 173
scenario planning 74, 76, 77, 78, 88, 91-102
Scully, Dr Dana 177-185
shareholders 142-143
shares 80
short-termism 143
Signal and The Noise, The: The Art and Science of Prediction 75
Silver Lake Resources 66
Silver, Nate 75
SinoCopper 90
Sirius Resources 66, 173, 209
Slade 127
Smyth, Erica 53
solvent-extraction-electrowinning (SXEW) 169, 184
Spotted Quoll nickel mine 172, 174
Stack, Jack 155
stakeholder engagement 7, 32, 254
stakeholder management 14
strategic guidance 7, 32
strategic management 37-73, 51, 70
Strategic Management of Resource Companies 51, 65

strategy 60, 62, 152, 203
– asset-level 45, 67
– business 41-42
– capability-led 138-141
– consultant 114-116
– corporate 125-126
– corporate level 45
– economics 46
– essentials 41-44
– exploration 165-195, 172, 189
strategy, innovation 67-73, 93
Strictly (Mining) Boardroom – Management Insights from Inside the Resources Sector 3
Sunter, Clem 87
Superforecasting 76
Sweet 127

tantalum 242
Telfer gold mine 172, 173
Tetlock, Philip 76, 87
Thinking, Fast and Slow 76
tin 59
Tintina Resources 66
Titanic 158
Toro Energy 53
Toronto Venture Exchange (TSX-V) 97
Toyota 50, 140
Trench, Morgan 83
T-Rex 127
Turnbull, Malcolm 93
Twain, Mark 32, 107
Tyrwhitt, David 173

Under Siege scenario 88-91

University of Western
  Australia, The (UWA) 103,
  173, 205, 231, 256
unknown knowns 76
unknown unknowns 76
uranium 59, 138, 145, 230,
  239-243

value accretion curve 55
value chain analysis 43
value creation 56
vanadium 242
Virginia City, Nevada 109
volcanic massive sulphide
  (VMS) 208

Waterman, Robert 159-160
Western Areas 96, 173
Western Australia goldfields
  184

White Dam gold mine 67
Wilkinson, Charles 173
WMC Resources 130, 133
women on boards 18-20, 74,
  83, 161-163
Wood, Dan 173
workload 23
Wright, Josh 31

X-Factor 198-199
X-Files, The 177-185
X-Files Movie, The: Fight the
  Future 179
Xstrata 67

YouTube 113

zinc 59, 184

Optiro is an advisory services firm that provides strategic, independent advice to mining and exploration companies, their advisors and investors.

Drawing on extensive geological, mining engineering, metallurgical and financial expertise, Optiro provides technical and commercial advice to assist clients with investment decisions at or before commencement, and maximise operational value throughout the mining cycle. The company's team of geologists, mining engineers and other mining professionals are among the most experienced consultants in the industry.

Find out more: www.optiro.com

Greenfields Research is the trading name of independent minerals-industry geologist, economist and strategist, John P. Sykes. The company name reflects John's industry research focus on exploration and mine project development (so called "greenfield" projects) and long term mineral economics and strategy.

Greenfields provides dynamic consultancy to the exploration, mining, financial and public sectors, specialising in work which requires a period of intense exploration, mining or commodities related research. Greenfields' services include exploration and mine project search, profiling and assessment; mine cost modelling; mineral market entry analysis; project, company and industry-scale scenario planning; strategic and decision-making advisory, cross-silo communication, boundary spanning and intra-company and inter-industry knowledge exchange; and executive and management assistance.

Greenfields high-quality, client-led service is quick, straightforward and competitively priced. In short, if you want to find something out about exploration and mining: Just ask Greenfields.

Find out more: www.greenfieldsresearch.com

The CRU Group is the world's leading independent business analysis and consultancy group focusing on the mining, metals and fertilizer sectors. Founded in the late 1960s, the group employs more than 250 experts in Sydney, Perth, Hong Kong, London, Beijing, Santiago, Sao Paulo, Mumbai and key centres in the United States. It comprises three major businesses:

- **CRU | Analysis** provides market analysis, price forecasts and cost models across the value chain for steel raw materials and steel, aluminium, base and precious metals, energy minerals and fertilizers.
- **CRU | Consulting** delivers solution-orientated advice in support of capital raisings, diversification, market decisions, pricing and a range of industry related negotiations.
- **CRU | Events** organises international conferences covering the aluminium, copper, steel, stainless steel, ferro-alloys and wire and cable, sulphur, nitrogen and phosphates industries.

More information can be obtained from www.crugroup.com

The Centre for Exploration Targeting (CET) is a unique research institution combining pure science and applied research to address the practical problems of the mineral exploration and mining industries.

Its driving vision is to be recognised as the global leader in research excellence, innovation, education and training in exploration targeting.

The mission of the Centre for Exploration Targeting (CET) is to apply scientific research to increasing both the rate and quality of discoveries made in mineral exploration, without relying on substantial increases in exploration expenditure.

www.cet.edu.au

The University of Western Australia Business School aims to advance the welfare and the prosperity of the people through excellence in business education and research.

Recognised as one of the premier business schools in the Asia-Pacific region, the UWA Business School offers a broad range of business and management courses. The School's flagship MBA suite has produced leaders across the public, private and not-for-profit sectors, and allows students to complete a range of specialisations, including in Natural Resources.

The UWA Business School holds international accreditation through both EQUIS (European Quality Improvement System) and AACSB (Association to Advance Collegiate Schools of Business). In addition, the School's commitment to corporate sustainability and social responsibility is cemented by its role as a signatory to the United Nations Principles of Responsible Management Education (PRME).

The University of Western Australia is one of the region's leading universities. UWA is the only Western Australian university to belong to the Group of Eight – a coalition of the top research universities in Australia – and it is one of only two Australian members of the Worldwide Universities Network, a partnership of 18 research-led universities from Europe, Africa, the Americas and the Asia-Pacific. The University is also a foundation member of the Matariki Network of high quality, research-intensive universities with a particular focus on student experience.

www.business.uwa.edu.au

www.ingramcontent.com/pod-product-compliance
Ingram Content Group UK Ltd.
Pitfield, Milton Keynes, MK11 3LW, UK
UKHW041414180426
11947UKWH00007B/126